Everyday Acts

Against Racism

Raising Children in a Multiracial World

edited by Maureen T. Reddy

SEAL PRESS
Seattle

Seal Press
3131 Western Avenue, Suite 410
Seattle, Washington 98121
Email: sealprss@scn.org

Library of Congress Cataloging-in-Publication Data
Everyday acts against racism: raising children in a multiracial world / edited by Maureen T. Reddy.
Includes bibliographic references.
1. Prejudices in children—United States—Prevention. 2. Race awareness in children—United States. 3. Child rearing—United States. I. Reddy, Maureen T.
BF723.P75E94   1996   305.8'0083—dc20   96-31501
ISBN 1-878067-85-0

Printed in the United States of America
First printing, October 1996
10 9 8 7 6 5 4 3 2 1

Distributed to the trade by Publishers Group West
In Canada: Publishers Group West Canada, Toronto, Canada
In Europe and the U.K.: Airlift Book Company, London, England

Cover design by Kate Thompson
Text design by Stacy M. Lewis

Acknowledgments

Many people helped to shape this book, and I am grateful to them all. First, thanks to the students in my introduction to women's studies course in the spring of 1993, whose questions about what they could do to end racism and sexism inspired the book in the first place. I also want to thank the many writers who responded to my call for essays on the topic of antiracism, mothering, and feminism; I learned something from each proposal I read, and only wish I could have used them all. Thanks to Faith Conlon of Seal Press for her enthusiasm for this project and for her thoughtful, sensitive editing of the essays. Thanks also to copyeditor Cathy Johnson, who helped enormously. Any errors that remain are my own. And, finally, thanks to my husband and son, who took turns reading sections of the book aloud to me while I proofread the galleys.

This book is truly a collaborative effort, and so I want to give it a collective dedication: for all of our children.

CONTENTS

Connections

Introduction

Like most parents, I want to pass my values on to my children. However, we parents are not the sole influences on our children, and passing along our values can be difficult when those values stand in opposition to social norms. In the United States, teaching antiracism to children is often arduous because racism is so deeply embedded in the culture that learning to stand against it may sometimes feel like learning to have no place to stand at all.

When I tell people that one of my central child-rearing goals is to teach my children to oppose racism, they sometimes misunderstand and remark that they, too, advocate "nonracist" parenting. But nonracist implies a completed process, the end point of a movement from racist to nonracist. It suggests that one has done the necessary work and has achieved a perfect state, that there is no further need to keep working. "Antiracism," in contrast, implies action and ongoing work against racism. More than a change in consciousness, although that also is necessary, antiracism is an ongoing, collaborative, collective struggle against the pervasive racism of this society. Like feminism, antiracism is revolutionary in its ideals and in its goals; each seeks to change a whole social system, not merely one individual's ideas. Raising antiracist children means not only avoiding inculcating racism, but also teaching children to be agents of change.

Few child-rearing books address helping children to understand, and to stand against, racism. For me, other mothers have often been a source of wisdom in this struggle to teach my children to be agents of change. I have found support, reassurance, inspiration and ideas for specific actions in mothers' stories of their own struggles. *Everyday Acts Against Racism* was born from mothers' stories and mothers' questions, and offers readers the opportunity to tap mothers' wisdom and to share it.

Why focus on mothers'—as opposed to mothers' *and* fathers'—attempts to learn and to teach antiracism to their children? One practical reason is that mothers are still the primary caregivers and, therefore, the first socializers of most children. A more philosophic reason comes from Sara Ruddick's *Maternal Thinking: Toward a Politics of Peace,* which identifies the ways in which mothering work has been undervalued and maternal thought has not been recognized *as* thought. I want to honor that work and thought. Ruddick details how a feminist, politicized maternal thought can lead to a politics of peace. There can be no peace without justice, and racial justice is long overdue. The contributors to this collection illustrate some of the multiple ways in which maternal thought and work can serve the cause of racial justice.

Like Ruddick, who points out that both men and women can engage in mothering work and therefore in maternal thought, I do not limit "mother" to women. The mothers who speak in this book are predominantly, but not exclusively, women who through birth or adoption have responsibility for the daily care of children. But one of these "mothers" is a man whose feminist mothering takes place in a college classroom, and many of the writers describe extensions of mothering work into teaching and mentoring.

Although my interest in maternal thought originated in mothering my two children, the uses of maternal thinking of course extend well beyond those children. For instance, like other writers in this volume, my teaching and my mothering often overlap. On the last day of an introductory class in women's studies I taught recently, for example, several students asked for my advice as the director of women's studies at their college. They knew what classes they could take next, but were much less sure about—and far more interested in—how they could act on what they had learned in class. "Now that we know more about how sexism and racism work together," one young woman said, "what can we *do* to change things?" As a class, we brainstormed to come up with some possibilities, including local groups students could join. Some of the students in the class were parents already, and many more believed children would be part of their futures. A number of these students spoke of their determination to do things differently than their own parents had, and of their belief that the best hope for ending racism and sexism lay in antiracist and antisexist parenting. They weren't sure, however, just how to put their ideals into practice.

I certainly did not have *the* answer for my students, but I did—and do—share their concerns. My students were looking for practical applications—"everyday uses"—for their new insights into racism and sexism, just as I have searched for such strategies for myself and for my children. The advice I offered my students then drew less on my expertise as a women's studies professor than on my life as a mother committed to antiracism. This book offers better answers to my students' questions than I was able to give at the time. One need not have daily responsibility for particular children to find in these essays helpful strategies against racism. Everyday mothering acts can take many forms, most of which put maternal thought into practice outside one's own home.

Those of us committed to antiracism need strategies for fighting racism that can be part of our daily lives, that are as essential to those lives as eating and sleeping. This collection's title—*Everyday Acts Against Racism*—emphasizes the daily, the ordinary, as opposed to the extraordinary. The title deliberately echoes one of my favorite short stories, Alice Walker's "Everyday Use," which tells of a conflict between the narrator, Mama, and her worldly daughter, Dee (as Mama named her)/Wangeroo (as she renamed herself). Venturing home to the country for a quick visit from the city, Dee announces that "it's a new day" for black people, explains that she has changed her name, and generally disrespects Mama and Dee's own sister, Maggie, telling them they are "backward." Dee/Wangeroo wants to take back to the city a number of items, including a quilt, to put on display as part of her heritage. But Maggie and Mama live this heritage every day; these "quaint" art objects are meant for "everyday use," not for museum-like preservation. At story's end, Mama finally stands up for herself and Maggie. Through Mama's actions and her compelling voice, the story celebrates the everyday, indeed insists on its central significance, as I believe this volume does as well.

When I first began to think about putting together an anthology on mothering and antiracism, I knew I wanted personal stories that could inspire constructive actions against racism. For the anthology to work as a catalyst for new ways of thinking leading to new ways of acting against racism, I knew that the perspectives included would have to be diverse. The contributors to *Everyday Acts Against Racism* indeed have varying life experiences and backgrounds. The writers whose work appears here identify as black, white, Asian, Latina, Tejana, and multiracial; we are heterosexual, lesbian, and bisexual; we range in age from our twenties to our sixties. As the essays in this collection illustrate, different strategies are needed to teach antiracism to white people (child or adult) and to people of color (child or adult), to men and boys and to women and girls. Racism is not simple, but complex and diverse in its workings and in its effects. Those likely to be racism's targets need ways of resisting not appropriate for those likely to be tempted as its beneficiaries. Racism operates differently for men and for women, and differently again for black men and for white men, for example. We need antiracist strategies at least as complex and multiple as the structures of racism.

Despite the diversity of the contributors' experiences and perspectives, there are some significant similarities: University professors, for example, are overrepresented, as are currently middle-class women, although many of our families of origin are working-class or poor. When I first contemplated editing this anthology, I anticipated that certain ideas would come up in more than one essay, and several themes do indeed recur. A number of writers talk about their own mothers, for instance, and many identify schools as important locations in transmitting racism and therefore as strategically important in fighting against racism. The essays fall into three overlapping but nonetheless distinct groups: The section titled "Starting Points" focuses on places to begin fighting racism, "Reading and Teaching" centers on classrooms (the writers' and their children's) and books, and "Connections" discusses building community across racial and ethnic divides.

The seven essays in "Starting Points" describe a number of different places to begin antiracist work. Martha Roth's "You Have to Start Somewhere" argues that perfection is not the point, rather *doing* and *trying* are. Nancy Butcher locates that starting point in her own internalized racism, against Japanese and African-American people. To mother her small son effectively, Butcher realizes she has to "undo the smile" she learned from her Japanese mother and allow her anger to work for change. Pauline A. Santos movingly describes mothering her daughter as a rebirth for herself. Taught self-hatred and acceptance of racism and sexism by her (white) mother, Santos vowed not to pass along that legacy to her (black) daughter; "A Mother's Birth" details how she kept that vow. Yolanda Flores Niemann, a Tejana married to a white man, writes about the pain of teaching her white-appearing children about racism. Jennifer E. Morales, a multiracial, bisexual mother of a white-appearing child, writes about living the ironies of American racism, sexism and homophobia, offering useful strategies for "race bending" as one tool against racism. Staci Swenson considers the myth of meritocracy as a barrier to racial justice and describes putting her daughter's innate sense of fairness to use against racism and other injustices. Daryl LaRoche's funny, scathing how-to manual on anti-racism and antisexism, "Trial and Error," closes this section while leading into the next with reflections on the author's work as an elementary school teacher.

The essays in "Reading and Teaching" look at mothering work's relationship to reading and to classrooms, our own and our children's. In "Confessions of a Witch with Limited Powers," Martha Satz reflects on her very different experiences raising her biracial adoptive son and daughter, and on taking the risk of bringing her personal life into her teaching. Andrea O'Reilly uses students' responses to Toni Morrison's portrayal of Eva Peace in *Sula* to examine the effects of codifying a dominant, white, middle-class definition of motherhood into "the official and only meaning of motherhood." The struggle against racism, O'Reilly shows, requires undoing that codification. Shawn R. Donaldson, in an essay titled in homage to Derrick Bell's *Faces at the Bottom of the Well: The Permanence of Racism*, describes how she dealt with several racist incidents at her child's school and questions whether racial equality is a realistic goal in the United States. Lynda Marín's "Bringing it on Home: Teaching/Mothering Antiracism" offers a painful, powerful exploration of the intertwined experiences of adopting a multiracial daughter and teaching a university course with an explosive history, "Women of Color in the U.S." Blanche Radford Curry, like Marín, links mothering and teaching, in this case offering the experiences of a black mother teaching antiracism to her young son and to her (mostly white) college students. Eileen de los Reyes examines the lessons she learned from what she considers her failures as a director of a college's learning center, laying bare the particular dynamics of divisions among people of color that tripped her up. Gary Lemons's essay on what it means to be a black male feminist professor, "Teaching the (Bi)Racial Space that Has No Name," rounds out this section by inviting readers to expand their definitions of mothering and to challenge their preconceptions about race.

Marguerite Guzman Bouvard opens the final section, "Connections," with an essay that reflects on her childhood as a refugee from Trieste and her adult work as a sponsor of Southeast Asian refugee families in the United States. Bouvard closes her essay with a story about a painful breach with a beloved niece, reminding us that sometimes mothering goes terribly wrong. Jane Lazarre's "Passing Over" juxtaposes a Passover seder and her son's surgery, concluding with her application of the biblical Ruth's promise to her mother-in-law that "your people shall be my people" to her own life as a white mother of black sons. Julia Epstein looks at her family position "between exiles": the daughter of a survivor of the Nazi's "Final Solution" and the adoptive mother (with her partner) of two Latina daughters, Epstein considers the dynamics of a family history of loss. Linda H. Southward and Phyllis Gray-Ray's essay is a dialogue between university professors—one white, one black—raised in the deep South during the aftermath of the *Brown v. Board of Education of Topeka, Kansas* Supreme Court decision, a dialogue on working as allies in the struggle against racism, for the sake of their children, their students and themselves. Shelley Park uses her own experience as a white adoptive mother of a child of color to argue for open (versus closed) adoption as a strategy in antiracist mothering work. My essay, "Working on Redemption," describes some of the ways that mothers can act on behalf of children not their own by birth or adoption, and how such actions might benefit their own children as well.

My goal was to create an anthology that could serve as a resource for those who share the desire to act against racism by teaching children to be antiracist. My hope was that the anthology would provide descriptions of actions mothers, especially feminist mothers, had taken against racism, actions that might inspire other actions or that could be emulated, turning good will into transformative action in the world. Thanks to the honest, direct maternal stories told by the contributors, that goal and that hope are realized. At a conference on ending childhood poverty, political scientist Howard Zinn said, "When changes take place in history, they are not the result of a few heroic deeds, but of many small actions—all that persistence creates a great social movement." This volume is a record of many small actions—often heroic deeds in themselves—toward ending racism.

Maureen T. Reddy
May 1996

Starting
Points

You Have to Start Somewhere

MARTHA ROTH

My mother was a liberal, and she taught me that racial prejudice, as she called it, was a mark of ignorance and vulgarity. To the end of her life she had a tendency to call working-class black and white women "girls," although she and my father leaned over backward to say "gentleman" when referring to a black man of any class.

She was born in 1907 and trained as a social worker, and most of the black people she knew to speak to were hired help or casework clients. My father, a high-school teacher of English and journalism, had black colleagues, but my mother didn't meet more than a few African Americans on terms of equality until she was past fifty. Still, she and my father did their best to rear my brother and me without the kinds of prejudice they considered vulgar. They made their attitudes devastatingly clear— they had a class prejudice against race prejudice—and they chose to live in the city, in a multiracial neighborhood, while their brothers and sisters all moved to the suburbs to raise their families.

My father taught at an all-black industrial-arts high school. His students were mostly uninterested in his subjects, and I think he took this as a personal slight, though I also think he grasped the social forces

acting on black adolescents in Chicago in the 1950s: de facto segregation of housing and education, lack of access to good jobs, and systematic corruption of black politicians by the Democratic machine.

There were no people of color among my parents' friends, but I didn't
think it odd; they had grown up among Jews and had few gentile friends.
They spoke disapprovingly of Dixiecrat politicans and Jim Crow. My
father recommended Richard Wright's books. So I was shocked, when I
was sixteen and first dated an African-American boy, that my father
asked me, grinding his teeth in shame, to meet my friend outside the
house so the neighbors wouldn't see. I refused. His prejudice shocked
me, but his shame shocked me more.

By the 1960s I was a young mother living in that same neighborhood on
Chicago's South Side, and I was delighted that my two tiny daughters
had the opportunity to play with children of different colors. I had married a graduate student, white and Jewish like me, and we lived in a
student apartment where our neighbors were Africans, Asians and Europeans as well as hyphenated Americans. We were left-liberals; we
gave money to the Student Non-violent Coordinating Committee (SNCC)
and the Congress on Racial Equality (CORE) and I put my babies in
stroller and carrier and marched for school desegregation and nuclear
disarmament.

My husband finished his degree and got a job teaching at the University of Minnesota. We moved to the Twin Cities and tried to find a
community that resembled Hyde Park. I didn't realize how rare it was
(especially for Chicago, which was then and still is the most residen-
tially segregated city in North America). Surely in Hubert Humphrey's
town, I thought, we would be able to buy a modest house in an integrated neighborhood.

When I first told a real estate agent that I wanted to live in a neighborhood where my children could play and go to school with children
of different colors, his face went blank. "That's real different," he said,
pleasantly enough, and made some notes.

I said, "I should think most people would want that." This was a bare
few years after the march on Selma and the murders of James Chaney,

Andrew Goodman, Michael Schwerner, Medgar Evers, and Viola Gregg Liuzzo. In my cocoon of youth and liberalism I assumed that other northern white people believed as I did, that living as neighbors with people of color and raising our children together was the best hope for healing the gaping wounds that our racist history had slashed in the body politic.

The child of secular Jewish parents, I knew something about "restricted" neighborhoods, clubs and schools. Jews didn't buy Ford cars because of Henry Ford's reputed anti-Semitism. One of my uncles changed his last name in order to get into medical school; he believed that universities had tacit quotas for Jewish students, especially students of medicine. There were restaurants my parents wouldn't patronize, but I never felt my own range of choices curtailed because of my ethnic heritage, and I was outraged that people of color should be denied equal housing, jobs and education.

The phrase "people of color" had a genteel Southern ring in 1965; white and black people still said "Negro" and "Oriental." I still believed in the metaphor of the melting pot. When barriers to open housing and schooling came down, I was sure, people would intermingle and produce a color-blind, vaguely beige society.

Of course I knew about the ugly housing riots in Chicago. I'd seen the distorted faces of white people on TV, screaming at black people who sought to buy and live in bungalows in Lawndale or Cicero. But I saw them with my mother's eyes, as ludicrous and pathetic as flat-earthers clinging to outmoded ways of thinking.

The realtor laughed. "You'd be wrong," he said. "As far as I can see, most families seem to want to live around families just like them." I couldn't imagine anything more stifling than for our children to grow up among white faculty children. I'd gone to public schools with children from families both richer and poorer than my own, Jews and gentiles, European refugees, Appalachian migrants, Filipino/as, Chinese, Japanese, Koreans and—after restrictive housing covenants were broken in the late 1940s—African Americans. I'd learned a lot from all of them, and I loved the variety in our school, in our neighborhood. I had black and Asian friends in high school and college, and I wanted the same for my kids.

We found Minneapolis depressingly white and Protestant, although more American Indians lived here than in any other U.S. city. Our first rented house nestled in a pretty little community on the edge of an old Jewish neighborhood. All our neighbors were white, but on Sunday mornings when we went up to Plymouth Avenue in the old neighborhood to buy bagels, we found streets that looked more like Chicago. That was because the area was "transitional"; a public housing project had been built on the edge of the neighborhood, some magic number of black property owners and renters had been reached and (like my aunts and uncles had) white homeowners began to flee to the first ring of suburbs. What looked like a mixed area soon became a black neighborhood. In the hot summer of 1966, there was rioting and burning along Plymouth Avenue. The bagel shop moved to the suburbs.

Neither my husband nor I wanted to buy a house on the North Side, in a neighborhood struggling with violent change. We had both grown up in cities, both played in the streets. We weren't afraid of ordinary city roughness, but we wanted our kids to be safe. Cities are hazardous enough, we thought, and we bought a charming old house in a neighborhood that looked okay: mixed houses and apartments, near a school, near a lake—in the Twin Cities you're almost always near a lake—and far from the university. No people of color lived on our block, but a Chinese family soon moved in two houses away.

Our children went to a nursery school where a few middle-class families of color sent their children. The school's director, Sophie, was a German Jew married to a non-Jewish German ethnomusicologist, and she had learned Pestalozzi-Froebel child-centered techniques in Berlin. After Sophie and Johannes left Germany for South America in the 1930s, she ran a nursery school in Quito, Ecuador. Now, in Minneapolis, she wanted more children of color in her school, and a number of parents supported her plan to provide scholarships for children from low-income black and Indian families. We raised tuition and asked for donations from rich parents, and we began to fumble with a well-intentioned but not particularly well-considered scholarship program.

How did we find the children who received scholarships to the School for Young Children? I think they were recommended through personal contacts—churches and social service agencies where Sophie had friends. The year was 1970. We had no experience of—or even language for—equal opportunity, and these privately gathered funds were expended in a tradition of strictly private benevolence. *All* our scholarship recipients were black and Indian.

What a little bastion of middle-class privilege we were! Because this was a private preschool, we mothers (and a few fathers) car-pooled our kids. I remember including an Indian child in my car pool, a silent little boy named Frank whose nose ran all the time. By then I knew a little bit about Twin Cities Indian families; for example, the complicated construction of tribal identity and entitlement knitted together by successive government bureaucracies had the effect of splitting up many families with small children. Families or parts of families would move down to the Twin Cities, where parents could get work and kids could go to school, and then move back up north to the reservation in the summer. Lacking "residency," they weren't eligible for social services in the Cities.

Frank lived with his mother, brother and sisters in a public housing project across the city from the preschool. I was so embarrassed by being a provider of charity that I could not hold an ordinary conversation with his mother. I thought it was polite to ignore the signs of poverty in their overheated, underfurnished apartment, and I have no idea what she thought of me or of the scholarship program. The family had no car in Minneapolis, so we richer mothers drove extra shifts. There had been talk, on the scholarship committee, of asking some scholarship parents to come to school and "talk about their culture" as a way of "giving something back," but I don't remember that it ever happened.

All one year Frank rode in my car pool, one of the disgruntled little live packages I stuffed into the back seat of my VW Beetle on arctic mornings. In that first year of the scholarship program—which depended on most of us being full-time, stay-at-home moms—parents' meetings began to simmer with acrimony as people balked at tuition raises. Only one mother of a scholarship student (not Frank) came to parents' meetings; she was a diffident woman, and she mostly supported Sophie against the more conservative parents—as did I.

A few of us sensed there was something wrong with our program; it seemed to humiliate the recipients and make the providers angry, and rather than breaking down barriers between rich white kids and poor kids of color it reinforced them. We didn't yet understand that programs for people of color should originate with people of color, and be run by them, but we saw dimly that our seat-of-the-pants benevolence wasn't working very well. We didn't have a clue about our own racism; in fact, we all would have claimed we weren't racist in the slightest. Weren't we putting ourselves out for the sake of giving our children an interracial (we didn't say "multicultural" yet) preschool experience?

When we turned to Sophie for guidance, she said emphatically, "It's a start. We have to start somewhere," and our token scholarship mother would agree. The school didn't have the resources for a more extensive program, and although I came to see our program as flawed and partial, it was after all just a nursery school; our kids were going to spend the next ten or twelve years in public schools, which had bigger, juicier problems. (The richer parents sent their children to private schools, but never mind.)

My kids went on to elementary school. The federal government issued guidelines for school desegregation, and at coffee mornings and PTA meetings I agreed with other mothers that the schools were being asked to fix problems that had been created by the larger United States society, especially by residential and job segregation. But we had to start somewhere; I joined a citywide parent-teacher committee to help work out solutions.

Minneapolis's solution, both to shrinking enrollment and to mandatory desegregation, was to redraw school districts and make sure several educational alternatives were available in each one. Some children could go to their neighborhood schools, but most would be bused. In the poorest schools, in neighborhoods where most African-American and Native American children lived, jazzy alternative programs were developed to appeal to middle-class white parents: open schools, continuous-progress schools, even a free school. Money was spent on building and remodeling, on carpets, computers and teachers' aides. Traditional schools were expected to appeal to families of all colors. High schools developed magnet programs. Busing was free to all; any child could choose any school in the district, as long as the school's population remained within desegregation guidelines.

Working this out took a few years, and meanwhile the city's school-age population kept decreasing as white families moved out to farther and farther suburbs, into housing developments made possible by federally funded highways and built with cheap Federal Housing Authority (FHA) money. Minnesota's populations of color increased during the decades after the Vietnam War as Vietnamese, Lao, Hmong and Latin-American families came, often with the sponsorship of local churches. During the 1970s, public schools opened and closed like the doors in *Laugh-In*'s joke wall.

Our daughters both graduated from West High, an old Minneapolis institution. Black kids from the North Side, many of whom had been bused to elementary schools in the district, were bused to West, but their participation in the sports and social life of the school was curtailed by busing schedules. In eighth and ninth grade, our eldest daughter had an African-American best friend, Tammy, but when the girls were in tenth grade Tammy's family moved to the suburbs. After our second daughter graduated, in 1982, West High closed.

Our son went to a different school almost every year of his life, graduating in 1985 from North High, in the old neighborhood near where we had first lived. The school now had about a three-fourths majority of African-American students. He had gone to North for the film and television magnet program, and his social life during high school concentrated on all-ages punk-rock shows. North was a locked school, with armed security guards, in a neighborhood where the extralegal drug business was the only equal-opportunity employer. At his graduation, most of the academic honors went to the minority of white and Asian-American students.

Everyone in our family understands that desegregating the schools alone can't desegregate U.S. society, and that liberals like us haven't yet come up with effective ways to combat racist policies and practices. You have to start somewhere, but it often seems as though every tiny gain we make is wiped out and every new start is from scratch.

I've also begun to understand the complicated ways that race, class and gender are braided together. My parents called black men "gentlemen" as their way of acknowledging the special, atrocious oppression of lynching, but they were not sensitive to the race-based sexual oppression of black women. As a feminist, I need to be clear about the ways in which race and class interact with sexual fantasies—I would call gender a sexual fantasy—in our violent culture.

When I asked my children to think about the messages they got about race and racism while they were growing up, they gave three very different answers—unsurprising, since even with the same parents, every child grows up in a different family. Our elder daughter, a graduate student of anthropology, said, "The fact that you had friends who were people of color—that we saw black and Asian faces in our house—was more important than anything you said." She has always had close friends of color, and she has chosen to concentrate on West Africa as her area of study.

Our younger daughter, the middle child, said, "You wouldn't ever let us use those words. I remember you didn't care that much if we swore, but we couldn't say racial names or call people white trash." She works in feature film production, which these days is a fairly multiracial, international business, and she hires associates from the Spike Lee production company, Forty Acres and a Mule.

Our son, a filmmaker, said, "You wanted to make sure we knew what was going on. I remember your telling us our teachers were wrong, the TV was wrong; you wanted us to know what was going on with black people and Indian people." He makes music videos for all kinds of groups—rap, hip-hop, funk, rock.

The day I wrote these words, I bicycled through a park near The School for Young Children, past a crocodile of children of different colors escorted by men and women teachers, white, black, and brown. Sophie died several years ago, but the school she founded has survived, and it finally looks as if it might be worthy of her high ideals.

When I'm around my friends' children and my children's friends, especially on the streets of New York or San Francisco, I can almost recapture that naive vision of a color-blind world—except that instead of a beige sameness, I see what my husband calls "world faces" on people who identify with many different forms of ethnic heritage. They seem like true citizens of the world. Then I remember that the world is convulsed with violence, and that the owners of mass media prefer to have us believe that racial and ethnic conflict produces violence, rather than the true culprit: the criminal maldistribution of abundance. So I'll treasure the small gains and go on doing liberal things, giving money, making phone calls, writing letters, going to meetings and demonstrations, and doing my best to make sure that any project I'm part of is racially inclusive. It won't solve the world's problems—it won't end racism—but you have to start somewhere.

Undoing the Smile

NANCY BUTCHER

My childhood was divided between Tokyo, Japan, and Akron, Ohio: two cities with little in common except for the fact that I didn't belong in either. If I'd been completely American or completely Japanese, things might have been a little simpler for me, but as it was, my American name, my Japanese face and my mixed parentage—American father, Japanese mother—didn't play well on either side of the Pacific. I tried not to dwell on that too much while I was growing up, though, attempting instead to accept my mother's philosophy of thinking only positive thoughts . . . and smiling a lot. It wasn't until I was much older that I was able to look at my life more clearly. It occurred to me then that my mother had never been a happy person.

Perhaps she was as unhappy as she was because of her relentless optimism. She always kept her troubles to herself, and she encouraged the rest of us, tacitly, to do the same. It was the Japanese way. Which is why, when I came face to face with racism for the first time, I didn't tell anybody about it. I suppressed the memory of that experience, and other experiences like it, for a very long time.

It happened in 1967. I was six years old. My parents had decided to send me to America for the summer; at the time, we lived in Musashi-Koganei, a residential area on the outskirts of Tokyo. The plan was for me to stay with my American grandparents in Ohio and improve my English. My father disliked my "pidgin English": English peppered with Japanese phrases, English like "More hamburgers *kudasai*" and "He is *honto-ni* stupid." And so I was packed off to Ohio, alone, with a stewardess hired to watch over me on the plane. It turned out to be a fruitful trip; by the end of the summer, I was extremely fluent in English, to the point where I had nearly forgotten my Japanese. And I loved America.

But America didn't exactly love me. One day, a girl I often played with—a slim, blond girl my age—came up to me in the park and said in a fierce voice: "You caused Pearl Harbor."

I was devastated. I had no idea what Pearl Harbor was, but I could tell that it was something bad. Looking back, I'm sure she had no idea what Pearl Harbor was, either. Most likely her parents had instructed her not to play with "that Jap girl." "The Japs are no good," they'd probably said to her at the dinner table. "At Pearl Harbor, they killed thousands of innocent people . . . "

That incident was the first of many that led to my complex about being an outsider. Being shunned by that girl was a terrible experience for me, and I developed a tremendous need to assimilate. It didn't occur to me then, or for a long time after that, to be angry, to fight back. In the face of racism, my reaction was shame—shame coupled with an intense desire to please, to make up for who I was. Somehow, my slanted eyes, dark hair and round cheeks were proof that the girl, and others like her, were right. I was different, inferior.

Three years later, we moved to America permanently. That is, my mother, my little brother Arthur and I did—my father stayed behind in Tokyo. He and my mother had been separated for a while and were just beginning divorce proceedings. That my parents decided to switch countries was explained to me this way: My father wanted to remain in Japan, where he felt more at home than in America, and my mother wanted to take advantage of American public schools, rather than continue to pay the exorbitant tuitions of private English-language schools in Japan.

When I was older, my mother told me what had really happened.

One day, while she was riding on the subway with blond-haired, almond-eyed Arthur in tow, some drunk old Japanese man had called her a *pan-pan:* the Japanese whore of an American G.I.

There were other factors prompting her to leave Japan, but that incident was the deciding one. And it wasn't because she couldn't bear the thought of coexisting with bigots like the drunk man. It was because she couldn't live with the shame of being labeled a *pan-pan*—couldn't impose this dishonor on her parents. Just as I had done with the little girl in the park, my mother had taken the dagger of racism and pointed it in the wrong direction.

Of course, moving to America didn't help matters much. My mother, now thousands of miles away from her parents, could shelter them from shame and dishonor, could sugar-coat her new life in her frequent, cheery letters, but the reality was there were even more racists in Ohio than in Japan, or at least they were more open about it. People either ostracized her outright or treated her as though she were stupid and helpless. Even her friends teased her frequently about her stilted English and Japanese accent. ("Mitsuko's favorite beer is *Lolling Lock*," they'd say to each other, howling.)

As for me, I was getting the same sort of treatment at school. The local paper decided to do a story about me and three of my fourth-grade classmates—a girl from Italy and two brothers from Guatemala—because we were all "foreigners." (The reporter asked me to wear a kimono for the accompanying photograph, as though this were something I wore to class every day.) And once the word was officially out that I was half Japanese, I never heard the end of it from my classmates. They began calling me "Chink," squinting their eyes and bowing whenever they saw me, and yelling "Ah-So!" I was devastated and humiliated by this, but determined not to show it, and so I simply smiled every time I got teased. I wanted to let my classmates know I could take a joke, that I could be pleasant and accommodating about it all, that I was really one of them.

As the years went by, my classmates outgrew the Chinks and the Ah-Sos. I, however, did not outgrow my smiling, pleasant, accommodating manner. In high school and college, my boyfriends were often asked what "Orientals" were like in bed, and it never occurred to me to be angry. And once, while riding in a cab in Chicago, the driver asked me where I was from. When I explained cheerfully that I was half Japanese, he informed me that he'd never had sex with a Japanese girl. By then, we had arrived at my apartment building, so I took this to mean that he would accept such an experience in lieu of payment. And my response? I handed him the full fare plus tip and scurried out of the cab.

Being the victim of racism doesn't necessarily prevent one from becoming a racist. This insight became very important when, at the age of thirty, I got married and started thinking about having children.

I never had any intention of marrying a Japanese man. As far as I was concerned, they were all cold and unemotional—like my Uncle Terukazu, who would come home at nine or ten o'clock at night and head straight for the living room without kissing my Aunt Yoko hello, without even uttering a greeting. He would hunker down in front of the television set or open up the paper and wordlessly scarf down the elaborate dinner my aunt had prepared and kept warm for him: a grilled steak, rice, *miso* soup, pickles and a great deal of *sake*.

Of course, it never occurred to me that I was generalizing like crazy. Or that men all over the world had problems being warm and cuddly and communicative. Never mind that my own father—a white man, born and raised in Ohio—was far colder and more unemotional than Uncle Terukazu. Never mind that many younger Japanese guys had no problems being loving and demonstrative.

There was also the issue of physical attractiveness. I did not find Japanese men attractive. I used to tell myself that there was no explaining it, that attraction was a mysterious thing. Who knew why I had a taste for tall, lanky men with blond hair and blue eyes? Or why, the only time I ever dated a Japanese-American man, he seemed to me more like a brother than a lover? It never dawned on me that my romantic archetypes had been shaped by years of conditioning, by countless hours of watching television shows and films in which the heroes were always white men (and the Japanese men were usually sexless computer nerds, machinelike business executives, or evil soldiers slaughtering Americans). It also didn't help that during my sexually formative years in Ohio, I didn't know any Japanese or Japanese-American boys. The most popular, desirable guys—all the guys, *period*—were white. Besides, I had learned from hard experience that being Japanese-American was a deficit, something that detracted from my power and worth as a human being. I must have known on some level that the way to achieve power and worth was to hook up with a *white* boyfriend—not with someone else like me.

When I first met my husband, Philip, I didn't think about the color of his skin. I didn't tell myself: "Wow, what a cute white guy." To me, whiteness was the norm, the given, the thing-to-be-taken-for-granted. But his whiteness, and his family's wealth and class, must have trickled into my awareness and increased his desirability in my eyes. This is not to say I didn't fall in love with him for who he is. It's just that "who he is" is a complicated thing, especially for people like me who aren't color- or class-blind.

Shortly after our marriage, Philip and I started talking about having children. The subject filled us with elation, anxiety, dread. He wasn't sure we were ready, financially or emotionally. I had the same concerns and an extra one as well. I was worried about having a baby with Asian features, a baby who might grow up to be teased, tormented and treated like some exotic sex toy just as I had been.

I tried to impress this upon Philip. "What are you going to do when our son comes home from school in tears because someone called him a 'Chink'?" I asked him. "What are you going to do when some sleazebag cab driver propositions our daughter?" I wanted to convince him of how *bad* it could feel, he who had never been the victim of prejudice. I wanted him to realize that we had a serious job ahead of us: raising our child to be able to fend off the blows of racism in a way I had never been able to do.

But Philip never seemed too fazed. He'd witnessed prejudice, but he wasn't me; he didn't have my history, my personal baggage. Racism got him angry, but he didn't lose sleep over it. He also didn't think it likely our baby would look very Asian.

It turned out he was right about the last part. In April 1995, I gave birth to our son, Christopher Kenji. He came after nine months of a blissfully easy pregnancy and a day of labor involving hellish medical complications. He was nine pounds seven ounces, twenty-three inches and about as far from an Asian baby as a baby can get: red hair, blue eyes, just the faintest golden suggestion of eyebrows and eyelashes, and porcelain-white skin. (Genetics is a strange thing: the woman in the labor room next to mine was half Japanese, and her husband was white. When I saw their baby, I was astonished: He looked completely Japanese, with fuzzy black hair, large, almond-shaped brown eyes and tawny skin.)

So much for all my worries. Christopher will pass through life like his father: a white (and, we hope, well-off) male, untouched by the sting of racism. We won't have to warn him about kids yelling "Ah-So!" or accusing him of causing Pearl Harbor. We won't have to condition him not to play doormat to bigots. And we won't have to teach him to be proud of his differentness rather than ashamed of it.

Or will we? Since we live in a predominantly white community, Christopher may get some flak for having a Japanese-American mother—echoes of what my mother and brother experienced on the Tokyo subway so many years ago. And of course, there are issues besides race. Christopher may end up preferring dolls to trucks, or poetry to sports, or otherwise behave in some way that sets him apart from his peers. When he is older, he may discover that he is gay or bisexual. Contrary to my deeply entrenched beliefs, being white and male isn't necessarily a ticket to an easy life (although it's a big help).

We will also have to teach Christopher how not to be a racist himself. For my part, this means taking a long, hard look at my own racism. I will have to undo the images and ideas I picked up from decades of mass-media brainwashing, from people I've met, from my parents and grandparents. I recoil now when I think about my American grandfather driving us home, instructing my brother and me to lock our doors because we were passing through the "colored" section; or my father insisting that blacks were genetically inferior to whites; or my mother saying about a Korean-American woman: "She's very pretty . . . for a Korean." And yet, despite my horrified reactions to these memories, I can't ignore the fact that I'm guilty, too. I still hold on to my stereotypes about Japanese men. I instinctively associate young black men with violence, and blacks in general with poverty. I have a habit of saying hello to the black strangers I pass on the street more than to anyone else. (I have this bizarre idea that they need my kindness.)

How will I get rid of my racism? Awareness, mostly—and writing about it, discussing the subject with my friends and family. I will also try to unlearn mistaken notions I have about people of color by reading books by and about them. And if these tools work for me, I can pass them on to Christopher.

And something else I want to pass on to Christopher is the idea that one must *fight* racism actively. I want Christopher—and Philip, too—to lose sleep over racism. I want to teach Christopher to write angry letters denouncing racist policies to newspapers, government officials, corporations and other institutions. When his friends make jokes or remarks at the expense of people of color, I want him to perform the awkward, separating act of speaking up.

I don't want Christopher to spend his life smiling in order to get along. I want him to develop a steely glare, a big mouth, some guts.

These days, I don't get harassed by racists much. Maybe it's because I don't exude raw masochism the way I used to; maybe it's because I hang out with a better crowd. I do meet a lot of what I call "benign" racists: people who are fascinated by my "exoticness," strangers who come up to me and ask me where I'm from. (When I reply "Ohio," just to be difficult, they sometimes persist: "No, I mean, where are you *from?*") I also get stared at a lot when I'm out strolling with Christopher. People stop, bend down toward the stroller with that googly grin they get when checking out babies, and do a double take: a quick glance at me, and then at him again. I'm sure they all think he's adopted or that I'm his nanny.

When Christopher was a few months old, Philip and I took him bowling. Our friends Jenn and Marc came along. A teenaged boy in the next lane kept watching us, at the way I would pick up Christopher when he cried. At one point, the boy frowned at Jenn—who is white and has red hair—and said in an accusing tone of voice: "Whose baby is that, anyway?" When Jenn quickly explained that I was Christopher's mother, he looked incredulous.

Sometime in the near future, I want to take Christopher to Tokyo to meet his Japanese relatives: his great-grandmother, his great aunts and uncles, his distant cousins. But deep down, I'm worried about what they'll think of him. Of course, they will be polite and kind; they're Japanese. When they met Philip for the first time—during a trip the two of us made to Tokyo in 1992—they bowed to him and thanked him profusely for my happiness. But will they accept Christopher as one of their own? Will they be able to see past his red hair and blue eyes and white skin, his unpronounceable name? Will they love him as much as they do my brother Arthur's two daughters, who are three-quarters Japanese?

But maybe these are my issues, not theirs. Maybe I'm the one who is fixated on skin color. I can't deny I'm still haunted by my history of being an outsider, of feeling too Japanese in America and too American in Japan. And as long as I anticipate every encounter, every situation with the belief that I (or Christopher or Philip) don't belong, I'm doomed to repeat the past. If and when the racist slight comes, I'll react with shame, not anger; with a smile, not a steely glare.

Christopher is almost a year old now: a beautiful, precocious baby. Looking at him, I'm sometimes overwhelmed by the responsibility of raising him. I want him to be happier than I was as a child, more confident, more secure. I want him never to know the pain of being ostracized, of being discriminated against because of who he is. I want him to grow up without a racist bone in his body.

And as for me? Nearly three decades have passed since I was six years old, staring with helpless bewilderment at the blond girl who accused me of causing Pearl Harbor. And yet that six-year-old self is still a part of me, as is the blond girl. But their voices are getting smaller, and the voice of my older, wiser self—the one who feels, finally, at home— is getting stronger all the time.

A Mother's Birth

PAULINE A. SANTOS

> *The night you were born I ceased*
> *being my father's boy and became*
> *my son's father.*
> —Henry G. Felsen, *To My Son in Uniform*

There is an irony in my commitment to use this quote. Obviously it would be more appropriate to my purposes had it been written by a mother about a daughter. Nonetheless, it is too fitting not to use, for it captures my transition from daughter to mother, a transition that dramatically altered my relationship with racism, with sexism and with my mother. This transition took place over the course of a decade, but it began with the birth of my daughter, when race and gender took on new meanings.

My earliest memory of racism came to me one day when Tonja, my first child, was just weeks old. I was bathing her in the kitchen sink of our apartment. Her small fists and legs were a blur of motion as she cooed and smiled her pleasure. I remember marveling at the perfection of her tiny body, the delicacy of her skin, as soft and as rich as coffee-colored satin. Gently covering her glistening body with the mildest soap on the softest cloth, I was suddenly overcome with sadness. As I squeezed my eyes shut against the unexpected tears, another bathing scene began to emerge.

A six-year-old black girl sits on the edge of a cracked, vinyl-padded chair in the center of a small kitchen. Her legs dangle as her feet do their best to reach the now nearly cold water in the galvanized tub in which she has just been given her Saturday night bath. She is shivering, and she, too, is squeezing her eyes shut. Perhaps this is because the oil stove cannot adequately heat the three small but drafty rooms. Then, too, it might be because she has just stepped out of the tub, beads of water still visible on her smooth brown skin. The towel she tries to wrap around her naked body is too small and threadbare to offer any absorbency or warmth.

Or perhaps the answer to her tears is somewhere else in the picture. There is a small but strong middle-aged white woman muttering under her breath and shaking her head disapprovingly as she scrubs the already-bathed black child—right knee, left knee, right ankle, left ankle—with a scouring pad. Timidly the black child tries to tell the white woman that maybe her knees and ankles are not still dirty—that maybe it's just her color. The white woman scrubs harder. It hurts, and tears begin to fall. This seems to make the white woman angrier, and she scrubs harder still. So the child just shivers and squeezes her eyes shut.

What is the relationship between this adult and this child? Who is this woman? A sadistic baby-sitter perhaps? No, the white woman is the black child's mother. Oh. Then she must be the proverbial mean stepmother or an adoptive parent gone bad. Perhaps a burned-out foster parent? No, she is the black child's biological white mother. Oh. Then, the white woman must hate the black man who fathered the child; maybe it was rape? No, the child's father has always been there; he and the woman are married. He's out right now, but it wouldn't make any difference if he were home. Oh. Maybe that's why the child shivers and squeezes her eyes shut against her tears.

My father was Cape Verdean (or black Portuguese, as natives of then-colony Cape Verde were called), and my mother was white Portuguese. They were married in a small New England town in the 1920s, a place where and a time when interracial unions were an aberration. My father worked until his retirement at a local textile mill; he died in 1983 at the age of eighty-nine. My mother was a housewife and a hypochondriac; she died in 1985 at the age of seventy-four.

I had always heard that when a woman becomes a mother, she develops a new appreciation of her own mother, more respect for a mother's sacrifices, a better understanding of a mother's love. My journey into motherhood took on different dynamics. The more comfortable I became with my role as mother, the more difficult the role of daughter became.

I was not aware of this shift as it occurred, or at least I convinced myself I was not. The quality of the two relationships became more and more polarized over a ten-year period, from 1975, the year Tonja was born, through 1985, the year my mother died. During that time, I managed to suppress any awareness or acknowledgment of what was happening. It was only with my mother's death that I was forced to confront my feelings because I found myself devoid of any emotion except anger. That scared me. What was I so angry about? How could I feel this way about my own mother? What horrible kind of daughter was I? How could I have such anger toward the woman who had "given me everything"?

This was not my first or last experience with death. My father had died two years earlier, and while my sense of loss was profound, our love and respect for each other helped ease my pain. My husband died two weeks before my mother. My grief, while great, was moderated by the anger I felt at the untimeliness of his death following what I still believe to have been an ill-advised liver biopsy. When my oldest friend informed me the following month that she had inoperable ovarian cancer, and when she died seven months later, I mourned the loss of that special relationship. Yet, when my mother died I felt nothing but anger—and guilt about that anger.

My difficulty coping with these feelings resulted in a new relationship. I started to see Sylvia, a therapist. With her sensitive and insightful guidance, I ever so slowly began to understand what had taken place over that past decade—that the more I witnessed how my love for my daughter nurtured her self-esteem and the more I saw her grow and flourish within the safety of that unconditional love, the more I was forced to acknowledge what I had not received from my mother. As bits of awareness rose to the surface, they were entangled in anger, resentment and an overwhelming sense of abandonment and deprivation. The knowing process has often been painful, but with Sylvia's gentle caring and her unwavering positive regard, it has been bearable. More important, it has been freeing.

My mother taught me that my blackness and my femaleness were two strikes against me. She convinced me these two "flaws" were somehow of my own making. She taught me I would get or not get what I deserved based on these two flaws, that I was to be thankful for whatever I did get and that I had to accept the limitations placed on me.

These teachings did not involve structured lessons on her part or conscious learning on mine. Rather, they were taught through the everyday interactions of our lives. Whether she was scrubbing my knees with a scouring pad, or scolding me for my "ashiness" or admonishing me to stay out of the summer sun so as not to get "even darker," the message was the same—my blackness was an embarrassing defect. Whether she was being less than hospitable to my father's relatives or calling him a "black bastard" when she was angry (which was often), the message was the same—the color of one's skin determines the respect to which she or he is entitled.

Sexism was blatant as well. My mother never hesitated to tell anyone, including me, that she wished all her children had been boys because girls were "nothing but trouble." When I turned sixteen, I had to beg to be allowed to complete high school because I was "just a girl." I had less success with my dream of attending college, however. Once again, I was told that not only was this "not necessary for a girl," but it was "foolish" as well.

As a result of this racist and sexist mothering, I fluctuated between no identity and an unacceptable identity. Being nursed on racism and sexism by someone so crucial to one's self-worth left me vulnerable to *anyone's* racism and sexism. In fact, "vulnerable" is too passive a word;

it was more an expectation and an acceptance of racism and sexism from whomever and wherever it came. The thought of fighting them, or even questioning them, was as foreign to me as was the thought of fighting or questioning my mother. After all, if you learn at your mother's breast that you are a second-class child, why would you question society's designation of you as a second-class citizen?

And then, on August 13, 1975, everything changed. It was the last time I did anything as my mother had done—I gave birth to a black female child. It was as if until that moment, until I was the birth mother of a black female child, I had been unaware of the impact my race and gender had had on my life. I have often thought that Tonja gave birth to me that day as much as I gave birth to her.

I knew Tonja's life had to be different. She had to be protected from racism and sexism. She had to be free to do as much as she could do, go as far as she could go, without any *one* or any *thing* putting barriers in her way. Initially I would provide that protection, but eventually she would have to protect herself. I had two major tasks. One was to overcome, at least on a functional level, my predisposition to accept racism and sexism, even if it meant acquiring bravado. I had to do this not only to protect Tonja, but to set an example for her as well. My second task was to arm her in such a way that she could protect herself against racism and sexism without limiting herself and without becoming embittered against the sometimes cruel world in which she would have to live. I could not change the external world, but I could help Tonja create an inner space within which self-inflicted racism and sexism could never take hold, and from which she could recognize, confront and defy external racism and sexism.

I was twenty-nine years old when Tonja was born, old enough to have figured out, to some degree, that it was neither my blackness nor my femaleness that made me such an easy mark for racism and sexism, but rather my low self-esteem and my lack of education. While I assumed it was too late for me (it was not, I would learn!), I vowed to arm Tonja with a positive sense of self and with the best education possible. My instincts told me that with these as a foundation, Tonja could build her life as she chose, not without *experiencing* racism and sexism, but *in spite* of them.

As best I knew how, I nurtured my daughter's self-esteem as she approached school-age. But it took only a moment one day to reinforce my instinct of how fragile a child's ego was. When Tonja was four or five years old, she said something to her older brother that I thought was especially inappropriate. I became very angry. She had stomped off into the living room and was perched, with arms folded across her chest, at the edge of a lounge chair. I marched up to her, bent over, firmly gripped each of her forearms with my strong hands, brought my face to within an inch of hers and asked, with squinting eyes and through clenched jaw, the proverbial "just who do you think you are!?" Unaccustomed to this bullying approach, Tonja instinctively cowered and said, in the smallest voice she could find, what she thought I wanted to hear—"Nobody, Mommy, I'm nobody!" For one horrific moment, I had become my mother, and it was me sitting there cowering. I recovered, and what had started out as a how-not-to-talk-to-your-brother-or-any one-else lecture was quickly edited into a how-you-are-never-to-believe-you-are-nobody lecture. The memory of that moment has stayed with me, however, as a reminder of the power we, as parents, have over our children's sense of worth. With one thoughtless question, I had risked destroying what had taken years to build.

Through a combination of our good fortune, my tenacity, Tonja's strong academic performance and the school's community scholarship program, I was able to enroll Tonja in Lincoln School, a private, all-female school, which she attended from the sixth through twelfth grades. Tonja's seven years at this exceptional school built on the foundation I had laid for her, teaching her not only to excel academically, but also to believe in herself and to strive to be a leader among women.

For me, those same seven years epitomized my precarious position in life. They highlighted the duality of my world and intensified my struggle to maintain balance as I walked with one foot in each sphere. One sphere was shaped by Tonja's and my day-to-day interactions with her predominantly white, predominantly affluent schoolmates and their families and the school's faculty and administrators, and by my own relationships, as legal secretary to an attorney specializing in estate planning, with a class of people who live very differently from me. The other was colored by my own issues with my race and gender and by the oppression and discrimination inherent in the double-jeopardy of being black and female in our society.

An incident on the day I was asked by the head of my daughter's school to consider serving on its board represents for me the reality of that double life. Although I was honored to have been asked, I knew I had to give it some serious thought, because as a single, working, schooling parent, I was perpetually short on time. I promised to make a decision within the next few days, and I thought about it on and off throughout that day. After work and before going home, I stopped at a local supermarket. As usual, I chose the checkout line that time forgot, and my mind wandered back to the question of whether or not I could effectively serve on this prestigious board. I am not sure how much time had passed when the young man at the register brought me re-soundingly back to earth with, "Hey, lady. You got any food stamps?"

So, while it took its toll in heart and soul, I assembled at assemblies, oohed and aahed at yet one more open house, patronized plays, applauded awards, conferred at conferences, grimaced at games, and partook of potlucks. I remember leaving work one day to attend a morning assembly at which Tonja, along with a number of her schoolmates, was to be recognized for some relatively small accomplishment. As she walked across the stage after receiving her ready-for-framing certificate, she lifted her head long enough to scan the audience quickly. I recognized the look; it brought me back to another ceremony many assemblies ago at which another thirteen-year-old girl scanned the audience with that same hopefulness in her eyes.

I still can't believe it. Any minute now Miss Carpenter's gonna call my name—my name! 1959 Senior Girl of the Year. I know she'll be here when they do. She just has to be. I mean, this is a real big deal. It isn't just the top award for this playground; it's the top award for every playground in the whole town of Bristol! Yeah, this is big. It's so hard to see into the crowd. The lights are too bright. That's why I can't see her. She's probably out there somewhere. Maybe if I look at each face really slowly I'll see her.

Oh, God, I think I'm gonna throw up. What'll I do if that happens? I'll just start running and never come back. Look how far away the table is. When they call my name, I have to walk all the way over there. What if I trip? Oh please, please, please, don't let me trip. I'll just die if I do. I can see my trophy! It's the one in the middle—the one that's taller than all the rest.

Wait 'til she sees it. I know she'll be proud.

What'll I say? I'll just say "Thank you." That's all I have to say.

Where is she? Please let me just see her once before they do it. But what if my voice doesn't work? What if I open my mouth and nothing comes out? Everyone will think I'm stupid.

Okay, God. I know I've been bothering you a lot today. But please, this is so important. Please don't let me trip or throw up or lose my voice, okay? I promise I'll be so, so good. I won't tease Rosemary, and I won't steal food in the middle of the night, and I won't say or do anything that'll make Mom have a sugar spell. Just please—this one night!

What? Hey, stop pushing, Sarah Paul. Oh, me? She's calling me? Oh my God—listen to them clap. I wonder if I'm blushing? Can they see my heart pounding? I hope not. The table is so far away. I have to watch where I'm going. I can't look around for her, or I'll fall.

Finally. It's mine. I'm holding it. Oh, no, she's telling me to stand here. Is it me she's saying all those nice things about? My shoelace is untied. Great. You know what, God? I'll trade— I'll take my chances with falling or throwing up or losing my voice. Just please, please, let her be here hearing this. Please.

It's over. All my friends want to see my trophy. That's okay because I'm gonna polish it when I get home anyway. It has my name on it. On a brass plate. Isn't it beautiful? My name will be in the Phoenix. *I still can't believe it.*

The lights aren't so bright now. And the crowd is smaller. I can see she's not here. Well, maybe my brother got in trouble again. Or maybe she had to yell at my sister for skipping out last night. Maybe her corns are hurting. I hope she didn't have one of her spells. Maybe she got company and wanted to come really bad but couldn't. I bet she's really sad she's not here. I'd better hurry up home. I bet she can hardly wait to see my trophy. I wonder where she'll put it? She's probably got a spot all picked out.

Tonja's eyes found mine; the soft, confident smile that appeared on her face said it all.

More than a few times I questioned my good intentions in placing Tonja at the Lincoln School. After all, I was forcing her, too, to straddle two worlds. Was it fair to place her in an atmosphere where she was always "different"? Was I misleading her into thinking that her female-ness would be as much a non-issue in the real world as it was at her school? Was I setting her up for disappointment by immersing her in this college-preparatory environment when I had no idea how I would finance a college education for her?

But my determination to provide her with the best education pos-sible won out, and Tonja graduated from Lincoln in 1993 on a picture-perfect summer's day. Parents, teachers, family and friends looked on proudly as twenty three young ladies in flowing white dresses crossed a green carpet of lawn to take their places beneath the protective branches of a majestic beech tree. The last vestiges of doubt evaporated into the sunlight as I listened to my daughter deliver the graduation address.

Earlier, in Tonja's junior year, I spent some time sitting across from her college advisor as she told me what a strong candidate Tonja was and how she would be able to almost pick her college. When I stam-mered something about tuitions, she said, "Mrs. Santos, certainly fi-nances are a consideration, but they should not be your first. I'm confident Tonja will be offered a number of attractive packages by the colleges to which I think she should apply—Mount Holyoke, Amherst, Smith, Bryn Mawr, Wellesley . . .

It is March 1963. A brown-skinned student sits across from Miss Bullock, college advisor. The office is suffocatingly small. The young girl finds it difficult to breathe, partly because of the smell of the polish that makes Miss Bullock's desk glisten, partly because of the overpowering smell of her perfume, which everyone hates, but mostly because the girl is terri-fied. A short but massively threatening woman, Miss Bullock makes most of the students cower. She glances at this student's file, one hand teasing

*the handkerchief she keeps tucked between her breasts, the other fondling
the chain around her neck that attaches to her glasses. The lump in the
young girl's throat swells as Miss Bullock lowers her head, slides her
glasses down to the edge of her nose, and peers over them at her:*

— *Well, Pauline, I assume you have a job to go to after you graduate?*
— *You mean for the summer, Miss Bullock? Not yet.*
— *No. No. Not just for the summer. A job. A full-time job. I heard they're
looking for help at Smith's. You're seventeen, aren't you?*
— *Not yet, Miss Bullock, but I will be next month. But, uhm, well, I was
thinking that maybe I could get a job just for the summer, and then
maybe I could go to college in September?*
— *College? For what? And where would you go?*
— *Uhm, maybe Bryant?*
— *Oh. Well. Hmm. I suppose you could get a secretarial job in the city.*
— *Well, umh, I was thinking that maybe I could go into the teacher edu-
cation program? I think I'd like to teach accounting? I love it, and Mr.
Candelmo says I'm really good . . .*
— *Teach? You want to teach? Where, Pauline? Where would you teach?
You certainly couldn't teach in Bristol. Perhaps in Providence, I sup-
pose . . .*
— *But, why . . . ?*
— *And anyway, how could you go to Bryant? Your family doesn't have
any money. And speaking of your family, your mother was supposed
to be here today!*

. . . Swarthmore, Colby, Bates, Haverford and Middlebury." And we visited each of those colleges that summer. Sometimes my then twelve-
year-old daughter came along; more often it was just Tonja and me, or
so we thought. It was a summer of rolling green hills, ivy-covered walls,
and parking lots that looked like Volvo dealerships. During each visit I
donned my bravado long enough to meet the people who were to interview Tonja, and then I would slip into the background (as much as that
is possible for a large black woman in such surroundings). Usually I

would find my way outdoors where I would wait for Tonja. I let her believe this was for her benefit, that I was giving her the space and the freedom to experience each college for herself. While this was partly true, I needed to be alone as much as Tonja needed to be left alone.

I would leave Tonja to fend for herself in order to deal with another child who managed to sneak along on every trip, no matter how hard I tried to leave her behind. My inner child made each of these trips a bittersweet mix of excitement and resentment, contentment and deprivation, pride and shame, faith and fear. No matter how I tried to reason with this stowaway child, she embarrassed the parent in me with her neediness. And then I remembered another parent who had always been embarrassed by this child. I remembered the origins of this child's neediness. So, instead of trying to send her away, I embraced her. I took what I had learned as a mother and began the ongoing task of undoing what I had learned as a daughter.

Nurturing Antiracism

A Permeation of Life

YOLANDA FLORES NIEMANN

As a Tejana, a Mexican-American woman who was raised in Texas, I have been aware of racism from the time I started school and was disciplined and ridiculed for speaking Spanish, my first language. Racism was something I took for granted until its effects began to shatter the innocence of my gentle, firstborn child. With salient awareness I then ceased to just "live and let live" and vowed to do all in my power to eradicate racism. Today I "mother" against racism as a marriage partner and parent of two children and as a college professor who teaches undergraduate students and is directly involved in the training of graduate students. This essay focuses on how this "mothering" takes place, and my successes and failures with it.

Mothering Children Against Racism

My initial keen awareness of the insidious effects of racism began when my firstborn child, then barely seven years old, referred to a busload of black school children as "niggers." As I gently questioned this loving child about the use of the racial slur, it became clear he did not know what it meant, that he knew only that his friends said it, and it meant something bad. He said, "I don't know what it means; it means *them;* they're niggers, that's all—everybody says so!" "Everybody," referred to his Catholic school friends. I was very surprised because a couple of his African-American male school buddies had attended his recent birthday party. I asked him then who else his friends talked about, and he replied that they also talked about "meskins." "Yeah," he said, "they make fun of niggers and meskins."

Before I proceed with this story, some explanation for my son's naiveté is in order. My children are biracial—Mexican-American (my ethnicity) and Anglo-American (their father's ethnicity). Both of them have much of their father's light coloring, especially my son, who has light skin, blond hair and green eyes. Without knowing who their mother is, most people would assume by looking at them that they are Anglo-American. Indeed, when my son was an infant, I was often asked if I was the family maid or nanny. It seemed inconceivable to people that an olive-skinned woman could be *that* child's mother.

My children have very close relationships with my extended family members, many of whom speak mostly Spanish, and of course, we had casually mentioned to our son that he was Mexican-American, but up until that point we had never deliberately discussed racial issues with our children. My husband and I had thought it best to put off these discussions until our children were more mature and better able to understand the complexity of the issues. But now I had no choice. I gently said to my son, "Don't you realize that you are Mexican-American; that *you* are one of the people you and your friends have been making fun of?" He was very still for about thirty seconds. Then he looked up and said, "I'm not Mexican, *you are!*" I replied, "No, you are my son, that makes *you* Mexican-American, too." Once again he was still for several seconds, and then he began sobbing—big, heart-wrenching tears running down his cheeks. I put my arms around him, and he said, "But I don't want to be one of *them;* everybody makes fun of them!"

I realized then it had been a mistake not to discuss my son's biracial identity with him. We could have instilled ethnic pride in him and warned him that not all people respect differences, bracing him somewhat for the cruel words he was sure to hear. Some loving preparedness might have made his pain less intense. Instead of protecting him, we had left him wide open, defenseless and taken by surprise. We might have predicted that, since he looks white, he would experience and hear about more racism than if he looked Latino. My husband and I know from experience that many racist white persons don't seem to monitor their behavior around whites as much as they do around people of color. I felt like I had failed my son.

For a short time after this incident we had several family discussions about racism. We answered our children's questions about members of different groups as best we knew how and spoke to them about the advantages of being biracial, such as having the best of both worlds. Our children quickly became bored with these discussions, and the topic was moved to the background, with other nonessential parts of daily life. It wasn't long, however, before racism caused pain in our family once again.

When our son was nine years old we moved to a different neighborhood. Most of the children from the area did their swimming at a private club most locals refer to as "The Lodge," which is about five minutes from the neighborhood. Our son was soon invited to join his new neighborhood friends for swimming. By this time, I knew of the racist, white only, policies of The Lodge. So, of course, I told my son he could not go there. My husband and I explained to him that a person who is of mixed racial heritage would not be welcomed at The Lodge. He naively replied that it would be okay, because he looks white, and besides, his friends wanted him along. We then explained to him that it would be against our values to support a racist organization. He begged and pleaded for us to let him go, even offering to insist that his new friends invite some of his black friends from school. As we held our ground, his loneliness on spring weekends and summers pained us. It was true that virtually all of the neighborhood boys his age, his playmates, spent their spring weekends and summer days at The Lodge, leaving him without playmates during the days and on some evenings. He was lonely on those days. Some of his friends also made fun of him for not being allowed to accompany them; he was once called a "nigger lover." After about a month, he stopped mentioning The Lodge. He seemed resigned to the fact that we would not change our minds, though it was clear that he often thought about his situation. For me and my husband, the summer days our son spent alone were a constant reminder of how racism was affecting our lives.

Over the years our son has grown to take pride in his ethnic heritage, usually identifying himself as a Mexican American on the first day of each school year. He jokes that he can't win. In middle school he was called a "wannabe," that is, someone who wants to be Mexican-American, by some of his Mexican-American schoolmates who had trouble believing that someone so blond was half Mexican-American. Now seventeen, he seems to take it all in stride, and sometimes expresses astonishment that so many people are overtly racist. He has internalized antiracist values and simply does not tolerate racism when he recognizes it. He holds his ground and defends people of color when those around him make racist statements. The patient and loving nurturance we gave him has allowed him to be secure in his identity.

Our daughter, three years younger than her brother, has taken everything in. Though she is not as blond as her brother, she has green eyes and is often asked "What are you?" This question at first confused her, but now she understands that people seem to need to categorize and label. She listened carefully throughout her brother's ordeal, and one day when she was about nine years old she told us she had been invited to The Lodge by a friend, but had said no. She had explained to her friend that her family believes that racism is wrong and does not support racist organizations. She, too, had to learn to spend time alone when her friends were at The Lodge.

I am proud of both of my children. They have learned from their personal pain that racism hurts. They have internalized antiracist values and attempt to pass them on to their peers. Letting our children understand that we hold our ground when it comes to our values has reaped rewards. Through these painful experiences, they have learned about values and their importance. They are mature beyond their years for consistently taking time to think about their values and those of others, and how those values are manifested through behavior. As a family, we share a bond around the issue of racism. As important, our "mothering" has given our children the confidence to "mother" others against racism. Ironically, dealing with this ugly and divisive issue together with love and patience has enriched our lives and strengthened our family unit.

Mothering a Marriage Against Racism

The ethnic differences between me and my husband have affected our nineteen-year marriage in unpredicted ways. We knew from the time we were dating that some differences which other couples take for granted we would have to be conscious of and discuss. For instance, we are worlds apart in our expression of emotion. In my traditional Mexican-American family, indulgent emotional expressiveness was the norm. In his German-American family, the norm was calm and "rational" verbalization. We learned early in our relationship that neither mode of expression was "right," they were just different, and we learned to value our cultural differences for the richness they added to our relationship. We learned to pay attention to each other, lest we miss some important piece of communication because it was not delivered in our familiar emotional mode. What has been more difficult for us to share is pain and frustration around overt and covert racism we both encounter.

My husband was raised by parents who seem to have internalized institutional racism, while believing they have rejected personal racism. That is, they do not behave in an overtly racist manner, yet they do not seem to question racial inequities in areas that affect quality of life, like employment, education and housing. As such, they seem to be unconscious of their own racism. Having been raised with that lack of conscious awareness, my husband had not given much thought to racism or to the effects of racism on members of nonwhite ethnic groups. Like many well-meaning, unaware whites, he naively believed that racism was a thing of the past, taken care of by the civil rights movement of the 1960s. However, through his relationship with me, he began to learn that racism was quite rampant in both subtle and overt forms.

For instance, when we were considering buying our first property, we separately stopped after work to make formal inquiries in an area we'd admired and discussed living in. Unplanned, we had both stopped on the same day, missing each other by about fifteen minutes. Meeting at home, we had very different tales to tell. I disappointedly reported that I'd stopped at the property and was told that all the homes were sold. My visit had been very short; I wasn't even shown the interior of any of the properties. Amazed, he told me that he, too, had stopped. He'd been shown *three* available properties! Since I was in business attire and wearing my wedding ring, nonracist reasons for the behavior of the property managers were ruled out. That was his first concrete evidence that racism was alive and well in Houston, his birthplace. However, that experience and others did not make him as vigilant as I'd hoped.

My husband is an avid golfer, and it often made me angry that he never inquired about the membership policies regarding race at the golf clubs he patronized. In spite of our experiences to the contrary, he wanted to continue to assume that club policies were nonracist, except when contradictory evidence was undeniable. For years, I failed our relationship by keeping my anger about his passive stance to myself. One day I surprised and challenged him by stating that anyone who didn't inquire about club membership policies vis-à-vis racism didn't care about the extent and effects of racism. He was hurt and frustrated. Thanks to our strong relationship, we very quickly began to discuss the issue more. When I explained I felt he didn't care about racism toward me, our children or my family when he patronized possibly racist clubs, he immediately became more sensitive, and began inquiring about club membership policies before accepting invitations to play. To his surprise, he learned of clubs in town with white-only policies. They had always been there; he had just never before had to know about them.

My husband now understands that white people have the privilege of not having to know about racism, while people of color must know, sometimes to survive. Still, challenging racist attitudes and behaviors is sometimes very awkward for him, since he both works and plays in networks of "good old white boys." His work is in the construction area, and he plays golf at country clubs. In both these domains it seems to be a given that a group member does not express disdain at racial jokes told in the context of that group. To go against this norm is risky, especially since the family's economic well-being is in the hands of some of these "good old boys," who are also racist.

The racism my husband has personally experienced against whites has usually been the direct result of my academic work, which deals with stereotypes and intergroup relations. He has participated in discussions in which *all* white males are blamed for past and current racism and accused of deliberate oppression of all other people, especially people of color. He is frustrated by such a stance and points out that stereotyping all whites as racist is also racism. And, of course, if I don't also point this out, he becomes frustrated with me and feels hurt by me and by the group.

Our success as a couple on the issue of racism has been in learning to share pain, anger and frustration. We have also succeeded in learning to support each other's antiracist attitudes, even if the expression of those attitudes is not always as open and consistent as we would each like for it to be. My husband's willingness to take risks by openly taking a stand against racism in unfriendly situations has enhanced my respect for him and our commitment to each other. Again, dealing openly with this painful and divisive issue has enriched my marriage by increasing our meaningful communication.

Mothering College Students Against Racism

As an assistant professor of psychology, I have developed a cultural psychology course at an urban university with an ethnic makeup that is approximately 60 percent white, 12 percent African-American, 13 percent Mexican-American, 10 percent Asian-American, and 6 percent foreign nationals. The theoretical underpinning of the course is the idea of subjective construal. That is, I emphasize the idea that understanding the perspective of the other is crucial to communicating, working and living together in harmony. I emphasize that it is especially important to understand how another's perspective is shaped by social, personal and institutional racism toward members of historically oppressed groups. The class is interactive by design. I facilitate, or mother, this learning; I do not lecture.

I begin each class by asking students their opinions of assigned readings, which include sometimes controversial theories about ethnic differences and racism. It is not a politically correct class. My success in mothering students against racism through this class has come through my courage to let students speak their minds. They are not tested in such a manner as to have to regurgitate information. Instead, grades are based on class participation, outlining of readings and group presentations. In that manner, students are encouraged to express their feelings and thoughts about theories and readings related to cultural differences.

Students express anger, hope, frustration and sorrow at what they hear from their peers in class. They don't often like what they hear, but they learn. For example, white students learn about black students' anger at white privilege; black students learn about young whites' frustration at being blamed for racism beyond their control. Latinas/os learn and talk about pride in their indigenous heritage, coupled with red, white and blue Americanism. All students learn about the pain and courage of homosexual identity. They begin to understand the quietness of Asian females, not as a weakness, but as a cultural value. Each semester I "mother," with pride, forty students in this class. Of course, this learning is transmuted, in one form or another, to all other psychology classes I teach, and from my students to other students.

Teaching a course that deals directly with racism takes an emotional toll on me. The hour and a half in front of the class is intense. I must be prepared to facilitate any situation in what is often an emotion-charged atmosphere. My reward comes from watching the students develop before my eyes. Their understanding of and respect for one another increase as the semester progresses. Many students have taken the time at the end of a semester to tell me how much they learned from the course and how they apply their learning to their daily lives. Since the vast majority of students respond very positively to the course, as evidenced by my excellent teaching evaluations, I consider my teaching of this course an incredible success.

Of course, an acceptance of and respect for differences is not a value incorporated by all my students. Nevertheless, I am one of only a few Mexican-American professors on campus, and thus I also serve as a role model of someone who does not fit the negative stereotype of Mexican Americans. As such, I can affect students' attitudes simply by behaving toward them in a professional, dignified and sensitive manner.

As a social psychologist working in a research institution, I also train graduate students. Students who work with me learn a great deal about racism through our research. My research, and theirs, centers on stereotypes and the effects of stereotypes on interethnic group relations and on self-identity. These graduate students, who come from all parts of the United States, are constantly amazed at the racist attitudes subjects relay in the laboratory and in our community research. This learning is creating in them a desire to focus their future research on understanding the underpinnings of racism, in hopes of helping to eliminate racism.

Once again, nurturing others through the pain of racism has enriched my life more than I can say. That I am facilitating vigilance of racism, and antiracist values and behaviors of my husband, children, students and future psychologists and academicians, which they are passing on to others, helps me to know that I am making a positive difference in the world. For me there can be few greater rewards.

Unpacking the White
Privilege Diaper Bag

JENNIFER E. MORALES

My husband called me at work one day last summer, hot and ticked off.

"The diaper bag's been stolen," he said.

"What?" I asked. "Who would steal a *diaper bag*?"

John had left the bag in the backyard next to the garage door as he put our son Anansi in the car. He drove away without the bag, and by the time he realized he didn't have it and returned, forty-five minutes had passed—long enough for someone going down our alley to find it and take it away. It was the thief's lucky day: Ours was probably the only diaper bag in the neighborhood with an expensive (and borrowed) video camera in it.

An hour later, with Anansi in a sling over my shoulder, I was walking down the alleys checking garbage cans. Of course they took the camera, I thought, but maybe they ditched the bag and the baby equipment inside.

We live in Riverwest, a multiracial, multigenerational neighborhood in Milwaukee, Wisconsin—an anomaly in one of the most intensely segregated cities in the United States. Riverwest is one of the few areas in the city where mixed-race families can settle in relative social comfort, and many do. We also have a melange of African-American, white, Latino and Asian-American households. Nevertheless, on the day our diaper bag was stolen, most of the neighbors I encountered were older whites who were happy to offer racist speculations about the kind of person who would steal a baby's bag.

I stopped every person I saw to ask if they had seen anything suspicious. Yes, they all had, but none of their suspicions had anything to do with our diaper bag in particular. If someone stole something, they told me, as a general rule that someone was black.

"You have to be careful because black people walk down this alley a lot," one white man warned me.

"White people steal things, too," I said, but it went right over his head.

I had said nothing radical, just a statement to signal to him that I was not going to play the Game. (The rules of the Game: You say something bad about black people; I say something bad about black people; we pat each other on the back and go our separate ways, affirmed and fulfilled.) Still, he couldn't hear me resisting his invitation to join in, and my reward was a blank stare, as if he were awaiting further instructions from a coach I couldn't see.

The next few neighbors were no better, though most confined themselves to euphemisms or a nod in a western direction, the direction of the inner city.

I never found the diaper bag, but I did find out something about how my life had changed since becoming a parent. As I rocked my son in his sling while my neighbors clouded the air around us, I realized that although I have worked against racism (as far as I was conscious of it) all my life, in becoming a mother I was now responsible for fighting racism "for two."

What Are You?

Not that our life, even in a less racist environment, would ever be uncomplicated by race. As a white-appearing, multiracial person, I have struggled with questions of racial identity for as long as I can remember. And by marrying a white-appearing man and producing white-appearing children, I have guaranteed all of us a long life of this struggle.

Consciousness of my racial heritage—a quarter Filipina, a quarter Mexican and one-half northern European—came early to me, and I reveled in it. As a child, I embraced the material and linguistic cultures of Mexico, the Philippines and, sometimes, Ireland, the country of origin of most of my European ancestors. I learned Spanish; I visited the islands; I baked broonie and boiled cabbage. To the question, "What are you?" I joyfully answered, "All of it."

My four sisters, all much older than I, found other answers to that question. One became an orthodox Jew, adopting a Jewish name and setting down roots in a closely knit Hassidic community in Chicago. Another, a lesbian who fought through a tumultuous adolescence to come to terms with her sexual orientation, lives as a person white by default. Issues of race do not challenge her, and she feels comfortable sharing in the racism that surrounds her as a white-appearing American. A third actively rejects our nonwhite ancestry, particularly the Mexican part, and the fourth claims our heritage proudly but apolitically.

I have the feeling that my sisters came to their identities in the same way I did, by battling with the painful reality that a multiracial individual belongs many places at once and nowhere completely.

I don't blame any of my sisters for making the choices they have, although they are not what I have chosen, which is to fight. I fight with myself over what cultural attributes and legacies I can honestly claim and what is merely wishful appropriation. I fight my own white privilege[1] and the systems that create and offer it to me. I fight the racism that has seeped into my consciousness and which the oppressor in me still sometimes subtly accepts. I even fight with the notion of race altogether and wrestle with the conflicting societal messages that race matters very much and shouldn't matter at all.

Many of these fights broke out in me when I entered college. I attended a fairly progressive liberal arts college in the Midwest. On my first registration form I was asked to mark a single box for my race/ethnicity. I marked "other." A few semesters later, my records stated that I was "Hispanic." I hadn't authorized the change. Some person on the registrar's staff had decided, presumably on the basis of my last name, what I am. Engrossed as I was in my studies and in my activism in the women's and environmental movements on campus, I didn't take the time to do anything about it. But I did store the implications in my memory for later: Your identity is fragile; others can define it for you.

In my junior year, I became involved in the multicultural curriculum movement. Fueled by an intense workshop with antiracist consultant Kesho Scott, a multiracial group of students formed an organization to promote the integration of multicultural materials into every department. When racial and sexual tensions within the group began to heat up (somehow the straight, white males had ended up running the show), I was invited to join the women of color caucus to help figure out what should be done. "I'm a woman of color?" I thought to myself. "Sure, why not?" But the designation didn't fit well. I went to a few meetings of the caucus, eventually retiring from the group altogether. I wasn't a woman of color; I was a multiracial woman. Some of the issues were different, and there was no getting around them for me just then.

After college there were more forms to fill out. On my marriage license application I am listed as "Hispanic" because the state would not process the form until we answered the "optional" race question at the bottom of the page—and selected only one. My husband, white-appearing though adopted and uncertain of his race, checked "white," and they accepted our application. On our children's birth certificates, again only one choice was available to each of us. John was not allowed to put "unknown."

Complicating my exploration of my racial identity was the slow realization that I am bisexual. I had had hints, but society trains us well to see nothing unusual in ourselves if it endangers the power structure. I didn't notice until I was completely infatuated with another woman that bisexual was indeed what I am.

I say that bisexuality complicated my exploration of race, mostly because of the fog that surrounds any discussion of sexuality in this culture, but the issues it raised for me neatly dovetailed with the concerns of a multiracial identity. As a married woman and a mother, am I "passing" for straight? Am I using heterosexual privilege to reap the rewards for acceptable behavior while living an unacceptable life? Where do I belong, and what am I *really*?

Each of these questions is unanswerable to a varying degree, and often I must content myself with uncertainty. It has helped to meet other bi women—some married, some single, some outside of those designations altogether—who share the same struggles and who have made a happy, if contested, peace with their sexuality and life choices.

Ironically, the lifelong wrestling match with my racial identity prepared me well for accepting the contradictions of a bisexual life. I know not only do I not *have* to fit into any one sexual (or racial) identity, I simply cannot.

Passing It On to the Children

I am as exhausted by these battles as I am committed to them. As a multiracial person, I know dislocation better than I know connection. As a bisexual woman, I am more familiar with isolation than with community. As a mother, I know the tension between wanting to make things easy for my sons and wanting to make things real.

I remember when, soon after Anansi was born, my mother and I were talking about his future. "Anansi," she said to his little face, "I sure hope you grow up to be straight. It's so much easier." It would be easier. It would be easier, too, if we just pretended he was "all white."[2] With his blond hair and white skin, it would be simple, but it wouldn't be honest. In spite of the costs, I know I must ask Anansi and his younger brother, Cedro, to take on the burden of finding out who they truly are, and why it matters so much.

Already my children are the recipients of white privilege. If the child in the baby sling hanging over my shoulder that day the diaper bag was taken had looked black or Asian, perhaps my neighbors would not have been so quick to assume they could say the things they did, or would not have said them at all. My sons have already been welcomed into the club. I want to teach them how to fight their way out.

One of the biggest challenges for John and me as we raise Anansi and Cedro will be finding ways to interject race into discussions with our families. My family's ambivalence about race and my in-laws' unabashed racism mean that any claim to nonwhite heritage is met with resistance of some sort.

My mother, for her part, cherishes her half Filipina, half European background, and her liberal upbringing in a multiracial Chicago neighborhood resulted in an antiracist atmosphere for my childhood. As she accepts my multiracial consciousness, she will accept her grandchildren's, should it develop.

John's family poses more of a problem. At our wedding, the older members seemed distinctly uncomfortable with my short, brown-skinned Filipino grandfather when they met him. "So your grandfather's Chinese?" John's grandmother asked me. That he is Filipino and not Chinese didn't seem to make any difference in the height of her arching eyebrow. Two years later, watching a *60 Minutes* report on Mexicans who cross the border for education and health care, John's family pointedly ignored my comments in defense of the Mexicans, as well as my revelation that my grandfather was an illegal immigrant. Their discomfort with my mixed heritage does not bode well for future discussions about our children's.

If I view their reluctance to discuss race in the best light, I can attribute it to an interest in making life as easy as possible for the family's children. That interest is indeed part of the reason, but denial is another. Because my children appear to be white, it makes it quite painless for other family members to treat them as such, as they have treated me. If we want race to be discussed, John and I must bring the subject into conversation ourselves and work to keep it there.

What's to Be Done?

My job in raising my boys as multiracial children cannot stop with making them aware of their mixed identity. I must also challenge them to wrestle with the conflicting messages they will receive about race and with their relationship to the power white skin brings. The task is complicated by their sex. Since in our society whiteness and maleness are given dominance, the combination is especially potent. But teaching them to reject racism, as we know, does not imply a rejection of other oppressive ways of thinking and behaving. Sexism is widespread in communities of color, as racism can be in feminist and sexual minority circles, and this contradiction is often unacknowledged and even more frequently unaddressed. John and I must require that Anansi and

Cedro take responsibility for their male privilege also so that it doesn't compound the power imbalance created by their "white" skin.

John and I have made efforts to expose our boys to a multicultural environment. Anansi attends a diverse daycare owned by a biracial couple. We read them books featuring stories and characters from a variety of cultures, races and family structures. We have chosen to live in the most integrated neighborhood we can find in this city.

Beyond these environmental choices, however, lie our actions. Our children must see that we are willing to work against racism in our daily lives. Some of the solutions I have found through my own experiences can be taught to them through observation of and participation in antiracist activities.

The single most important action we as parents can take against racism is to dismantle the taboo against addressing race. When I went to the Philippines I was warned never to bring up politics, gambling or cock-fighting at the dinner table, for fear of causing intrafamily strife. In the United States, of course, the taboos are politics and race. As difficult as it is, we must model for our children a willingness to talk about the hard stuff, while respecting the desire for family harmony. Even if race can't easily be brought up at extended family gatherings, discussions around the dinner table should not shy away from the topic of racism and what can be done to overcome it. By creating an atmosphere of open exchange, we make it comfortable for our children to return to us with questions and their own observations of the interplay of race and power.

On the other hand, it is also vitally important to confront racism as it presents itself, even if that means addressing a relative's racist joke at a family function. "Confronting" does not have to mean yelling or fisticuffs, of course. A quiet but firm response to racist words and actions may not change anyone's mind, but it does illustrate to children in two ways that all people are to be respected: first, by not humiliating the family member to make your point, and second, by demonstrating that racism will not be tolerated.

Another tactic to model for children, particularly for white and white-appearing children, is "race bending," a racial equivalent to the "gender fuck," the politicized variant of gender bending. Bisexual activists promote the gender fuck as a way to eliminate strict gender roles in both the hetero- and homosexual communities. Gender fuck is a conscious decision to act outside of the assigned sociocultural limitations of your apparent sex. Politically active transsexuals and transvestites are the most obvious practitioners, but other, less dramatic actions are gender fuck, too. For example, John chose to take my surname when we got married, in part for this limitation-challenging quality. Any conscious, public (or semipublic) choice of clothes, habits, language, activities or roles of the other sex is gender fuck.

Race bending is more complicated than gender bending, of course. While there are only two apparent sexes, there are many races, and while it is possible to be biologically a blend of two or more races, individuals are generally considered to be physically only one sex. In addition, the power struggle between the sexes is less heated than that among the races. A boy learning to cook gourmet meals might be considered charming, but a white teenager's use of black English raises concerns of appropriation of the minority's culture by the oppressor.

For these reasons, race bending is probably most effectively employed by multiracial individuals, including children. Multiracial people have the ability and the responsibility to move back and forth across the lines of race. Blurring those lines is both a survival technique for multiracial children and an educational tactic for others. Participating in the constant race sorting we as a society and as individuals do forces us to decide who belongs to what group and, in our racist environment, who is on top. Race bending confronts this sorting and asks the questions: What is race? Why does it matter? Should it matter?

Multiracial people can race bend by attending people-of-color-only events. Just as the gender fuck works to liberate both hetero- and homosexual communities, sensitive race bending can destroy barriers in both white and people-of-color groups. When I attend conferences, I make a point of joining the people-of-color workshops and caucuses. I have come some distance from my initial discomfort with being a part of the women-of-color caucus in college. Over the years I have realized that, as a multiracial woman, I belong as much in a people-of-color-only group as I do in the white-dominated groups of which I have been a part. My experiences have borne out my choice to join minority groups. I have always been welcomed and felt my point of view honored as a provocative challenge to the polar, us-against-them mentality that any closed group—majority or minority—can foster.

The well-timed revelation of one's mixed heritage can be an extremely effective race bender. For a white-appearing, multiracial person to allow a white to engage in uninterrupted racist speech for a time and then to reveal membership in the maligned group requires the racist speaker to explain away his or her comments. The act of explaining cannot be done without some reflection on the meaning of race and the impact of racism.

People of mixed race should also check all the boxes that apply on census and other official forms. The U.S. Census Bureau is currently investigating the possibility of inclusion of an "other" or "multiracial" box on its forms. Until then, marking all the races and ethnicities that apply, and writing down why, is a way to dismantle the idea that we must belong only to one.

None of the above is to suggest that white people cannot commit race bending. Whites can create and wear a "Don't assume I'm white" T-shirt, calling into question white privilege for themselves for the time it is worn. On official forms, they can designate themselves a race they seem obviously not to be, thus interfering with the efforts of government agencies to sort people by race. Asking people what race they are, especially if it seems obvious, is another way of challenging the notion of a race-sorted society.

A Challenge, An Opportunity

For antiracist parents, white-appearing, multiracial children pose a special challenge and an opportunity. Carrying both the badge of power in our society (white skin) and the legacy of the oppressed, they can suffer from white guilt *and* minority rage. Even before they can articulate what they feel about race, their identities are forming. It is essential that parents give their multiracial children an environment that honors all of their "parts" and allows them room to talk about the tensions they are discovering inside.

As an adult I can appreciate the conflict that my mixed background brought me as a child and adolescent, and the lessons I learned from it. The advantages and disadvantages of multiracial identity inform my day-to-day efforts against racism in a way that a single-race heritage would not. I live the ironies of race in a racist society. I feel a responsibility to pass on this legacy to my sons, even if it means more work for them. It's the only honest thing I could do, and the best thing I can do against racism.

Notes

1. I am indebted to the work of Peggy McIntosh for the title and concept of this essay. For an introduction to the notion of white privilege, I highly recommend her essay, "White Privilege: Unpacking the Invisible Knapsack," published in *Peace and Freedom* (July/August 1989).

2. Of course, no one is "all white." I am submitting here to the cultural fantasy of white racial purity not because it is real or possible, but because it is widely accepted. Most people seem to believe that a child *could* be all white, and that he or she should be raised as such if physical characteristics permit.

"That Wouldn't Be Fair"

STACI SWENSON

How do white mothers rear white children to respect and honor diversity in a society that insists on stereotypes and prejudice? As a white, lesbian, multicultural feminist, I have found raising a white child and teaching young adults in this racist society to be complex and demanding and to involve a never-ending expenditure of energy. Yet not actively to attempt such a feat is unbearable for me as a feminist mother.

I have tried to plant the seeds of racial awareness in my daughter since she was very young, though I have often made uninformed mistakes. Because she and I did many years of growing up in the Appalachian mountains of North Carolina, we had no explicit role models or examples of how to be white females working toward an antiracist society. I did not learn to take responsibility for my situation of privilege as a white person or how to channel and release the anger I often felt toward unfair situations.

Not wanting my child to grow up with the racist attitudes blatantly flowing through the South, I did what was easy to do in a town less than 3 percent African American—I ignored the issue of racial difference. My thinking at the time went: *We aren't any different aside from skin*

color, so we should just ignore the color difference and all will be well.
When Kendalyn was three years old, I started noticing the absence of racial descriptions in her vocabulary. Kendalyn spoke frequently of her favorite playmate, James, who was black. She would describe his brown eyes, his blue tennis shoes and his favorite color of crayons, but she never mentioned his skin color. This thrilled me, because I assumed that avoidance of racial or ethnic differences was a positive way of raising an antiracist child.

The autumn before Kendalyn turned five, I stumbled into a women's studies class. If someone had asked me at the time, I would have said I was a feminist, though I did not have a concrete concept of what that meant. Barbara and Beverly Smith examine "the click" that many white women experience in their early adulthood when exposed to the ways oppression affects them.[1] I was clicking all over the place that fall. I changed my major to women's studies. This new information excited me, and I wanted to share what I had been learning with my daughter. Through listening to my discussions with others, Kendalyn, too, became sensitive to the sexism in our culture. Many times she overheard the word "sexist" thrown around during conversations between my sister and me while we watched and analyzed television shows and commercials.

Only on the brink of seeing sexism, homophobia and racism as part of the same system, I was not willing to shelter my child from sexism, homophobia or my sexuality, yet continued to evade the issue of racial difference. My way of handling racial diversity had been by trying to ignore it. By stating that we are all the same, I made the common presupposition that we can all be "white" regardless of skin color. I was unaware of any distinctions and I, therefore, did not encourage my daughter to appreciate differences in culture or experience. I had unintentionally, though effectively, passed this form of racism on to my daughter.

As a positive consequence of reading about and acknowledging my own racism, I began to notice the exclusion of people of color in Kendalyn's books, coloring books and assignments from school. Admitting I was wrong to avoid discussions of racial difference, I began pointing out to her exclusions based on race. She, too, became aware of the racism signified by absence. Watching television together was one way we raised our awareness of blatant as well as subtle examples of racism pulsing through this medium.

Analyzing cartoons and television shows is a great "assignment" for parents and children to do together. We count the number of male versus female, middle- and upper-class versus working-class, whites versus people of color, straight versus queer, able-bodied versus people who are disabled and young versus older characters. Children can see the disproportionate recognition given dominant characters in most forms of popular culture. Almost all child-oriented sitcoms, as well as cartoons, are especially imbalanced, so teaching children this method of analysis is a good way of helping them to become aware as well as keeping them active while watching. Kendalyn and I created charts at first so we could really "keep score." I have even overheard Kendalyn mention these character discrepancies while watching TV with her friends.

When Kendalyn was seven, I helped her to make the link between homophobia (which she was already aware of) and racism (about which she knew less). She had a solid sense of the social unacceptability of homosexuality. I "came out" to Kendalyn when I first began dating women, when she was five. Even then, she was able to understand homophobia in the surrounding society. She had seen too many sitcoms not to be well versed in what "dating" meant. When I told her I would be dating a friend of whom she was quite fond, she said, "Good, just don't date in front of my friends."

One weekend while visiting her father, Kendalyn heard that one of her paternal uncles was angry with her father because he was allowing his daughter to live with a lesbian. He insisted her father should try to obtain custody of Kendalyn because of the negative influence I would have on her. Soon after, a lesbian living in Virginia had her child taken from her by the court. Indeed, homophobic prejudice was (and remains) a concrete fear for both of us.

Kendalyn heard this same uncle use the word "nigger" when referring to a relative who is multiracial. Recapping the story later, she said that she didn't know why, but it made her angry. "Uncle Nick was mean about Larry the way he is mean about you being a lesbian. I was mad, but I didn't tell him." I shuddered with the knowledge that it would not be the last time she would hear *that* word or feel silenced and angered by prejudice. I then realized I could use her uncanny understanding of homophobia to help her further understand racism.

I told Kendalyn that when her father and I were dating, I often heard her Uncle Nick yell expletives like "stupid pussy nigger" at the TV when certain football or basketball players made mistakes. I told her that her father would tell him to "shut up" because he knew it bothered me. Part of Nick's delight in using this language in my presence stemmed from his disgust that I had dated a black schoolmate a year earlier. I told Kendalyn that, though his racism and sexism made me furious, I felt unable to say anything to him. I was terrified of what might happen if I opened my mouth and expressed my anger. I don't want my daughter to go through her life choking on this silencing fear and anger. I asked Kendalyn what she would say to Uncle Nick if she could do it over. We role-played, pretending that I was Uncle Nick. She yelled at Nick, "You're a jerk!" She and I talked about what might be a more productive way to verbalize her anger if the situation arose again.

Role-playing is an effective method for inspiring children to express their feelings and for helping them to respond when they come in contact with difficult situations. Role-playing also prepares them to handle situations *before* they arise and to channel their anger in a constructive direction. Because many of us, adults and children alike, are often silenced by prejudice, it is imperative to prepare children for encounters with prejudice so they will be more likely to speak up as allies for one another. Kendalyn said, "I could tell him that Larry is wonderful and he shouldn't be racist. It makes me sick and it's not fair." I asked her if this is the same type of comment she could make if Uncle Nick made homophobic or sexist remarks. "Yeah, it's almost the same." She was already beginning to recognize the importance of voicing her anger as well as the relation between different forms of oppression.

In addition to learning to express and to channel their anger, children also need to validate the anger members of oppressed groups may harbor for those responsible for or benefiting from that oppression. In her essay "The Uses of Anger: Women Responding to Racism," Audre Lorde proposes anger as a "response to racist attitudes and to the actions and presumptions that arise out of those attitudes."[2] A common response to oppression is for the oppressed people to become angry. If the oppressor respects this anger, it can be a learning tool for changing behavior.

One evening last year while Kendalyn and I were reading to each other, she told me that she had experienced racism earlier that day in school. Uncertain of what she meant, I questioned her for clarification. She explained that while walking with her friend Janay, who is black, several black boys bumped into Kendalyn and called her a "skinny little white girl." She concluded that "they were being racist to me because I'm white."

Carefully trying to validate the anger the two boys have toward whites while not invalidating my daughter's hurt over the name-calling experience was tricky. I told her sometimes people of color get really angry because there are so many unfair situations for them. "This is similar to how we get angry when someone is homophobic." I continued by telling her that our criminal justice system places many more black men in correction institutes, either for crimes they haven't committed or for the same crimes for which white men have not undergone punishment.

After much wary tip-toeing through examples for fear she would not understand or that I would mess up this fragile area of comprehension, Kendalyn shared an epiphany, much to my relief: "It's kinda like when I get in trouble for doing something that the boys do all the time and they don't get sent to the office. It's okay for them to do it because they're boys, but the second a girl does it, it's not allowed. We [girls] get sent to the office if we push them [boys] even a little bit. But they push us all the time and never get in trouble."

"Exactly, and how do you feel when those unfair situations happen?"

"I get really mad at all the stupid boys—and the teacher [on the playground who sends her to the office]."

I then asked Kendalyn what happens when she argues with the teacher about the circumstance. She responded, "I only get in more trouble." "So, what do you do?" She looked down at her hands, and I could tell she was unsure if she should tell me—"I push Donald when the teacher isn't looking."

I explained that it isn't *all* the boys who push others and get away with it, or even that push at all; nevertheless, in those moments she gets mad at all of them and at the teacher who is allowing such inequality. Kendalyn takes her anger out when it's safe, "when the teacher isn't looking." She understood the similarity between her anger and the anger of the two boys that teased her. It was safe for those boys to take their anger out on her because they are not able to take their anger out on their oppressors. In Kendalyn's words, they'd only get in "more trouble." I suggested there might have been more constructive ways for those boys to handle their anger, comparable to the more constructive ways she found to channel her anger at Uncle Nick when we role-played: "Sometimes we react because we're angry, without thinking about more productive ways to deal with that anger. It's okay that we're angry at homophobic or sexist people, just like it's okay those boys have a lot of anger at white people."

Lorde explains that when anger is directed at us, the oppressors, if we respond to that anger with our own, "the substance of our exchange" is moved away from "effective action."[3] I don't want Kendalyn to feel hurt by or defensive about that anger, but rather to understand and respect it so she might be better able to work against the situations that trigger the anger.

In an attempt to empower children to use their anger to speak out and to respect anger when it is directed at them, parents must be careful not to reinforce themes of meritocracy. Children (and adults as well) are constantly fed the myth that our capitalist society equally distributes rewards based on merit. For instance, Kendalyn has often arrived home from school clutching stories and poems that reflect the morals "if you try hard, you will succeed" and "if you believe with all your heart, you can make your dreams come true." Such simplistic meritocracy is the basis on which western hegemonic culture, including schools in the United States, is founded. It is also the lie by which society and American institutions perpetuate sexism, racism, classism and other oppressive ills. This optimistic dogma places the burden of overcoming oppression on the oppressed and not on the oppressors. Essentially, meritocracy is indirect victim blaming and lets oppressors off the hook. I have to remind Kendalyn (as well as myself) that merit is by no means a guarantee of success or rewards.

One example of this myth is one of Kendalyn's favorite books, *Amazing Grace*. This wonderfully illustrated book tells of a young, imaginative girl who is black. Grace loves acting out stories she's heard and casts herself as the star. One day, her teacher announces that the class will perform the play *Peter Pan.* A classmate, a boy of color, tells her she can't be Peter because "that's a boy's name." Another classmate, a white girl, tells her that she can't be Peter Pan because he "isn't black." Though Grace's feelings are hurt, she practices all weekend, telling herself, *I can be anything I want.* Her mother and Nana tell her, "You can be anything you want, Grace, if you put your mind to it." When she auditions, Grace is so good that everyone realizes she is perfect for the part and her classmates vote for her to be Peter. Her class performs the play, and, as she had hoped, she is the star of the show.

At story's end, Kendalyn and I have often been filled with the joy and wonder of meritocracy. Despite the warmth we felt when we read the story, it occurred to me that Kendalyn and I needed to question the realism of this plot in this sexist and racist society. At one point I asked her, "What would you think if she didn't get the part *because* she is black or *because* she's a girl?" Kendalyn was quick to respond, "That wouldn't be fair. I would be mad." I told her that I would be mad, too, and that we *should* be angry because such unfair situations happen all the time. I want her to be aware of what would probably happen to Grace as a black female, and to stimulate her sense of anger about unjust situations so she will notice them when they happen to her friends and to herself, as indeed they will. Now when she is given a story to read that contains such an ethic of "good hard-working American values," I will ask her why the story is problematic. At age eight, she can tell me that sometimes, no matter how hard we try or believe, we may not be able to succeed because of prejudices.

I recently used *Amazing Grace* as an example of meritocracy in the Women, Culture, and Society course I teach. Some of my students were resistant to understanding meritocracy as a myth. They saw themselves as in college to achieve a goal, which they were *earning.* They saw the outcome of their achievement as solely based on their brains and motivation. Several white students with high grades in my class wanted to argue that hard work in school has rewarded them with good grades. Secure futures would be the payoff to this hard work. Some of their protests against my descriptions of meritocracy were rooted in the fear not only that they might have gained grades they didn't deserve, but also that they might *not* receive what they do deserve.

One white female student said she had more training and experience than a new male employee with whom she worked in a bank. She heard that he was already making $1.50 more an hour than she was. This personal example stimulated a discussion of the unspoken impetus behind most institutional policies forbidding open discussions of employee pay rates. Finally, a white male student resistantly admitted that "If we got paid based on experience and talent alone, they wouldn't care if we talk about how much we make." His point that pay often reveals discrepancies based on prejudicial attitudes helped establish for the rest of the class the point I was trying to make about Grace. Kendalyn had not had as difficult a time as my students had grasping and accepting the message about unfairness.

Educators working against prejudice and discrimination can employ children's active sense of fairness to our advantage. We often see their disgruntlement with unfairness when they get the smaller piece of cake or have to go to bed before their parents. This sense of fairness, however, is something parents and the surrounding society usually teach them to ignore instead of using it to stimulate their sense of justice. After seeing a movie or reading a book, Kendalyn and I sometimes play a game where we will take turns saying how we would change the movie or book to make it "better"—more fair. We name what is unfair. This is a good way to encourage children's sense of fairness in a productive way. "Was it fair that all the people in that action scene were white men?" A typical response from Kendalyn is to substitute one of her friends for the hero: "I would have Yishin be the pilot." Kids are perceptive, and I am often impressed at the details she notices or connections she makes, ones I sometimes miss.

One evening, a television news magazine segment discussed the insistence of many white, English-speaking United States citizens (especially in areas of California, New York and Florida) on a requirement of English as the "official" language of the United States. This requirement would include eliminating translations on governmental forms, thereby making life in this country virtually impossible for immigrants who are unable to speak English. Interviewed on the show was a man of color who spoke English as a second language. He argued that the refusal to accept other languages in this country is a form of racism.

After the segment concluded, we turned off the TV, and I asked Kendalyn what she thought about the man's idea that excluding certain ethnic groups who are unable to speak English is an act of racism. She angrily agreed, stating that "it's not only what language you speak, it's what color your skin is. That's why they don't want them to speak other languages. It's just like when the slaves weren't allowed to speak their own language. They were made to speak English, too. That way the white people could understand what the slaves said." I had overlooked the connection Kendalyn made between the enforcement of English as a way of once controlling African slaves and a way now of controlling non-English-speaking immigrants.

Children can learn to fight against oppression not only by recognizing and speaking out against others who are prejudiced, but also by taking responsibility for themselves—owning their mistakes, facing the truth when they're wrong, and being responsible for their own positions of privilege. This kind of responsibility takes on a new meaning when the child is a potential oppressor. After reading Peggy McIntosh's list of privileges,[4] I related to Kendalyn a simplified version of what it means to have privilege. Together, she and I developed a list of privileges we have as white people. She understood McIntosh's example of Band-Aids matching the skin tones of whites but not the varied skin tones of people of color. We went to a card store and visually "shopped" for cards, wondering if we would be able to find representations of ourselves if we were African-American or Asian-American. We also looked in the video store and saw how limited representations of people of color are. These exercises were telling examples of the hyperprevalence of white faces on cards and videos to the exclusion of other racial and ethnic groups.

While learning quotes from "Great Americans," Kendalyn noted that she had one privilege over the students of color in her class—most of those quoted were white. Out of a list of thirty-five, only two were black, and both of these were men. She said there were no women of any race represented on her list of "Great Americans." She and I then talked about how we are privileged as white people. Racially we can see our image consistently represented, yet our privilege is limited because we are female. We investigated our own "Great Americans" and found several quotes from females, which Kendalyn took to school. Her favorite was from Sojourner Truth's speech, "Ain't I a Woman," which metaphorically illustrated the situation we had confronted: "If my cup won't hold but a pint, and yours holds a quart, wouldn't you be mean not to let me have my little half-measure?" As it turned out, her teacher was delighted to have the new quotes from women. She shared them with her class and had the other teachers add these new quotes to their lists as well.

This identification of privileges is also an assignment I give to my students in the course I teach. The students create their own lists of privileges that dominant groups of people have, often at the expense of other groups. This assignment helps the students become aware of any positions of privilege they may occupy. Defensiveness, anger and guilt frequently arise among my students during these discussions.

Not surprisingly, I have noticed a marked difference between the reactions of younger children and the adults in my classes. Adults have had many years of learning patriarchal American values; consequently, their hate, prejudice and/or ignorance are more deeply implanted and more difficult to excavate. Children, however, are more easily able to learn about and acknowledge their positions of privilege without the defensive resistance exhibited by many of my students. Women students often feel threatened by my suggestion that it is *not* only men who can be oppressors. The white women especially feel disconcerted by my request that they list, become aware of and, consequently, become accountable for their positions of privilege. The men, who usually enter a women's studies class feeling like the "bad guys," are relieved that it is not only they who are responsible for oppression. Many women, however, are quite reluctant to acknowledge their place in the scope of oppression. As bell hooks mentions in her essay "Feminism: A Transformational Politic," women often see men as the perpetrators of all evil and themselves as innocent victims. She goes on to posit that women interrogate their role "in the perpetuation and maintenance of systems of domination."[5]

In a final evaluation of my class, one white woman wrote what many students have said. While she loved the class, she was bothered because she "felt disgusted about being white." Her disgust stems from her awareness that racism exists partly through her privilege as a white person, and, therefore, she not only contributes to that racism but also benefits from it. Yet as Audre Lorde suggests, it is "corrective surgery" that is needed for change and not guilt.[6] I try to convey to my students that though prejudice and discrimination negatively affect the oppressed persons, they are not only the problems of those who are oppressed. Prejudice and discrimination are the problems of the oppressors as well and not merely in support of the adages that "sexism hurts men" and "racism hurts whites," for acknowledging prejudice in this vein only repositions these groups in the center of importance. Rather, it is because of men and whites that sexism and racism even exist, and they endure because they benefit men and whites. Therefore, whites working against racism need to see racism not as the problem of people of color.

Racism is the problem of the white woman who asks me after class whether or not she should have to worry about racism if Alice Walker's definition of "womanism" does not include her.[7] Racism is the problem of the white woman, and all the other white students, who feel guilty because they don't know what else to do. I explain how often whites expect people of color to "solve" racism, so that we, as privileged whites, will not be burdened by such guilt—but they are not accountable for the solution. We whites are the ones who have caused racism's existence. If we whites collectively chose to give up our privilege and demanded an end to discrimination, it would be eliminated. Yet rather than forgo such comfortable unearned extras, white students often want to relieve their need for responsibility and action with guilt. They believe, much as I used to, that if we feel guilty, we do not need to be responsible for our position as oppressors. We use feelings, and verbalizations of these feelings of guilt, to assuage our need to take responsibility and to effect change.

I have found, however, that white students find accountability easier to swallow if I, as a white, able-bodied, primarily middle-class woman, take responsibility for my positions of privilege. As mothers and as teachers, taking responsibility and being actively involved in issues that do not negatively affect us in a direct way are good ways of being active role models for children and students in privileged positions. It's well past time for white feminists to take responsibility for racism and for all of us who are mothers to teach our children the importance of accepting responsibility for their positions as well. We must teach them that to be antiracist and antiprejudice is to wade through covert as well as blatant racism and discrimination, which is everywhere in our society. We must also teach them to respect the anger oppressed people feel toward the oppressor (which may include themselves), in addition to respecting and channeling their own anger—toward their oppressors when they themselves are oppressed, and, as allies, toward the oppressors of others.

Notes

1. Beverly Smith and Barbara Smith, "Across the Kitchen Table: A Sister-to-Sister Dialogue," in *This Bridge Called My Back*, ed. Cherríe Moraga and Gloria Anzaldúa (New York: Kitchen Table: Women of Color Press, 1983). Barbara and Beverly Smith explain that racial and class oppression start "from Day One." White women, however, usually do not notice their gender oppression until it is expressed to them in an "intellectual manner. It's something that's pointed out to them. It's something that they read about and say 'Oh, yeah!'" (114).

2. Audre Lorde, "The Uses of Anger: Women Responding to Racism," in *Sister Outsider* (Freedom, CA: The Crossing Press, 1984), 124.

3. Ibid., 128.

4. Peggy McIntosh, "White Privilege: Unpacking the Invisible Knapsack," in *Peace and Freedom*, (July/August 1989): 10–12. McIntosh establishes most privilege as being a "package of unearned assets" about which the privileged are to remain "oblivious." We are all taught *not* to recognize our situations of privilege. So that she can be actively aware of her "unearned assets," McIntosh lists the privileges she has as a white woman. Privileges are also held by those in other dominant groups, i.e. men of all races, heterosexuals, able-bodied people, financially-secure people, etc. and she suggests they move towards recognizing their privileges as well.

5. bell hooks, "Feminism: A Transformational Politic," in *Talking Back: Thinking Feminist, Thinking Black* (Boston: South End Press, 1989), 20.

6. Lorde, "The Uses of Anger: Women Responding to Racism," 124.

7. Alice Walker, *In Search of Our Mothers' Gardens* (San Diego: Harcourt, Brace & Jovanovich, 1983), xi–xii. Walker defines a "womanist" as a "black feminist or feminist of color" who usually has "outrageous, audacious, courageous or *willful* behavior" (Walker's emphasis).

Trial and Error

DARYL LAROCHE

If you live in a small southern city, even one that's just been awarded a National Football League franchise and has "The Bold New City of the South" on its police cars, do not give up your weekly outing to Village Inn to feast on the belly-buster special in order to write a reasoned letter to the editor explaining that you have a little problem with the article in the *Florida Times-Union*, 30 April 1995, that states, "White people and black people don't talk the same."

Do not encourage your teenage daughter, a young woman of color, to spend an hour writing her own reasoned, logical letter protesting both the tone and the content of the article. Do not scan the editorial page every day for the next week searching for your letters. You will only strain your eyes trying to read the fine print. You will find out information that may be useful to you, though, so I can't totally discourage you in this regard. It will slowly dawn on you that the newspaper's editorial staff will print your letter lickety-split if you write criticizing anyone but a reporter.

Do not bother trying to educate the newspaper reporters who seem to think black is a synonym for ghetto and illiterate, even if your daughter has just gotten back from a two-week, all-expenses-paid trip to England, courtesy of *Parade* magazine and the *Florida Times-Union*, because her essay was picked as the best out of all high school students in the city, grades nine through twelve, even though she is just in ninth grade, and the youngest one in her class. They will not be amused. And they will not print your letters.

The following Sunday, out of frustration, do not dig the paper out of the trash to look up the phone number for the Reader's Advocate, who, when you call, promises that if you leave your name and number, he will get back to you. He will not. Maybe it wasn't appropriate for my daughter and me to respond to an article demeaning black people, since I'm white and my daughter is therefore not 100 percent black. But most nominally black people are not 100 percent black. And isn't racism everyone's problem?

Both my parents are white—my father of French descent, my mother half Portuguese. My skin has yellowish undertones and turns the color of light honey in the summer. I say this with certainty, having just checked my kitchen cabinet and discovered that I'm lighter than both pretzels and cinnamon and darker than garlic powder. I have light brown eyes and black hair.

My ex-husband's parents are black. His paternal grandfather was a Cherokee Indian from North Carolina, and my ex-husband has Hershey's Kisses skin, black hair and dark brown eyes. I thought my daughter's eyes were the same color as her father's until I saw daughter and father side by side when she was a week old. Her eyes are black, a wonderful deep Cherokee Indian black, much darker than either his or mine. Her hair is also black. I welcome the day when, as Dr. Martin Luther King, Jr., said, people are judged by the content of their character and not by the (exact) shade of their skin.

The President has the advantage of being briefed before every encounter with the press. His advisors have learned from bitter experience that if they send him to face the White House press corps without briefing him on what questions to expect and what stock answers he should give, he'll be in for a less than wonderful experience. If the reporters sense indecision or the slightest hesitation on his part, the gloves will come off and they'll gang up and start to bully him. Human nature being remarkably consistent, the same can also be said of the sandbox gang.

Give your young child the same benefit the President enjoys. Otherwise, when you go to pick her up at the end of the day, you'll have to answer the five-year-olds' questions yourself, thus providing an unplanned and unwelcome distraction at story time. "Are you her mommy?" "What color is her daddy?" "Are you really in the Army?" "Are you really a mechanic?"

Ignoring their questions only leads the toddlers to think she must be guilty of the crime with which they are charging her, that of being different. Protesting that it's none of their business affirms their sneaking suspicion that she should be, and is, ashamed of who she is. After much trial and error, we've found that "My mommy's white, my daddy's black, and I'm brown" works quite nicely, especially when delivered by a gregarious child who doesn't shrink from life, but embraces it, and most of the people in it, with enthusiasm.

Be grateful your mother goes to such great lengths to find not only black and white baby dolls for this little girl to embrace, but brown ones as well. Appreciate the box of Christmas cards with brown angels and a brown Baby Jesus that she proudly shows you, while gently questioning the wisdom of racing another woman down the aisle to get the last box of them.

My daughter's an only child. To say she's an extrovert would be an understatement. After kids get past the temporary blindness caused by their reaction to her color, they begin to see her as an individual, one that's smart, kind, funny and fun to be with.

So when you pick your child up that first day of preschool, don't feel worried if she's not instantly accepted, few of us are. Be sensitive. Understand that toddlers can absorb only so much information at a time. Promise to answer their questions about the Army and tanks another day.

Understand that racists can be any size, shape and color. Try not to threaten with bodily harm the little white child who hurls racial epithets at your daughter. Practice the same discipline with the little yellow, brown and black children who do the same. If they find out that it really upsets you, they'll happily repeat them over and over whenever they see her.

Understand that children are creative and that new language is being born every day. Learn to practice deep breathing when your child comes home and tells you two boys on her bus have been calling her "wigger" every day. Try to admire the ingenuity of a mind that can come up with a word meaning "white nigger" while deploring the use to which this level of intelligence is being put.

Trial and error. Do not waste twenty minutes looking up the boys' parents in the phone book, calling them and then trying to engage them in an open, friendly exchange of ideas. Be patient. Wait. Distract yourself with the Tuesday night Movie of the Week. A six-mile run at a brisk pace is also a good idea. Remind yourself that people don't change their minds about something because they are yelled at, and recognize that racists are rehabilitated the same way they were deformed: one at a time and slowly.

Make sure you get to bed early so you can pick up the phone first thing in the morning and speak to the principal. Derive pleasure from the fact that she is a black woman who assures you in a tone that conveys both righteous indignation and a firm sense of purpose that she "will see to this immediately." Try not to engage in vengeful fantasies that the boys will be put on a rack in the dean's office and stretched until they cry out for mercy, or that their next field trip will be to the alligator farm just down the road in Saint Augustine, where they'll be accessorized with porkchop necklaces and bracelets just prior to being thrown into the pit.

Be mature. Satisfy yourself with the fact that the dean of boys calls your daughter in to find out what happened and then calls the boys in and gives them a referral and the promise of suspension if it happens again. Try not to gloat when they are studiously polite to your daughter for the rest of the year.

Exercise patience when your child comes home and tells you about certain black children who accuse her of trying to be white because she speaks standard English. Head for the closet and pull out your running shorts once more when you hear they've told her she's stuck-up, even though they've steadfastly rebuffed a year's worth of overtures to friendship, or when they assume she thinks she's better than they are because she has lighter skin, but it is they who do not deign to talk to her. Do not bother to look up their parents' phone number, either, and ask how the same person who cries racism picks up that same hateful weapon to use against another. Racism, whether directed at another, or internalized, is a horrible sight.

Here's the scene: Two junior high girls are scheduled to see the school psychologist, an immaculately dressed black woman. The girls are brought down to the guidance office by a white guidance counselor. As the students enter the office, the psychologist approaches your daughter, smiles warmly, extends her hand and says, "Hi. You must be here for the ZIP Team." The ZIP Team, another one of those groups that educators cannot resist assigning acronyms to, counsels at-risk students who are in danger of dropping out or being expelled. Your daughter shakes her hand (her mother's always taught her to be polite) while the white guidance counselor nervously pushes the white teenager forward and says, "Uh, this is the student for the ZIP team. Maria is here to be evaluated for the gifted program."

When your daughter is evaluated and admitted to the program, pick out something nice to wear to the staffing. Try not to sound too strident when you ask what percentage of the white students are in the gifted program, and they tell you proudly, "Five or six percent, at least." Remember Miss Manners' advice and use modulated tones when asking what percentage of the minority students are in the program. Practice deep breathing while the school psychologist, the guidance counselor and the teacher look at each other, nonplussed. "Well, less than 1 percent, I think," the counselor answers hopefully. After all, they've let your daughter into the program, isn't that enough? You should be happy now, right? Practice flashing a smile in the mirror the night before so it will seem natural and not strained when you say, "When I got my degree in education, we were taught that at least 2 percent of any population is considered gifted. I'm sure you're going to work very hard to identify all the other minority students in this school of twelve hundred who you previously might have missed." Sign the papers, shake their hands and smile warmly at them once more before leaving the room.

Trust everyone you play cards with, but always cut the deck. Wait a few months. Ask your daughter if she is still one of the few minorities in the program. Attend a meeting given by a state legislator you know to be of sterling character. Listen attentively to her remarks. Get a cup of coffee afterwards. Help yourself to the oatmeal cookies and a few more of the chocolate chip. Wait for most of the people to clear out, and then take her aside and explain the situation. Express profound appreciation over her assurance she'll look into the matter. Try not to gloat when your daughter informs you the next week that the school is pulling minority kids out of class right and left to test them for the gifted program.

If you have a biracial daughter, pray for one thing. Pray she will not be interested in fashion and one day decide to shave off all her hair as some of the new exotic models have done. Because if she does, you may find yourself holding her close and consoling her as she sobs, "Mommy, my skin is white!" There is a chance that her beautiful little cinnamon face will indeed be capped by what appears to be a white hat.

To look like an exotic model is one thing, to become a laughingstock is another. Offer to let her stay home from school for a few days until her hair grows out a little bit or she gets a tan on her head, whichever comes first. Be proud of her when she refuses to take you up on the offer, squares her shoulders and bravely ventures out into the world with the courage and grace of which you are so proud.

When your daughter comes home and tells you that two boys in your apartment complex, one white and one black, accost her every day as she's walking home from the bus, asking repeatedly in menacing tones, "Why's your hair so short? You look like a man," recognize that they are probably not hairstyle interns from *Elle*. Reexamine your stand on non violence. Recognize that good, polite little girls often turn into obedient, battered women. Buy a copy of the *National Enquirer*. Withhold judgment on whether O.J. killed Nicole and Ron, but do look at the pictures of what no one disputes he did do to her. Take in the blackened eyes, the ravaged face. Take a deep breath. Talk to your daughter about the importance of standing up for herself.

Once again, give her the benefit of a briefing. Discuss possible answers. Settle on the one she's most comfortable with, and demonstrate saying it for her in assertive tones: "Look, I wear my hair short because I like it that way, and I don't appreciate your comments." Model how not to say it, timid voice barely eking out the words.

Ask if she wants you to enroll her in a karate class. Discuss with her the feasibility of your talking to the boys' parents. Realize once again that talking to parents is generally useless, because it's almost always the parent who's deformed the child in the first place. Tell her it's her choice to say something or to remain silent. Discuss the possibility that if she says something they may hit her and continue taunting her. Discuss the possibility that if she says nothing they may hit her and continue taunting her. Finally, recognize that she's almost fifteen and it's her decision to make. Tell her you trust her judgment.

Tell her in stern tones, order her, command her: if they hit you, drop your bookbag and beat the tar out of them. Do not pass go, do not collect two hundred dollars, immediately kick them in the privates. This is not dirty pool. Initiating a verbal or physical assault on another is what's reprehensible.

Keep yourself very busy the next day. Try not to look at the clock. Do rush through work, however, so you can be home when her bus arrives. Stop at the store, and buy that pepper spray on a key ring you've been meaning to get for both of you. When you get home, practice using it, so you can demonstrate it for her later. Refrain from meeting her at the bus stop. It is permitted to peer out the window nervously every five seconds, however.

Breathe a sigh of relief when she walks in the door. Beam with pride as she tells you that when the boys taunted her, she turned around, drew herself up, took a deep breath and delivered her statement. Note with satisfaction that the boys did not dare touch her, and that they leave her alone after that. Thank God it didn't turn out differently. Demonstrate the proper pepper spray technique for her.

Go for another run, say seven or eight miles, when your daughter comes home and tells you about the lengths the English teacher goes to (commendably) to help the boys understand her subject, while the science teacher refuses to answer the girls' questions. Go in and talk to the science teacher; give her the benefit of the doubt, but tell her that your daughter is an A student and is capable of that in her class. Refrain from envisioning an alligator-farm field trip for the teacher when your daughter comes home and tells you the situation has not changed. Resolve to file an official complaint about this teacher as soon as your daughter is assigned her senior science teacher and there's no longer any possibility this woman can punish her with a poor grade. Beam with pride when your daughter is picked to represent her school at the citywide science fair. Try not to smile too broadly when she walks away with second place in her division.

The next year, when your daughter comes home from school and tells you she has a fair science teacher and an excellent math teacher, breathe a sigh of relief. Chastise her, however, when she slowly seems to fall behind in math. Do not let her feel sorry for herself. Have a talk with her. Discover that the boys in her class are very assertive about demanding help in the subjects in which they are weak and that they refuse to be labeled slow or backward for doing so. Remind her you can hardly get any writing done at night because boys are continually calling your house in search of appropriate thesis statements and competent editorial help. Insist that she be assertive and demand the same cooperation for herself and that she reject being labeled as well.

Send her to school the next day with firm instructions not to return home until she has the phone numbers of five math whizzes in her notebook. Hound her until she calls them. Breathe a sigh of relief when she brings home an A in math, one of only two girls to do so.

Encourage her to get after-school tutoring once a week in math to further ensure a solid foundation in the subject. Try not to cringe when she comes home and tells you the only guy she could find to do it is one assigned to after-school detention. Be proud of her creativity in bartering with him; he tutors her every Wednesday, and she agrees to go over his essays with a fine-tooth comb. Be happy that this is the school for the gifted and so even the after-school detainees are competent to offer math tutoring. Count your blessings that his offense was not bringing a gun to school, but holding a lighter to the spray from an aerosol can during an overzealous display of school spirit at a pep rally.

Practice not being surprised when lesbian acquaintances decry homophobia in one breath and nonchalantly make racist remarks in the next. At a social gathering, a potluck dinner, perhaps, a couple tells you they've been dating for a year and that one of the women has four children for whom her ex-husband refuses to pay child support. Maybe her partner makes a remark to the effect that she'd like to "arrange to have some dark-colored stranger pay him a visit," while the mother looks on and smiles approvingly. Congratulate yourself. You've been practicing, and you're ready when this ball is hit across the net to you. You bat it back: "I find that remark extremely offensive. My husband was black, and my daughter's biracial." Try not to recoil in horror when the mother then tells you that her ex is black and her four daughters are also biracial. Try not to cringe when you think about what twisted racist messages these four beautiful girls are getting from their mother and her partner.

Take a deep breath and count to ten when you're sitting behind a row of black women at the movie theater who nudge each other, shake their heads and whisper ugly things when a black lesbian and her date sit down in front of them. Quietly ask your partner to take off her sweater and reveal her gay pride T-shirt underneath. Restrain yourself from asking if she'll go to the bathroom and switch shirts with you. Cough loudly once the sweater is off, and stare boldly into the eyes that change targets and now stare at you and your partner with disapproval. As you walk to your car after the movie, be sure to thank your partner for braving the cold in the chilly theater. And wonder aloud how the same people who ask for unconditional acceptance for themselves continually deny it to others.

When you teach elementary school and 90 percent of the students are black, refuse to be one of the crowd. When you get an obviously bright girl the previous teacher refused to promote, look past her skin color and sex to see her spirit. Realize with a sinking heart after a few weeks that the teacher probably failed her because she didn't like tomboys and so labeled this aggressive girl a troublemaker instead of a leader.

Shake your head in disbelief when you give her the first reading test and she fails it, your best reader. Realize that "mother" is just a title, and that you have the opportunity to nurture every child with whom you come into contact. Call this child up to your desk, look her squarely in the eye and say, "You're my best reader, and I know you can do this. Why don't you sit over here and try it again?" Smile with satisfaction and praise her lavishly when she returns the test with every answer correct.

A normally compliant girl, young woman actually, violates the no-one-upstairs-before-the-bell-rings rule to stand quietly outside your door clutching her stomach. After conferring with her for a minute you discover three things:

1. She's started her period.
2. Her father, a single parent, has sent her to school with no information about what is happening to her body, and only one Kotex pad.
3. This young woman standing before you has terrible cramps, but believes she is sick with some unknown disease and is bleeding to death.

Realize that the Duval County School Board policy that restricts what can be taught in sex education, and when, is absurd when applied to the real world. Think back to your high school days when you broke a rule or two just for the fun of it. Decide to break another rule, this time for a more important reason than mere thrill-seeking. Open your mouth and hear yourself saying, "When a woman's body is physically developed enough to have a baby, her uterus lines itself with nourishment for a baby if needed. If the lining isn't used, it washes itself out of your body, and that's your period. If you have sex with a boy, the egg may become fertilized and you'll become pregnant.

"Just because your body's physically ready to have a baby doesn't mean you're emotionally or economically ready to take care of a baby. Do you understand?" She nods her head solemnly.

Go on to tell her about the wonders of Midol, and tell her to ask her dad to get some for her tonight. Casually mention that if he for some reason isn't able to get it for her that it only costs two or three dollars and she can buy it herself at the Winn-Dixie or Pic 'N' Save down the street.

Realize you made the right decision when this young woman asks in an exasperated tone, "Ms. LaRoche, is this going to last all day?" Tell her that, yes, as a matter of fact, her period is going to go on all day and will probably last for the next five days. Gently break it to her that this phenomenon will probably occur once a month for the next thirty years. Give her a hug and comfort her when you see the look of shock that appears on her face. Resolve to go for a very long run after school when you think about the fact that if menstruation and pregnancy happened to the males of the species, no way would they be forced to wander around in such pain, fear and ignorance.

Finally, be thankful for the opportunity each child represents to get it right this time—to raise a generation not hampered by any "-ism" or limited vision.

Reading and

Teaching

Confessions of a Witch with Limited Powers

MARTHA SATZ

Don't we all brag with the pictures on our mantel? Currently, my son's wedding picture sits above my fireplace, the photo including my young daughter as well, flanked by the wedding couple. The English departmental secretary at my university remarked that the photograph should adorn the syllabus of every course I teach. Indeed, the picture does seem to exemplify a triumph of multicultural values. On the left, stands my son, his olive complexion contrasting with his white naval officer's uniform, festooned with medals; he is an incarnation of the stereotypical fairy-tale prince—tall, dark, and handsome. Equally evocative of storybook images is his petite Japanese bride, her long, dramatic black hair crowned with white lilies. Between them, her arms around the bride and groom, a bright smile on her face, proud of the thin, tight braids to which I consented for the occasion, stands my eight-year-old daughter, her bright pink dress setting off her caramel-colored skin. There the three stand under the Jewish wedding *chuppah*.

I did not include myself in this photograph for fear of detracting from the image of radiant beauty projected by the others. In the photos taken, I looked very much like what I was, an overweight, middle-aged Jewish mother. I was proud that day, and the event seemed to celebrate the unconventional way I had chosen to live. I felt powerful and exultant when, by way of a toast, I told the assembled wedding guests a story from my son's earliest history.

Michael

Twenty-five years ago, when I adopted my two-and-a-half-year-old bi-racial son, Michael, the social worker kept plaguing me with questions, trying to sort out my attitudes toward race. She kept insisting on one, "Do you think he will marry a white woman or a black woman?" Disgusted with the question and its repetition, I finally blurted, "Japanese, he will marry a Japanese woman." The social worker balked at my reply, but recollecting that story on the occasion, I felt like a witch, prescient in foreseeing the future of my son, powerful in shaping him into the altogether satisfactory man he was. But examining my life realistically, I have to admit that I am a witch with limited powers.

Certainly, I relish my son's success in reconciling his complex identities. Often in trying to convey his comfort with his background, I allude to the fact that in college he simultaneously held the office of vice-president in the Jewish Student Association and the Black Student Association. I explain how he mounted a protest concerning racism on campus in the same month that he represented the university at a Jewish student conference, where he became the catalyst on a session concerning the relations between Jews and blacks.

I also tell of the law school application essay he recently wrote describing his first naval assignment. Arriving on the ship, he became its first African-American officer, and minority sailors immediately began coming to him complaining that the situation aboard was acutely racist. He was in a quandary—he knew that sailors sometimes tried to take advantage of new officers, and he knew also that he was very green. But as he became more acquainted with the facts, he went to his commanding officer. He detailed the evidence of discrimination. But the commanding officer, barely allowing him to finish his story, threw him out of the office. In the essay, Michael describes his ambivalent feeling of self-doubt on the one hand ("He nuked me. I ruined my career in the first month.") and confidence in his decision on the other. As it happened, the officer changed his mind and a few days later made Michael both the legal officer and the equal opportunity officer. Indeed, in a few months the ship's racial practices had been reversed. And at quite a young age, Michael could write to law schools describing his pride in making a difference.

When I read this essay I felt triumphant. It seemed as if I really had done with my son what I had set out to do. I wanted to wave his essay in the face of all those who had doubted the wisdom of my undertaking, particularly a supervisor at the public human service agency, where I had initially inquired about a child. When my application to adopt a child as a single woman was being considered in 1970 by the Dallas Department of Welfare, the first such case that it had considered, my caseworker reported the response of her supervisor: "It's odd in this society for a woman not to be married. And it's odd for someone to be Jewish. And it's odd for a white woman to teach in a black college. And it's odd for a single person to adopt a child. And it's odd to adopt a biracial child. And a boy. How odd does this woman want to be?"

The woman had been right. I was odd. But I was not the random conglomeration of oddities that she had enumerated. I had always felt an outsider—bookish, awkward and idealistic. I had never felt at home talking about hairstyles or engaging in flirting. I enjoyed serious books, discussions and ideas. My values had led me to where I was at that point, a white woman teaching philosophy at a black college. My general sense of being an outsider freed me from any desire for superficial conformity. So, passionately wanting a child, I undertook adopting one when I was twenty-six and single.

Living on the campus of a black college, I found it natural when requesting to adopt a child not to make race a restriction. I told the agency I didn't care what sex the child was, but secretly I hoped for a boy, afraid I would be stymied by braids and hair bows. I realize now my ways of raising my son were a result of my own idiosyncrasies, the times, his personality and my relation to him. I realize these things only in retrospect. Then I thought it was simply a matter of enacting my convictions. Now I know the particularity of my experience because I am having quite another with my daughter, Miriam.

When I adopted Michael we lived on the campus of an historically black college. Most of the people we saw every day were African-American. In this situation, I could easily explain Michael's mixed racial heritage to him. I could say he was black and white, black like his babysitter, Fred, and like Ruthie, our much loved artist friend, and white like me.

I bought him black dolls and action figures. And books soon became a major tool for me to deal with racism and oppression. My son was charmed by narrative. I harnessed his interests for pedagogical purposes, turning to Greek, Norse and African myths and legends, concentrating on the heroic and the monstrous. And beyond being sure that the picture books I read included a racial mix of characters and that the fairy tales came from African, Asian and Native-American backgrounds as well as European, I soon began reading books explicitly concerned with oppression and liberation. When my six-year-old son in the season of Passover explained to me why a book jacket referred to Harriet Tubman as the Moses of her people, I rejoiced. All of the reading had paid off. He had been able to link different oppressions.

And I vigilantly kept books away from him that even fleetingly expressed racism. Sometimes it broke my heart. When he loved the Babar books, I sadly withheld one of the best, *The Travels of Babar*, because of one page that depicted Africans as grotesque cannibals. I wrote a children's book for him, offering a mythological account of the origin of racism.

School opened the door to the sometimes disturbing influences of the greater world, but, on the whole, his experience was not an unhappy one. When he began elementary school, he went to a school that was by court order 50 percent black and 50 percent white. Michael explained this fact in a striking way: "My school is half black and half white," he said, "and I (making the shape of a triangle with his hands) am at the top." My children's book became a part of the "tolerance curriculum" of his school. This school, however, was a bit difficult for him. Some of the black boys were more physically combative than he was, and some of the white boys called him "nigger." But Michael was a boy with a mind and a tongue. He formulated his retort for a number of days and then delivered it: "You can't call me nigger because I'm a honky, too, so you'd have to call me 'nigronky,' and you can't pronounce that so you'd just better shut up."

He found his circle of friends in school—a mixture of black and white. His best friend, Ruben, a bookish African-American boy, remained his friend through high school. Last summer, Ruben honored his junior high school promise to be the best man at Michael's wedding.

But there were moments in those elementary school years that tested my parental wisdom. One summer morning when he was seven, I waited with my son for the YMCA bus to take him to day camp. He told me that the day before some boys had called him "nigger," but he had responded that he wasn't black, he was Mexican. There were five minutes until the bus was due. What to say? With a dazzling sweep of history and in terms that were certainly too lofty for him, I began an account that had quite an historical sweep—beginning with Jews in Roman times and ending with Martin Luther King. "So, Michael," I ended, "Do you see why you can never deny who you are? Don't say you are Mexican when you are not." He looked up, assenting seriously, "Yeah, I figured that out. They've got bad names for Mexicans, too."

Although he did confront explicit racism in those years, the incidents were relatively rare, at least those he reported to me. And when he and I went about in the world together, we almost never heard negative remarks. Rather, we encountered an eery benevolence. I recall a white colleague commenting of Michael at three that he would be "a leader of his people." I remember the white woman who invited Michael to play, saying it would be good for her son because he had never played with a black child before. But mostly I remember that many people conveyed the idea that I had nobly rescued an unfortunate child.

I always found this strange. Perhaps his needs had been met, but what I noticed more was that mine had. Michael was the quintessential child, showing wild, infectious enthusiasm for everything. I, who never had celebrated any holiday with my parents, recouped my own childhood with him, finally getting to go trick or treating and bake chocolate chip cookies. And he willingly listened to my lectures on racism, accepting my explanations and categories.

Once, when he was in junior high school, I found him glued to the television, watching a documentary on the Ku Klux Klan, taking notes. "Look at how they describe me, 'half-breed, bastard, mongrel,'" he said with sardonic relish.

I basked in Michael's successes, unaware that I ignored certain things. Michael never dated in junior or senior high school. A trumpet player, he hung out with a large coeducational group of musicians. I knew of his crush on Crystal, a fellow trumpet player, a blond girl from a conservative Christian family. That he never dated her I attributed to his immaturity. It was puppy love. Only years later did I learn that her parents had forbidden her to go out with him. And he dated only rarely in college.

Miriam

I suddenly recalled these things when I adopted my daughter, Miriam. When my son was eighteen and poised for college, I again yearned for a child. Although I had doubts about whether I had the emotional and physical energy to combine a career with mothering again, I had no doubt that I could successfully raise a biracial child. It was clear I was equal to the task. Besides, this child would have Michael as a big brother to show the way.

Once again, in the adoption application, I said I was indifferent about the sex of the child, but this time I inwardly leaned toward a girl. Motherhood, feminism and the intervening years had changed my attitudes about my own femininity. I had not gotten any better at sewing, flirting, ironing or other traditional feminine skills; however, I came to appreciate my capacities for nurturing and emotional warmth as deeply feminine.

But a week after my application had been approved, the agency called to say they had a ten-month-old boy named Teddy for me to visit. It's hard to describe the emotions I felt the morning I prepared to go see the baby who would undoubtedly be mine that afternoon, for I had never seen a baby I didn't love. I paced the baby aisle at Toys R Us looking for just the right first gift from me to my new son. After hours of deliberation, I finally settled on a baby vehicle—it dinged, it honked, it moved. I knew it was just the sort of thing Michael would have loved as a baby. I went to see Teddy. He was a good-looking, sturdy, light-skinned boy with broad shoulders. In some ways, he resembled Michael. I picked him up and played with him. He smiled at me. But then I turned away and left. He was not my son. I would never have predicted that I could have refused any child. I can only guess that unconsciously I suspected that raising Teddy would be very much like raising Michael. And I wanted to do something different.

That day, I told the agency I wanted a girl. The social worker tried to dissuade me. Maybe I wouldn't get a baby at all. But I remained firm.

While I waited for my daughter, some of my friends expressed their views on my decision, rather forcefully. One, in particular, the mother of two boys, an old friend who very well knew all my vulnerabilities said, "Don't do it. She'll torture you. She'll criticize your hair." She referred to a very sensitive area of my psyche. All my life, my friends and relatives had said, "You would look very nice if only you would do something with your hair." My hair was curly, wild. I tried—straightening it, setting it—but always I was ineffectual. After I had expended my best efforts, someone would inevitably say, "Why don't you do something with your hair?" I ignored my friend's comments, attributing them in part to sour grapes. Probably she would have liked to have a girl.

The adoption agency called one day with the news of my three-day-old daughter, Miriam. But even while immersed in the unprecedented bliss I felt holding her, I began to worry. Friends who had adopted biracial girls had had terribly sad experiences with their teenage daughters, who were unhappy and self-destructive. Was there something about being a biracial girl in a white family? Were females in spite of everything too much identified with their bodies in adolescence to psychically survive that kind of difference in the family?

Miriam lay in the crib, and I paced the floor. So anxiety-ridden was I that when Miriam was one month old, I made an appointment with a child psychologist who specialized in adoption. She tactfully showed little shock that I was consulting her about a one-month-old, reassured me and made some suggestions about Miriam's development.

I continued to worry about Miriam until she revealed her personality. When she was three months old, my worry abated, and by the time she was five months old, it had disappeared. I had learned who Miriam was. One of the happiest children I had ever seen, she met the world with complete openness and confidence. She was peculiarly attentive to all, adjusting her manner to suit them.

One of my most vivid memories pictures her as a baby in an oncologist's office. When Miriam was eight months old, I quite often drove our friend Roberta, who had metastasized breast cancer, to her treatments. Miriam accompanied us. When we entered the doctor's office, Miriam seemingly sensed the atmosphere. She responded by turning her most winning smiles on each waiting patient in turn. Gradually, the mood lifted, as the patients smiled and talked to Miriam. But even as a roomful of people focused on her, if there was one patient who remained withdrawn, she wouldn't rest until she had engaged and charmed that one, too.

Yes, it was hard to worry about Miriam's future, when she seemed to have such a grounded personality. A friend of mine, steeped in eastern religions, said of Miriam that she had an old soul. I have no affinity for such a metaphysical framework, but the judgment resonated with me. It seemed absurd to say of a baby that she was wise, but yet . . .

As Michael had been hungry for books and narration, Miriam craved social interaction, and her play always involved people visiting each other. In tune with the wider society, she became fixated on hair when she was three. She had beautiful short, curly hair, but she yearned for long hair. She began placing the neck of a T-shirt over her head, fastening it with a rubber band or hair fastener and calling it her long hair. She had a Nefertiti look. She mastered all the long hair gestures of little girls and practiced them with her T-shirt. I could have let her hair grow, fixing it in multiple braids, but I doubted my ability to do so. Besides, what she wanted was long, straight hair; she wanted to possess society's ideal of beauty, which in spite of my best efforts, she had absorbed at the age of three. I felt terrible.

It was in the midst of this stage that we visited Carol, the friend who had originally made the pronouncement about my potential daughter torturing me with hair. As she watched Miriam going through her "long hair" rituals, my friend fixed me with a significant "told you so" look. I felt I had been captured in a fairy tale at the moment when Sleeping Beauty pricks her finger; the curse of the evil fairy had in spite of all efforts been realized.

Miriam was also troubled by her color. I now taught in a predominantly white university, perhaps unconsciously following the advice given to me so long ago by my black radical colleagues—be a missionary to your own people. Consequently, although we had black friends, most of the people we saw on a daily basis were white. Occasionally, when I held Miriam's hand in mine or our arms were entwined, she would say, "I wish we were the same color. I wish I were your color." I would reply saying, "If we were the same color, I would choose yours. It's much prettier." But Miriam was adamant. She insisted that white was better.

I tried every means at my disposal to dislodge her from this attitude—books, lectures, stories, toys and talks from her brother. But all the techniques that had worked so well with Michael were futile with her. She did not respond to narration or words. With Michael, I had placed an ideological screen on the world, and he saw the world through the filter I imposed. Miriam refused such interventions; she directly imbibed the social world. By the time she was three, she knew that in society white was better.

As I learned that my words and stories were useless with Miriam, I learned also that the boundaries between us were more permeable than those with Michael. He and I had communicated quite satisfactorily with each other through stories. Miriam and I had direct access to each other's psyches. Once, when she was four, I learned that one of her best friends was having a small birthday party to which she had not been invited. The party's theme was ludicrous and distasteful—a makeover for four-year-olds complete with manicures, makeup, and new hairdos. I certainly would have been outraged if she had been invited. But she hadn't, and I sank into a deep depression, spiraling down to the despair of my own childhood isolation.

Maternal Powers and Their Limitations

My identification with Miriam has put me in a strange position in the racial nexus, and recently I have found myself occupying and using that position self-consciously, but with mixed results. For example, in preparing a talk on Toni Morrison's *The Bluest Eye* for a community group, I contemplated what felt like a risky strategy. I would talk about Miriam, her struggles with her hair, and my own anguish in watching those struggles as a way of vividly conveying the torment of Morrison's character, eleven-year-old Pecola Breedlove. Finding herself ugly because she is black, Pecola desires the most quintessentially white attribute—blue eyes. But immediately after conceiving the strategy, I felt terribly anxious and immensely vulnerable. The women I'd be lecturing to were financially comfortable and politically conservative. Would they feel revulsion for the way I had chosen to live my life? I couldn't accurately assess their racial attitudes, for, although I had lived in Dallas a long time, I was still essentially a Yankee, a stranger in the South. So I consulted a new friend, Lark, a native southerner, whose judgment I nevertheless trusted implicitly. She had kindly been attending my lectures, even acting as a kind of undercover agent for me, hitting the ladies' room at the end of each talk, learning what the critics were saying there.

"These women," she said, with a voice of genuine authority, "remind me of my mother. My mother does not believe in racial mixing, but she is always polite."

"And so how would your mother respond to Miriam and me?" I asked.

"I just don't know. I don't know how closed off she is, how much she would allow herself to learn. But you should try it."

With much shaking and trepidation, I did try it. I thought that I had established a relationship with these women, that they liked me, and so I asserted the authority of experience. I, as a white woman, had had the unusual sensation of feeling racism directly in a way these women would recognize as valid—by living it through my daughter. I talked about hair—their hair, my hair and Miriam's hair. More than a conversation about racism, it felt like a direct communication of racism.

In the end, I don't know how I succeeded because the women *were* polite, but they did seem more attentive than usual when I spoke about hair. After the lecture, several women approached me confidentially, talking about conversations with their maids or black children in their class that bothered or puzzled them. It seems that suddenly I had made a realm of experience accessible and a possible topic of discussion.

But had I exploited Miriam in this talk? Was I aggrandizing myself, thinking that I, a "privileged" white person who had experienced racism through my child, could bridge the races? I know that I can get terribly confused in these situations. My encounter with Lark's mother was a telling example.

At the time of her mother's visit, both Miriam and I were enthusiastic about Lark's family. Miriam was best friends with Katy, Lark's daughter, and I was elated by acquiring a new friend, on terms of intimacy that I had despaired of having with anyone whom I met for the first time in middle age.

As Miriam and I were getting ready to meet Lark's mother, Cokie (a childhood name that had stuck), I found myself acting very peculiarly. I was issuing strange directions to Miriam: Fix your hair again, tuck in your shirt, don't wear that outfit. Finally, Miriam said, "We're not going to a party, only to Katy's house." I tried to figure out what was going on. I knew a great deal about Cokie. I had heard, for example, that one day at Toys R Us, Cokie had promised to buy her then five-year-old granddaughter anything she wanted. But when Katy picked out a black Barbie, Cokie refused to buy it in spite of the tearful protests of her beloved granddaughter. Cokie was a racist, but one I couldn't dismiss because of her importance to someone important to me.

I realized I was falling under the spell of Cokie's racism. I carefully attended to Miriam's grooming because I didn't want her to fulfill Cokie's racist stereotype. When we arrived at Lark's house, Miriam immediately darted off to play with Katy, and I enjoyed myself talking to Cokie, trying to figure out how my friend resembled her mother. Then, Cokie said she wanted to meet "my family." Miriam was summoned. She took the moment of introduction as an opportunity to demonstrate her recently acquired burping skills. I became furious at Miriam, and then instantly at myself. Why was I placing on Miriam the burden of overcoming anyone's racism? No doubt, I had unconsciously fantasized that Cokie, taken in by Miriam's charms, would begin altering her attitudes. I realized, too, that led by Miriam, my views of combating racism had changed. It was no longer a matter of explaining positions but rather influencing experiences.

There are certain experiences I simply don't want Miriam to have. Katy, for example, suggested that Miriam go with her to visit her grandmother in Arkadelphia. I said, "No, Miriam, you can never go there." Taken aback by the absolute nature of my prohibition, Miriam asked why. I answered, "because Arkansas just has too many racists." Ever adaptive, Miriam said, "Well, there must be some people who like blacks, and I'll just hang out with them."

I have continued to try to supply Miriam with the conceptual ammunition she needs. I continue to read with her about black history . . . with varying degrees of success. When she was five, I purchased Faith Ringgold's beautiful *Aunt Harriet's Underground in the Sky*, an imaginative rendering of Harriet Tubman and the Underground Railroad, but when I began to read it, Miriam quickly stopped me as we reached the page depicting the block at a slave auction, saying, "Close the book, Mommy, it's too scary." But recently when Miriam attended a conference with me, we saw Faith Ringgold, a striking figure in an imaginative combination of African and western garb. Miriam immediately wanted to talk to her and tell her that we had read her book.

Miriam is getting older now, and she cannot shut history out forever. Last year, I made her continue to listen to a child's biography of Martin Luther King, Jr., even when the stories of segregation made her once again plead with me to shut the book. "Hold on, Miriam," I told her, "it's about to get very good." I was glad I insisted. Inspired by the protests, she played civil rights march all afternoon, carrying "Jim Crow Must Go" signs up and down the living room. She revisited Martin Luther King this year as part of a school project. In the middle of the book, she sadly shook her head, "I guess white people are mean." "No, Miriam," I replied, "lots of white people marched with King. I marched with his friends."

A week later, I found myself talking to Miriam about the Holocaust. When I briefly related the horrors of that period to her, explaining how they had affected my family and the families of our friends, Miriam surprised me by saying, "I wish I had been alive then." "But why?" I asked, "It was horrible." "I want to fight evil people. I want to fight the Nazis. I wish I could have marched with Martin Luther King." "Oh, but Miriam," I replied "there are still things to fight against." "Okay," she said, "help me find them."

Miriam remains dissatisfied with her hair. The kids in her class call her "Afro-puff." The picture on the mantel with her in long braids reflects a fleeting idyllic moment. Soon after, her braids began loosening.

I panicked because we were setting out for Taos, New Mexico, where I was to teach a course. I anticipated that there wouldn't be a black person for five hundred miles. What was I going to do if Miriam's braids were half in and half out? The first night at the isolated campus, however, a beautiful black woman in her forties with a hairdo identical to Miriam's approached us, saying she had heard wonderful things about my teaching. Inwardly I rejoiced. Soon I became fast friends with Matilda, and she took an interest in Miriam and her hair.

This semester Matilda decided to take a class of mine. Last week I mentioned a gesture of reconciliation between the races at the end of Bebe Moore Campbell's *Brothers and Sisters*. The angry black female protagonist decides to fix the hair of the little biracial girl next door, forgiving her white mother who didn't know how. Suddenly I heard a loud giggle in the class. I looked up and burst into laughter myself, sharing the moment with Matilda, both of us wondering if Miriam would ever fix her hair to her satisfaction.

"Ain't That Love?"

Antiracism and Racial Constructions of Motherhood

ANDREA O'REILLY

Dominant ideologies and discourses of mothering and motherhood are racialized and racist; that is, they represent only one experience of mothering, that of white middle-class women, and position this experience as the real, natural and universal one. Any discussion of mothers and antiracism must, therefore, begin with an understanding of how discourses of motherhood become racially codified and constructed. This essay explores how the development and dissemination of one normative discourse of motherhood—that of so-called sensitive mothering—causes other experiences of mothering—working class, ethnic— to be marginalized and delegitimized.

Motherhood is a cultural construction that varies with time and place; there is no one essential or universal experience of motherhood. However, the diverse meanings and experiences of mothering become marginalized and erased through the construction of an official definition of motherhood. Through a complex process of intersecting forces— economics, politics, cultural institutions (what Teresa de Lauretis would call social technologies)—the dominant definition of motherhood is codified as the official and only meaning of motherhood.[1] Alternative meanings of mothering are marginalized and rendered illegitimate. The dominant definition is able to suppress its own construction as an ideology and thus naturalizes its specific construction of motherhood as the universal, real, natural maternal experience.

The dominant discourse of motherhood is, however, historically determined and thus variable. In the Victorian era, for example, the ideology of moral motherhood that saw mothers as naturally pure, pious and chaste emerged as the dominant discourse. This ideology, however, was race- and class-specific: Only white and middle-class women could wear the halo of the madonna and transform the world through their moral influence and social housekeeping. Slave mothers, in contrast, were defined as breeders, placed not on a pedestal, as white women were, but on the auction block.

After World War II, the discourse of the happy homemaker made the "stay-at-home mom and apple pie" mode of mothering the normal and natural motherhood experience. Again, only white and middle-class women could, in fact, experience what discursively was inscribed as natural and universal. In the 1970s, the era in which many baby boomers became parents, a new hegemonic discourse of motherhood began to take shape, one that authors Valerie Walkerdine and Helen Lucey appropriately term "sensitive mothering" in their landmark book *Democracy in the Kitchen: Regulating Mothers and Socialising Daughters.*

Walkerdine and Lucey examine how the maternal behavior of the middle-class became culturally constructed and codified as the real, normal and natural way to mother. Natural mothering begins with the ideological presupposition that children have needs that are met by the mother. To mother, therefore, is to be sensitive to the needs of children, that is, to engage in sensitive mothering. The first characteristic of the sensitive mother, Walkerdine and Lucey explain,

is that her domestic life is centred around her children and not around her housework. The boundaries between this work and children's play have to be blurred . . . While the mother is being sensitive to the child's needs, she is not doing any housework. She has to be available and ready to meet demands, and those household tasks which she undertakes have to become pedagogic tasks . . . The second feature of the sensitive mother is the way she regulates her children. Essentially there should be no overt regulation; regulation should go underground; no power battles, no insensitive sanctions as these would interfere with the child's illusion that she is the source of her wishes, that she has "free will." [2]

This mode of mothering is drawn from the parenting styles of the so-called baby-boom generation. Today good mothering is defined as child-centered and is characterized by flexibility, spontaneity, democracy, affection, nurturance and playfulness. This mode of mothering is contrasted to the earlier stern, rigid, authoritative, "a child should be seen and not heard" variety of parenting. Today's ideal mother is not only expected to be "at home" with her children—as her mother was with her in the fifties—she is also required to spend, in the language of eighties' parenting books, "quality time" with her children. While the fifties mom would put her children in the pram or playpen to tend to her household chores, today's mom is to "be with" her child at all times physically and, most importantly, psychologically. Whether the activity is one of the numerous structured moms-and-tots programs—swimming, kindergym, dance—or an at-home activity—reading, gardening, cooking, playing—the mother's day is to revolve around the child, not her housework as it was in the fifties, and is to be centered upon the child's educational development. The child is to be involved in any domestic labor performed and the chore at hand is be transformed into a learning experience for the child.

Working-class mothers, Walkerdine and Lucey emphasize, do not practice so-called sensitive mothering; work does not become play nor do power and conflict go underground. Working-class mothers, in the authors' study, do play with their children but only after domestic chores have been tended to. In working-class households, the boundaries between mothering and domestic labor are maintained and the very real work of domestic labor is not transformed—or trivialized—into a game for the child's benefit. Nor does the mother abdicate her power and authority to create the illusion of a family democracy. This type of mothering, however, becomes pathologized as deficiency and deviance because the middle-class style of sensitive mothering has been codified, both socially and discursively, as natural. Working-class mothering is, thus, not simply different, it is deemed unnatural, and working-class mothers are deemed unfit mothers in need of regulation. In other words, "there is something wrong with working-class mothering which should be put right by making it more middle-class."[3]

Lucey and Walkerdine do not specifically look at African-American mothering in their book. The research that has been done on black mothering, however, does suggest that Lucey and Walkerdine's observations may be applied to black women's experiences of mothering, at least among working-class families.[4] Patricia Hill Collins, for example, argues, in her many works on black mothering, that there is a distinct African-American experience of mothering. African-American mothering, what she calls mother-work, is about "maintain[ing] family life in the face of forces that undermine family integrity" while "recognizing that individual survival, empowerment, and identity require group survival, empowerment, and identity."[5] Central concerns of "racial ethnic" (Collins's term) mothers include keeping the children born to you, the physical survival of those children, teaching the children resistance and how to survive in a racist world, giving to those children their racial/cultural history and identity, and a social activism and communal mothering on behalf of all the community's children. What the research on black mothering suggests is that sensitive mothering is not valued or practiced by African-American mothers, particularly if the family in question is urban and working-class.

In her brilliant book *Maternal Thinking*, Sara Ruddick argues that the first duty of mothers is to protect and preserve their children: "to keep safe whatever is vulnerable and valuable in a child."[6] "Preserving the lives of children," Ruddick writes, "is the central constitutive, invariant aim of maternal practice."[7] "To be committed to meeting children's demand for preservation," Ruddick continues, "does not require enthusiasm or even love; it simply means to see vulnerability and to respond to it with care rather than abuse, indifference, or flight."[8] Though maternal practice is composed of two other demands—nurturance and training—this first demand, what Ruddick calls preservative love, is what describes much of economically disadvantaged African-American women's mother-work. For many African-American women, securing food, shelter and clothing, building safe neighborhoods, and fighting a racist world is what defines both the meaning and experience of their mother-work and mother-love. However, because sensitive mothering has been naturalized as the universal normal experience of motherhood, preservative love is not regarded as real, legitimate or "good enough" mothering.

In the mothering of my children and in my teaching on motherhood, I seek to challenge the normative discourse of sensitive mothering by inscribing mothering as a culturally determined experience. I bring to this struggle the experience of being raised in a white, middle-class family by a working-class mother. The stories my mother tells me of my early childhood indicate that my mother's mode of mothering was clearly that of working-class 1950s culture. She used to "air" me on the front porch in the pram and, later, in the playpen each morning—summers and winters—as she tended to her housework and the caring of my infant sister. It was the early 1960s, and my mother had an eight-year-old daughter from her first marriage and three children under the age of three from her second marriage.

My mother grew up poor in a working-class family from, what was called in my hometown of Hamilton, Ontario, the "wrong side of the tracks." In the 1950s she found herself divorced with a young baby to raise. At twenty-eight she married my father, a man from an established middle-class family, and moved to middle-class suburbia. My mother has often told me she never really felt she was a part of the suburban culture of young motherhood—the morning coffees in each other's kitchens, afternoons in the park, recipe sharing, and the borrowing of that cup of sugar.

Having had my children in graduate school with no one to share young motherhood with, I envied my mother and could not understand why she kept herself apart from what I imagined to be a feminist utopia of female solidarity. Only recently have I been able to see my mother's experience for what it was: It was the 1950s, and she was an older divorcee with a young daughter, from a poor, working-class family, among young, newly married women from "good" middle-class families. I can only imagine the culture shock she must have experienced and speculate upon how she was received by those "good" middle-class neighbors of hers. The memories of my later childhood reveal that my mother eventually became part of that middle-class culture and practiced, at least occasionally, the so-called sensitive mothering Walkerdine and Lucey discuss.

The struggles of my mother were replayed when I became a mother thirty years later at the relatively young age of twenty-three. While my class affiliation was middle-class, my spouse was working-class; and though we were educated—both of us were pursuing graduate degrees at the time—we were also very poor. At that time, though, my energies were focused on challenging the oppressiveness of motherhood as a patriarchal institution. As a student of women's studies, my perspective was decidedly feminist, and I sought to imagine and achieve an experience of mothering that was empowering or, at the very least, not oppressive to me or my children. What I had not considered in my feminist practice of mothering was how the philosophy of so-called sensitive mothering to which I subscribed was a regulatory discourse as oppressive as the patriarchal one with which I was familiar.

I became conscious of the class and racial dimensions of discourses on mothering only upon reading *Democracy in the Kitchen* and Toni Morrison's novel *Sula* midway through my early mothering years.[9] What these readings forced me to recognize is that although so-called sensitive mothering is neither real nor universal, it results in the regulation of middle-class mothers and the pathologizing of working-class mothering.

I planned to use the novel *Sula* in my teaching as a way to talk about racist constructions of motherhood and to arrive at an antiracist perspective in the way we perceive and practice mothering. I became more and more convinced that any attempt at teaching antiracism to children and students was doomed to failure as long as our perceptions and practices of mothering were racialized and racist. How can a white middle-class woman who sees her sensitive mothering as more real— and hence superior—possibly teach antiracism to her child? In turn, how can a black mother empower her child to resist racism when that child is encouraged to see her own mother's mode of mothering as insufficient? With these questions in mind I set to work.

I presented a lecture on *Sula* at the conclusion of a first-year humanities course entitled "Concepts of the Male and Female in Western

Culture" in March 1995, a class made up mostly of mature and returning students. The perspective of the course was thoroughly feminist and issues of race and racism had been discussed in the classroom. My audience was, thus, a highly informed and, for the most part, receptive one.

I spoke with much passion on how the mother's preservative love in the novel had been pathologized by the critics because it did not fit the bill of sensitive mothering. I stressed the need to deconstruct the hegemony of sensitive mothering so that other expressions of mothering are given legitimacy and validity. With this lecture I hoped to generate discussion on the ways in which black and working-class women's mothering is often delegitimized and how white middle-class women are regulated in trying to achieve this sensitive mothering. Instead, what I got was a hazy fog of incomprehension, bewilderment and indifference.

Interestingly, when I moved from the topic of mothering to other themes in *Sula*—women's friendship, growing up female—I could feel—almost see—a shift in the students' response to my lecture: Suddenly there was connection, interest and understanding. I also observed, though could not account for, a noticeable change in the emotional climate of the lecture hall. Inexplicably, during the first part of my lecture on motherhood the atmosphere was serious and noticeably tense, yet in the latter section the mood was lighthearted and relaxed. When we talked about the lecture and text later in tutorial, the students, much to my dismay, replicated the patronizing stance of the critics regarding Eva's mothering—we can't be too hard on her, it wasn't her fault, she would have done it differently had she had the choice and so on. They had missed the whole point of my lecture.

I was troubled, dismayed and perplexed by my students' misunderstanding/incomprehension; eventually though I attributed it to a weak lecture. Not until I started working on this essay did I think about the experience again and see it from a different perspective. At the same time, a Caribbean student in a course I was teaching told the class about her family experience. This student's mother, like many Caribbean women, came to Canada in the early 1970s to secure work and left her children back home with her parents in the hope of creating a better life for them. The mother sent her earnings home, visited her children on holidays, and several years later, when she had good, permanent work, had her children join her in Canada. The eldest sister had great difficulty adjusting to this change and blamed her mother for being absent all those years. Good mothers, the daughter told her mother, don't leave their children for a day, let alone for many years. Good mothers, like those of her Canadian friends, did things with their kids, were not always so tired and away so much working. What the daughter was saying is: Why can't you be more like other mothers? Why can't you be normal?

Hearing this student's story I began to make sense of my former students' reaction to my lecture. Though sensitive mothering is a recent ideological construction of motherhood—having been around only two decades—it has very successfully taken up residence in the dominant culture. (It reminds one of the aliens in *The Invasion of the Body Snatchers* who enter and take over, en masse, the human population.) Good mothers read to their children, enroll them in ballet and piano lessons, enrich them with theatre, art and culture; they are patient, nurturing, spontaneous, sensitive and—most importantly—child-centered, transforming even the most mundane task into an entertaining and educational experience for their children.

Now no mother can actually live the ideological script of sensitive mothering, though all mothers are judged by it and many mothers seek to achieve it. And most children, very much cultural creatures, interpret their own mother's mothering from the discourse of sensitive mothering. On several occasions my children have responded to my behavior or comments with the statement: Mothers don't do, or say, that. We have embraced so completely this discourse of mothering that we see it as the best, ideal, normal and, ultimately, only way to mother. Hence my students' confusion: Why would I problematize something so good, so natural? Why wouldn't I want the characters in this book to partake in such mothering, given how good it is? And why shouldn't we help others to achieve the same experience of sensitive mothering? Why not indeed?

With my own children I struggle to make conscious to them the ways in which mothering is overdetermined and regulated by cultural discourses, such as sensitive mothering. Discussions about racism and antiracism have always been part of our children's upbringing. What is more difficult to work through with our growing children is, I think, how practices of mothering are racialized and class-specific. After all, kids don't see mothering as a practice. I strive to challenge that perception in my mothering. What I seek to emphasize to my children, both in word and deed, is that my experience of mothering and their experience of being mothered are culturally determined. I want them to know that children are mothered differently and that one way is not any more real, natural or legitimate than any other way.

When my kids respond to something I have said or done with the line "Mothers don't do that" or, conversely, "All the other mothers are . . . so why can't you?" I remind them that there is no one way to mother or be mothered. As I seek to free myself from the regulation of sensitive mothering, I share with my children my critique of this discourse by giving concrete examples of how this discourse is oppressive to me— and by implication to them—and how it results in the "putting down" of other mothers.

In my critique of sensitive mothering I am not suggesting that I am against reading to your child or playing, every now and then, "let's wash the floors" to make enjoyable an otherwise tedious chore. However, what I do find deeply disturbing is the codification of this discourse as the official and only way to mother. Walkerdine and Lucey argue that sensitive mothering is ultimately bad for both mother and child: It trivializes women's domestic labor, causes the mother's workday to be never-ending and compels her to be manipulative with her children— to make them believe that her wishes are really their own—so as to avoid authoritarianism and conflict. It causes the child to confuse work with play and to see the self as completely in control of circumstances— somewhat problematic lessons, particularly for black and working-class kids in a racist and capitalist world. While I agree with Lucey and Walkerdine's observations, I am less interested in debating the pros and cons of sensitive mothering than in deconstructing any normative discourse of mothering that pathologizes difference and seeks to regulate it.

What has this to do with mothers acting against racism? My students' incomprehension at my lecture and my student's moving story have brought home to me the intricate relationship between mothering and racism; mothering and antiracism. If that mother could have told her daughter that her survivalist type of mother-love—mothering as separation—*was* an expression of mothering, as good as, if not better than, the dominant mode, perhaps there would have been less blame and more understanding between mother and daughter. With my own lecture I would have been able to talk about an antiracist perspective with respect to mothering far more effectively had the students not been so thoroughly identified with the dominant discourse of mothering.

Adrienne Rich in her ovarian work *Of Woman Born* discusses how motherhood is an institution that is defined and controlled by patriarchy. I would add that ideologies of mothering, and the institutions they create, are also thoroughly racialized and racist. I believe that the teaching and practice of antiracism through mothering can happen if, and only if, the dominant mode of mothering is identified and challenged as racist. It does not help to build an antiracist household on foundations that are racist.

—The author wishes to acknowledge the Contract Faculty Research Grants Fund of York University, Toronto, Canada, for support of this work.

Notes

1. Teresa de Lauretis, "The Technology of Gender," in *Technologies of Gender* (Bloomington: Indiana University Press, 1987), 1–30.

2. Valerie Walkerdine and Helen Lucey, *Democracy in the Kitchen: Regulating Mothers and Socialising Daughters* (London: Virago Press, 1989) 20, 23–24.

3. Ibid., taken from the back cover.

4. See, for example: Valora Washington, "The Black Mother in the United States: History, Theory, Research, and Issues," in *The Different Faces of Motherhood,* ed. Beverly Birns and Dale F. Hay (New York: Plenum Press, 1988), 185–213; Filomina Chioma Steady, ed., *The Black Woman Cross-Culturally* (Rochester, VT: Schenkman Books, 1981); Patricia Bell-Scott et al., *Double Stitch: Black Women Write About Mothers and Daughters* (New York: HarperPerennial, 1991); Carol B. Stack, *All Our Kin: Strategies for Survival in a Black Community* (New York: Harper & Row, 1974); Patricia

Hill Collins, *Black Feminist Thought: Knowledge, Consciousness and the Politics of Empowerment* (New York: Unwin Hyman, 1990); bell hooks, "Revolutionary Parenting" in *Feminist Theory: From Margin to Center* (Boston: South End Press, 1984), 133–46, and "Homeplace" in *Yearning: Race, Gender, and Cultural Politics* (Boston: South End Press, 1990), 41–49.

5. Patricia Hill Collins, "Shifting the Center: Race, Class, and Feminist Theorizing About Motherhood" in *Mothering: Ideology, Experience, and Agency,* ed. Evelyn Nakano Glenn, Grace Chang and Linda Rennie Forcey (New York: Routledge, 1994), 47.

6. Sara Ruddick, *Maternal Thinking: Toward a Politics of Peace* (Boston: Beacon, 1989), 80.

7. Ibid., 19.

8. Ibid.

9. Toni Morrison, *Sula* (New York: New American Library, 1973). The contemporary critical responses to a dialogue in the novel brought home to me how thoroughly identified our culture is with the discourse of sensitive mothering. In this novel, Eva, the mother, is left by her husband in 1895 with "$1.65, five eggs, three beets" and three children to feed. After her baby son nearly dies from constipation Eva leaves her children in the care of a neighbor, saying she will be back the next day, only to return eighteen months later with money and one of her legs gone. It was rumored that Eva placed her leg under a train in order to collect insurance money to support her children. Years later, her now adult daughter, Hannah, asks her mother if "[She] ever love[d] us?" The mother responds: "You settin' here with your healthy-ass self and ax me did I love you? Them big old eyes in your head would a been two holes full of maggots if I hadn't." The daughter then asks: "Did you ever, you know, play with us?" Eva replies: "Play? Wasn't nobody playin' in 1895. Just 'cause you got it good now you think it was always this good? 1895 was a killer, girl. Things was bad. Niggers was dying like flies . . . Don't that count? Ain't that love? You want me to tinkle you under the jaw and forget 'bout them sores in your mouth?" (67–69). Many readers of the novel question, with Hannah, whether Eva did in fact mother her children. Her mothering has been called unnatural and untraditional. The words unnatural and untraditional, however, accrue meaning only if both the speaker (writer) and listener (reader) know what is meant by their opposites, the normative terms—in this instance, natural and traditional. When a critic, like Dayle Delancy, laments that Eva has "no time to lavish traditional displays of affection upon her children" or that "she has to work for the survival of her offspring at the expense of having fun with them" ["Motherlove Is a Killer" in *Sage* 8 (fall 1990): 15–18] she is working from a very specific discourse of what constitutes good mothering—namely that of sensitive mothering.

When Our Faces Are at the Bottom of the Well[1]

SHAWN R. DONALDSON

At this opportunity to "speak my piece," I am overwhelmed with emotions: elation that such a volume exists; frustration that I have been fighting racism "since since," constantly responding to its chameleon nature; anger because of the unfairness of it all. I share the life experience of Hannah Nelson in that she remarked, "I have grown to womanhood in a world where the saner you are, the madder you are made to appear."[2] Indeed, hopeful hopelessness is the result of living in a society suffering from "racial schizophrenia."[3]

I find some solace in my professional work. In fact, I chose sociology as my major and area of scholarly pursuit because it permitted me to make sense of the world on both the micro and macro levels. I recall the initial excitement of every disclosure concerning social stratification, authority and social control. In discovering the invisible yet potent influences that condition behavior and attitudes, I became self-accepting and self-assured. It is precisely this inner strength and confidence that I want to instill in my daughters, Layla and Ayanna, presently two and seven, respectively.

As a parent, an educator, a scholar and a woman of African descent,

I knew I would eventually have to address the issue of white supremacy as well as other types of oppression with my children, but my responsibility in this regard seemed overwhelming. Thus like many parents, I attempted to insulate my elder daughter, Ayanna, from the ugliness of the world. When this effort failed, I changed my tactic, planning to handle racist or sexist attacks on her personhood as they occurred, which I hoped would not be often. In essence, why focus on the issue of oppression when it is not necessary and so unpleasant? However, are we ever truly prepared for the moment when we see the distress/puzzlement/hurt conveyed on that wonderful once-sparkling face because of a racial slur? And so when we respond to such incidents, how do we walk the tightrope between realism and idealism? How do we therapeutically heal our children and subsequently ourselves in order to move on? Do we educate our children as to the permanence of racism in America and the righteousness of struggle for the sake of struggle or have them literally (figuratively?) dream about an end to the madness while suffering disappointment after disappointment? What are parents to do when our "faces are at the bottom of the well"?

As I view the tremendous losses in the civil and human rights struggles on the horizon—the dismantling of affirmative action, the rise of socially acceptable levels of expressed racial hatred, police brutality disproportionately targeted at people of color and/or the poor, the coded racial overtones of anti-poor sentiments—deep-rooted pessimism sets in. Consequently, I am reminded of Derrick Bell's assertions on the profitability and permanence of racism in America as discussed in *Faces at the Bottom of the Well*:

> To initiate the reconsideration, I want to set forth this proposition, which will be easier to reject than refute: *Blacks will never gain full equality in this country. Even those herculean efforts we hail as successful will produce no more than temporary "peaks of progress," short-lived victories that slide into irrelevance as racial patterns adapt in ways to maintain white dominance. This is a hard-to-accept fact that all history verifies. We must acknowledge it, not as a sign of submission, but as an act of ultimate defiance.*[4]

So, finally, someone has given voice to my hollow feelings while singing "We Shall Overcome" at local programs, churches and tributes. We shall overcome what? Racism in America? Get real. Hasn't this song been our somber rallying cry for decades? Where are we now? Where are we headed in respect to the pre-1960s civil rights movement? Again, I am compelled to reconsider Bell's bone-chilling assessment of our status in America—past, present and future. If we accept Bell's position as the gospel, a bitter pill we must/should swallow, a profound statement on America at the macro sociopolitical and economic levels, then what of hope? Hope for the future and particularly the hope of and for our children to thrive, excel or even merely survive in such a society?

In response, Bell advocates a rather noble approach: struggle for the sake of struggle. Struggle as an end rather than a means to an end. Struggle as a moral responsibility. To quote Bell:

> Struggle to gain full acceptance in this country, for all black people—as opposed to some black individuals—is virtually impossible in the society as we know it. But the obligation to try and improve the lot of blacks and other victims of injustice (including whites) does not end because final victory over racism is unlikely, even impossible. The essence of life fulfilled—a succession of actions undertaken in righteous causes—is a victory in itself.[5]

Therefore, I feel victorious for taking a stand as my oldest child began the rites of passage into being not-white in America.

It was a day just like any other day—or so I thought. Juggling my multiple professional and domestic roles and attempting to organize the family at the onset of another academic year, I asked Ayanna about her day at school. In essence, she was excited about being a first grader, somewhat bored with the review of subject matter extensively covered in kindergarten and happy to be reunited with her friends from kindergarten. Overall, I had been pleased with her academic performance (particularly reading aptitude), the diversity of the student population and the caring environment of the Catholic school she attended.

Nothing appeared to be wrong until my husband approached me the next day. Apparently, Ayanna had come to him the night before because she was confused, bewildered and hurt about an event the previous day. Beatrice, a white friend from kindergarten—"friend" as in having hung out during recess, eaten lunch together, called each other at home and attended each other's birthday parties—stated that she could no longer have black friends. Her father had made it quite clear. After getting over the initial shock, I asked Ayanna to recollect in detail exactly what had transpired. The revelation did not come out in a private conversation but a declaration to the class. At recess, some of the black girls asked her for clarification. "Does it mean that we can't play together anymore?" they inquired. But, they had observed, Beatrice was already playing with a black girl from their class. Obviously confused by the situation, Beatrice declared that she would indeed play with black girls, but her daddy could not know. I can recall myself repeatedly saying, "What?!?" in total disbelief at the disclosure of every minute detail. Poor, poor Beatrice. The child had made a bold but perhaps dangerous decision. In her own childish wisdom she had decided to defy her father's mandate. Was Sister Joyce present when Beatrice made the initial statement? And, what was her response? Well, she said that she thought Beatrice's father was wrong. Thank God, I thought to myself, but no follow-up? No discussion of racism or prejudice? No contact with the parents since this attitude clearly undermines the mission of the school?

Exhausted yet invigorated, I verbally and physically hugged my child who was obviously injured by the experience. Reassuring her that she was wonderful and a fine friend, I asked her why she didn't tell me about her day when I asked. Her "I don't know" was sufficient for the moment. Perhaps she thought I would get Beatrice in trouble if she shared the secret. I explained to her how ridiculous—no, downright stupid—people could be to choose their friends simply on the way they looked rather than how they were treated or behaved. Then we played the "What If . . . " game and role-played a number of scenarios for her to understand prejudice in different forms (that is, due to physical size, ability, scarification, gender). We concluded that prejudice wasn't right and didn't feel nice, but what of her immediate concern—her endangered relationship with Beatrice? Would she still be her friend? I could not answer that question, but I was determined to get an answer, some answers, from someone.

That evening I called Beatrice's parents and their teacher but initially I called my best friend to calm me down. How dare he, I thought. This ignorant man has damaged, possibly destroyed a caring, loving relationship between two innocent children with his bigotry. And, my child is left to ponder why her race suddenly has become so repugnant as to warrant rejection from her friend's father. In face of this aggressive attack, it doesn't matter that our household decorum, our behavior, our hairstyles, our holiday celebrations, our storytelling, our playthings, even our wardrobes are African-centered and consequently reinforce a pride in self, race, ancestry and family. Ayanna was made to feel inferior, less than, simply because of the color of her skin. Now, she was unworthy of having Beatrice as a friend.

Composed, I relayed to Beatrice's mother, Shirley, Ayanna's account of what happened. Immediately, she insisted there must have been a misunderstanding. Of course, she knew my child. Of course, our children had been playmates since kindergarten. Shirley made a point of telling me over and over again that she was not prejudiced. After all, she socializes with the black "girls" on her job and invites their children to her children's birthday parties. Translation: I am a liberal. I'm okay. Interpretation: I am an "unintentional/unaware racist."[6] I get along with you people. I go out of my way to be "nice." In addition, I am married to an "aware/blatant racist"[7] whom I can't control or convert, which is why I haven't even tried to deny the possibility of my husband's making such a statement. Shirley babbled on about not being able to talk to Beatrice because it was past her bedtime (time: 8:20 p.m.) but maybe it had something to do with her dad and a little [black] boy she liked/kissed. But still, Beatrice must have misunderstood. Alarms went off! So, Daddy had nightmares of permanently tanned grandchildren calling him "pop-pop," eh?, I thought in silence. Shirley would talk to Beatrice in the morning, and we would meet—our girls included—in the playground the next day at 8:15 a.m. so we could get to the bottom of this "misunderstanding."

Soon thereafter, Sister Joyce returned my call. She confirmed

Ayanna's story about what had happened in the classroom. Sister Joyce had decided not to make a big fuss over the incident. Likewise, she assured me she was not prejudiced while giving me story after story of her positive, saintlike interaction with people of color and similar experiences of her family members. Translation 2: See Translation 1. Interpretation 2: I am also an unaware/unintentional racist. My father clandestinely risked everything to save a black man from sure death by allowing him to exchange work for a night's accommodation in my father's general store on a bitter cold night in the Midwest. I am of this stock. This is the example I live by. I wanted to break out into Janet Jackson's song "What Have You Done for Me Lately?"

I expressed my concerns about the here and now, future interaction between the children, the poisonous atmosphere created in her classroom and the school's mission. I told her about my and Ayanna's meeting tomorrow with Shirley and Beatrice. Finally, I was referred to the principal, Sister Patricia. I decided to talk to her after school the next day.

Ayanna and I were prompt for our meeting. Shirley and Beatrice were not. Again, I had to deal with my child's utter disappointment and confusion before kissing her and sending her into the school building moments before the late bell sounded. For a few minutes I stood in the courtyard, furious that I had been made a fool of. Then, a bleached blond woman tugging along a toddler tried to get past me to deliver her son to the preschool. Our eyes met momentarily and I knew it was Shirley. Flustered. Uneasy. Attempting to avoid all eye contact. Then it dawned on me. Beatrice was already at her desk. Shirley had arrived early and escorted her child inside, but her toddler was another matter since the youngest children could not gain access to the building until much later. Shirley played the waiting game with me and lost because I—like the problem—did not go away. In the brief minutes of interaction as she handed her toddler over to the teacher, Shirley was in perpetual motion, never apologizing for her lateness. It was fine with her that they remain friends. She didn't know what had happened. She would call me later. The end. I was dismissed.

"So, Ayanna, how was your day at school?" I asked cautiously that afternoon. Ayanna, Beatrice and other girls—both black and white—played together. Beatrice's mother said it was all right. And, Sister Joyce talked about slavery and Dr. Martin Luther King, Jr. . . . What? I just had to hear it from Sister Joyce, so I called her. Yes, she had decided to make a more formal response to the question of race by drawing a time line chronicling world history which included American slavery, the civil rights movement and, of course, Dr. Martin Luther King, Jr. No doubt, this exercise was cognitively beyond their age group. But, Sister Joyce assured me, some of the children grasped the idea. But, if my child who is in the top reading group in the class and scored in the 90 percentiles in vocabulary and reading in the Iowa's came away with vague ideas about slavery and Dr. Martin Luther King, Jr., Sister Joyce missed the mark. Beyond the issue of age appropriateness, if the time line was of world history, why was the African presence emphasized around the time of/during enslavement and on? Why not during periods of greatness and marked achievements before Christ?

Next, I called Sister Patricia, who was knowledgeable about the circumstances surrounding the last few days. I filled in the blanks: my brief meeting with Shirley, the lesson plan for the day and my displeasure with the way Sister Joyce dealt with the racial issue. First of all, Sister Patricia said, since I had dealt with Beatrice's mother, there would be a parent conference should *another* incident of racism arise. This type of racial attitude is counter to school and church doctrine; therefore, if Beatrice's family feels that strongly about race, she would ask them to find another school for Beatrice. Second, Sister Patricia was present during some of today's lecture and personally would not have selected that format, but Sister Joyce had tried. She's been teaching for forty-five years. Translation 3: Sister Joyce is highly respected and my senior in the sisterhood. Her heart is in the right place. It's done. The children are playing together again.

At the end of the conversation (perhaps to appease me), Sister Patricia agreed that cultural diversity training for her faculty would be a good idea. Yet to date, some ten months since, Sister Patricia has refused to respond to correspondence and telephone calls attempting to schedule a free faculty workshop on multiculturalism offered by a distinguished leader in the field of education. I will continue to pursue this matter in the next academic year and become more active in the P.T.A. in coming years.

Shirley has called a few times: Once, a few days after our meeting, to invite Ayanna to go with her family roller-skating at the local rink. Ayanna was also invited to Beatrice's birthday sleepover as an after-thought (as in the night before). Absolutely not. My friends and I laughed at the thought of sending my daughter to spend the night in the belly of the beast. Finally, Shirley and I served as chaperones for the class trip to Storybook Land. The girls preferred to go with Shirley rather than to have me and particularly baby sister Layla slow them down. Every time I see Shirley, I simply can't forget. And, I will never entrust the welfare of my child to her family on unsupervised outings or visits.

In retrospect, the entire ordeal was both emotionally and physically draining not to mention time-consuming. Troubled minds never really rest. My husband and I sat up nights and discussed lifetimes of racial experiences—his in rural Alabama, mine in Connecticut, ours separately at different locations in New Jersey, "up South," down South, various forms (covert and overt). And then, we realized the obvious. Ayanna and Layla would also have their stories to share well into the twenty-first century because we live in a society where white privilege is assumed. These entitlements were implicit in the race question raised by W.E.B. Du Bois nearly a century ago. Wisdom, history and experience tells us that Du Bois's prophetic statement—"the problem of the twentieth century is the problem of the color-line" will ring true in the twenty-first century as well.[8]

As Peggy McIntosh so keenly observed, most whites, even the well intentioned, are clueless and/or in denial as to the extent that they are placed at an advantage on a daily basis by virtue of their race. Benefits based on race are part of America's culture and psyche. For example, McIntosh's list includes:

- "I can go shopping alone most of the time, fairly well assured that I will not be followed or harassed by store detectives."

- "I can turn on the television or open to the front page of the paper and see people of my race widely and positively represented."

- "I can be sure that my children will be given curricular materials that testify to the existence of their race."

- "I could arrange to protect my young children most of the time from people who might not like them."

- "I did not have to educate my children to be aware of systemic racism for their own daily physical protection."

- "I can be pretty sure that my children's teachers and employers will tolerate them if they fit school and workplace norms; my chief worries about them do not concern others' attitudes towards their race."

- "I can easily buy posters, post cards, picture books, greeting cards, dolls, toys and children's magazines featuring people of my race."

- "I can arrange my activities so that I will never have to experience feelings of rejection owing to my race."[9]

As a result, we must reconcile the reality of our situation with parenting two confident, competent African-American women of the future. The positive reinforcements about self, race, ancestry and family will surely continue. Likewise, we will instill in them—like our elders and ancestors did in us—the mind-set that *no one* is better than they are. When they are injured and/or become unsure because of racial attacks, we will reassure them—but not that Dr. King's dream may be realized in their lifetime. Rather, we are a people who have survived every physical and psychological assault imaginable. And, they too will survive if they only access their reservoir of ancestral strength and spirituality to move on. It's fine to be angry as opposed to hostile. As stated by Comer and Poussaint, "Anger is a healthy human emotion . . . Hostility is not like healthy anger. It is a fixed mind-set rather than a healthy emotional reaction. It is not helpful in the fight against racism."[10] Accordingly, we must help our children channel their negatively generated energy into positive activism for the sake of activism because, simply put, it is the right thing to do.

I hope that as my children come into their own they will be pro-black, which is not synonymous with anti-white. As Dr. King so eloquently stated, "To develop a sense of black consciousness and people-hood does not require that we scorn the white race as a whole. It is not the race per se that we fight but the policies and ideologies that leaders of that race have formulated to perpetuate oppression."[11] Foremost, we must give them the tools to assess and manage difficult and perhaps potentially explosive racial situations. It follows that they need to be able to defend themselves verbally and physically if necessary.

Last, but not least, self-respect fosters respect for others. My children are already learning about the dignity and worth of every human being when I raise questions about depictions, behavior and attitudes that seem to denigrate another tradition, language, people or group. In later life, my daughters will be able to clearly see the interconnectedness of different types of oppression because the issues will have always been a topic of candid discussion.

In all my life, I would like nothing more than to have Bell's dismal hypothesis proven wrong. But in the meantime, I must prepare my children for the journey that surely lies ahead.

Notes

1. The essay title refers to Derrick Bell's *Faces at the Bottom of the Well: The Permanence of Racism* (New York: Basic Books, 1992).

2. John Gwaltney, *Drylongso* (New York: New Press, 1993), 7.

3. Bell, *Faces at the Bottom of the Well*, 6.

4. Ibid., 14.

5. Ibid., xi.

6. Gloria Yamato, "Something About the Subject Makes It Hard to Name," in *Race Class and Gender: An Anthology*, 2d ed., ed. Margaret Andersen and Patricia Hill Collins (Belmont, CA: Wadsworth, 1995), 71–75.

7. Ibid.

8. W.E.B. Du Bois, *The Souls of Black Folk*. In *Three Negro Classics*. (New York: Avon Books, 1965), 221.

9. Peggy McIntosh, "White Privilege and Male Privilege: A Personal Account of Coming to See Correspondences Through Work in Women's Studies," in *Race, Class and Gender: An Anthology*, 2d ed., ed. Margaret Andersen and Patricia Hill Collins (Belmont, CA: Wadsworth, 1995), 76–87.

10. James P. Comer and Alvin F. Poussaint, *Raising Black Children* (New York:

Plume, 1992), 61.

11. Coretta Scott King, comp., *The Words of Martin Luther King, Jr.* (New York: Newmarket Press, 1983), 33.

Bringing it on Home

Teaching/Mothering Antiracism

LYNDA MARÍN

I am not sure whether parenting has been a foundation for my teaching, or whether teaching laid the groundwork for the parenting I began late in my thirties. Certainly I have been teaching longer than I have been doing anything else, save breathing, eating and sleeping. But in retrospect, it seems to me I have always used parenting skills in teaching. It just took actual parenting to recognize that fact. How race fits into this relationship is entirely more complicated, circuitous. Yet it is teaching, parenting and race that I wish to speak of all at once. And even as I write that sentence, I feel the way race points metonymically to class, and gender, and sexuality. So it is all of that and more that demands simultaneous attention. The only way I can proceed at a task like this is by way of stories.

As most of us who write about racism do, I have a memory of the first time "it happened" to me. I was seven. I was walking home from a new school, in a new neighborhood, to a new house and even a seemingly new mother, since we had been estranged for the last four years and had only recently been reunited. I had a new Toni-Perm, too, deftly applied in the apartment kitchen of the woman who had taken me in during those years. I had been walking alone and I first felt rather than heard a boy insinuate himself alongside. "Are you negro?" he asked. His eyes squinted up at me, and I think he was missing teeth. "I don't know," I answered right back. I wasn't exactly sure if "negro" was a name or a condition or an affiliation, and at that stage of my life I was loathe to turn down any opportunity to belong to something. "You are; I can tell." And off he loped, to the other side of the street.

"Mother," I said, that unwieldy word in my mouth making me feel too old and too young, "am I negro?" She had been helping me take off my sweater, and now she threw it hard upon the floor and raised her voice. "Who said that to you?" she demanded. "I don't know," I said again. "Some boy on the way home from school." She got down on the floor in front of me, something I don't remember her ever doing again, and leveled her eyes at mine. "Lynda, you are *not* a Negro, and don't ever let anyone call you that! You are as white as I am." But my brown hand resting on her pale shoulder cast everything she had just said into doubt. That doubt only grew stronger and thornier with the passing of the seasons. In summer, especially, my mother continuously warned me about the darkening dangers of the sun. "You don't want to look like a Mexican," she would say conspiratorially. My father, never legally married to my mother but the more present parent in my life up until then, had come from Nicaragua. I had always known this. But my mother collapsed all people south of the U.S. border into the category "Mexicans," and the point was that, like Negroes, my father's race was undesirable.

Yet I do not mean to suggest that my mother was the only parent who taught me my racism. My father came at it from a different angle, not being white the way she was, but having internalized every negative thing my mother meant when she said "Mexican." Without ever using pejorative terms, and rarely any terms at all that denoted racial difference, my father taught me the value of my mother's hue. Even in the heat of summer with the sun having darkened me to a nutty brown, my father praised my relative lightness. "See," he would say, stretching his smoky dark arm next to mine, "how nice and light you are." For no matter how brown I appeared to myself, my father was always browner. And this difference seemed to be both wonderful and awful at the same time. Wonderful that my skin pleased him, that it was the right color, and effortlessly, too. Awful that his skin was bad in its darkness, and irreversibly so. So much said with so few words.

The only time I remember my father even alluding to black people (he worked alongside of them daily in the garages where he parked cars for a living) was after he had received the prom photo I'd sent him, my "date" and I posing together with exaggerated, frozen smiles. Without referring to the actual boy there in the photo, a mixed-race boy who never himself alluded to his racial composition but who seemed to be the only person of visibly black ancestry in the school, my father simply said, "I hope you're dating white boys, Lynda. Anybody else would be a mistake." I can still recall the clipped quality of those words, quietly delivered in his almost accentless English. That moment, in his basement apartment, staring into the dark face that I loved unfathomably, I felt as though I myself were the mistake—an impossible half and half—and that nothing anybody did or said could right it.

Thirty years later I was vividly reminded of this moment when the media reported that Hulond Humphries, a high school principal in Alabama, had stood at the school podium and denounced one of the students there as another such "mistake." Revonda Bowen, who has a white father and a black mother, had inquired what people like herself were supposed to do about the prom if, as Hulond Humphries was insisting, no "interracial dating" would be allowed. Humphries did not apologize, nor did the school board fire him. A protest prom was held for students of all colors, and a few months later, the school mysteriously burned. Revonda Bowen eventually won a small award of damages against Hulond Humphries and the Randolph County School District in a court of law. What compelled me to keep track of the Revonda Bowen case was that here, in this post-colonial, post-civil rights, politically correct era, loomed the possibility that nothing ever really changes. Humphries, with all the righteousness of one who has no reason to doubt his own position, had expressed publicly the wrongness of racial mixing that I had always privately known was at the heart of my own "mistake." So the outcome of the trial felt terribly important to me. Indeed, her award, though far too small for the immeasurable meanness she had endured, resituated (yet again) the "mistake" not in terms of her racial identity (nor anybody's) but in terms of the social context in which it had been constructed, defined, valued.

But here I need to outline a personal conundrum. I have long been predisposed to mentally inserting quotation marks around the word "race" whenever I encounter or use it. Though I do not discount in any way the very real effects of racial differences in a racist society, I do discount any biologistic fact of pure race and therefore racial differ-ence. (Just recently, a front-page story reported that science had yet again proved that no race gene exists. Science has proved that point many times now, yet every generation or so it makes headlines.) Never-theless, I find myself staring—to a degree that I have to consciously con-trol it—at all persons of mixed-race heritage. In fact the way I determine that they are mixed-race is because I am staring, unable to stop looking until I can put ambiguity to rest, *know* what race it is, call it something.

And of course that's the problem. If race rests on the concept that racial difference is absolute, then to be mixed-race is not really pos-sible. So I keep staring. It's more socially acceptable to stare at the chil-dren, of course, because they are endlessly doing something engaging, even if they are being simply awful (I know how it feels to be that kid and the parent of that kid too). It's trickier to look long at the adults, because they look back, demand accountability. Of course many people in the United States might justifiably claim a "mixed heritage," but I am speaking here of people who visually defy the either-or category, even as this society still so rigorously requires it. I look at these people for the sheer mind-boggling effort of seeing them. I see, even as I look, that I don't see them. I see the features I associate with one race, and then I see sometimes these very same features slip into the features I associ-ate with the "other" race. Each time the image slips from one race to the other, I know I've lost at least half of it, and so I need to keep looking, for what? Am I waiting for some amorphous homeostatic moment when the images will coalesce as neither this nor that but something else entirely? Sort of like a Magic Eye exercise.

I realized only recently, though, that I have forever done this same kind of looking at myself, in every mirror, literal or figurative. "A

Mediterranean type," I heard myself described by a college boyfriend who had never met my father. In my twenties, I was grappling with enough other developmental issues to let myself pass for whatever racial designation I was assigned so long as it wasn't mean-spirited. When another, cruder boyfriend called me his taco belle, I was not so sanguine. And when three girls on my dorm floor admitted they had mistaken me for Jewish at first (although now they knew otherwise) and were sorry they had snubbed me, I remember the pleasure I felt in assuring them that my Jewish boyfriend (the one who billed me as Mediterranean) would get a good laugh over that. "Aren't you just white?" my well-meaning Anglo roommate asked when I told her about the "Jewish mistake." The thing about people who visually defy either-or categories is that we will take up positions within them anyway, no matter how inappropriately, uselessly, painfully. And the reason we do this fancy footwork is racism, pure and not so simple. Our own and everyone else's.

In my late thirties, when I learned from amniocentesis that I was carrying a boy, I slipped into shock. A boy? What did I know about boys? The possibility of mothering a boy-child had just not occurred to me. A similar surprise about race came my way after my son was born: Michael was translucently white. My brown hands stood out in stark relief against the unmistakable pallor of his tiny tummy, fingers, face. I quietly resigned myself to this difference in our skin color as a temporary condition. When his first hair grew in golden, I felt disoriented. I could explain his white skin—after all his father is white, and so was my mother—but no one I had ever heard of on either side of my parents' families nor on my partner's side had been blond. Michael's father and I joked about that color, made the usual not-so-funny speculations about baby-switching in the hospital, and assumed the blond hair would darken in time.

And, in time, Michael's hair did darken. But for the first two years of my son's life, I was at odds with what he looked like, even though he looked perfectly scrumptious. I knew better than to admit this worry to anyone, except in an offhand, joking way, but the truth was something else: I felt genuinely troubled that every bit of the Latino seemed to have disappeared in just one generation. I had racial anxiety about my son, and consequently about myself, because I saw myself as the conduit of that disappearance, as if I were not really who I thought I was. Without my father alive to assure me of where I had come from (and with a personal history of repeated displacements and interrupted stories), I had fixed—erroneously—on my father's Latino heritage as the one thing that racially defined me. And I had done this in a deep and private way, so that I could not even admit it to myself. For of all the things I could have chosen, this racial anchoring in brownness would be most antithetical to the liberating possibilities my father had envisioned in my whiteness.

We adopted our daughter. Race played a key role. After two years of working with lawyers, birth mothers (black, white, and brown), agencies, networks, referral services, and consultants, we got an unlikely call from a social worker in another county. She had heard of us because we were looking for a "special needs" child. "What do *you* mean by 'special needs?'" I asked her, having heard this term defined in many different ways in the adoption arena by then. Because of the child's background, the woman explained, because her mother had been on various drugs and had a history of mental illness. Had there been evidence of drugs or alcohol in the baby's blood at birth? "No," she stated. Was the baby of low birth weight? "No, no, nothing like that," she assured. Did the baby, by now a toddler, exhibit symptoms like those of children exposed to drugs or alcohol in utero? "Not exactly," she revealed. So what was it, I asked, that made this little girl a "special needs" child? Well, it was complicated, she explained, because even though children Rana's age didn't necessarily demonstrate symptoms of prenatal exposure to toxic substances, the effects of that exposure could show up later, around age five or so, when they entered school. And, too, her father was Mexican.

For a moment I was utterly stopped. I tried to think of some information I must have forgotten about a genetic predisposition to something or other that is common to people of Mexican ancestry. Like Tay-Sachs for Jews or sickle-cell anemia for blacks. All I could think of was milk allergy, something I have myself. In the silence, the social worker explained that the birth father had waived his rights and returned to Mexico, so that wouldn't really be a problem. Still, I was searching for continuity in this conversation. Finally I blurted out, "What does being Mexican have to do with it?" "With being 'special needs'?" She picked up the thread as if it had always been there. "Only that the county is required to locate adoptive parents of similar racial backgrounds for all children who are biracial. That's a smaller group, you know, where at least one parent is Mexican." I was struck by a number of things at once: that the child's birth mother must be white, since her race had gone unmentioned; that social services protocol must have collapsed the same categories that my mother had in order to allow my Nicaraguan father to qualify me as Mexican, and that this child was as many months old as I had been searching for her. My special half-and-half daughter.

When Michael was born I had "given up" teaching for six months. But when we adopted Rana seven years later, I stopped teaching indefinitely. That is, I didn't even pretend I knew when I might go back. Her transition, at age two, into our family became the most harrowing, demanding, exhausting challenge I had ever faced. Rana is a girl of extraordinary will and physical strength. And I was forty-five. So while my mothering of her benefited from every ounce of experience I had acquired up until then, it suffered from my waning stamina. I saw it as serendipitous that during this time, the writing seminars I usually taught were being reabsorbed by the Women's Studies Program in such a way that they would no longer be offered in the form I had been teaching them. Therefore I wasn't actually missing my classes. They had simply ended with the arrival of my daughter. Nevertheless, I speculated occasionally about what I would teach when I returned, for I imagined that I would someday do that.

Just when it seemed as though our family had braved the tempest of transformation that Rana's arrival had touched off—two years in counting time—I got a call from the department chair of Women's Studies asking if I'd like to teach a class I'd never taught before. "Which one?" I asked eagerly—that moment before destiny strikes and anything is possible. "Women of Color in the U.S.," she said evenly, betraying nothing of what she and I, and everyone else associated with Women's Studies, knew about the problematic nature and history of that course on our campus. "Hmmmmmmm," I stretched it out.

With surprising immediacy, scenes from "Women of Color in the U.S." and its predecessors replayed themselves in quick time: *Eight years earlier when I audit the class for the first time, the professor requires a divided seating arrangement for the thirty or so students, women of color on one side, white women on the other. Not being able to assign myself to either, I stand through a few classes and then stop going. A few years later in a large hall where the course now brims to its 150-seat capacity, a white woman stands up in the middle of a lecture and tearfully pleads to be educated about the condition of being colored and female on our campus and in this culture; a woman of color, fully exasperated, responds indignantly that she has no responsibility to teach white women anything; a white woman screechingly refutes the notion that she is racist just because she is white; a woman of color dramatically "gives up" (walks out of the lecture hall) on white women who are only in the class to assuage their "white guilt"; a man of color gingerly exits, inaudibly mumbling something like, "I'm not gonna learn anything here. I'm just gonna get kicked around"; a teaching assistant of color shouts, "Look at us! Look! We can't even have a conversation together!" A professor of color admits sadly to the students that she feels sick every time she has to come to this class. A mixed-race Women's Studies major I am tutoring in writing says she doesn't want to take "Women of Color in the U.S." because "it's too violent."*

My time away from the university had not softened my sense of the inevitable foibles and disasters that teachers, teaching assistants and students of "Women of Color in the U.S." had encountered over the years. I had no reason to think I could do it any better. I had never even taught a lecture course. But I thought about how important it was to make good use of the opportunities to stretch myself that life (and my department head) was offering me. After all, I had just stretched considerably to complete an adoption that had seemed at times against all odds, and in the process I had even located resources in myself that I had never imagined. Wasn't that equally possible about teaching "Women of Color in the U.S."? And, too, I thought about how much I missed teaching, how much I longed to reconnect with a community that had gone on without me for the last two years. And so I said yes.

Friends and family construed my "going back to teaching" as a positive move in the professional direction. Their well-wishing comments reinforced yet again that in the world of parenting everything is understood to be personal. And it is true that parenting, by and large, is a private endeavor, subject to the protections of the adult individual under law. Except for injurious neglect or obvious endangerment, most parenting is left to the privacy of the home, and even in public, a taboo is in force about intervening into child-parent interactions that appear to exceed the bounds of reasonable or safe practice. When Rana first arrived in our home, I recognized more deeply than ever the good and bad news about this fact. The rage she felt at being ejected from her foster home—that such a thing was even possible—often overwhelmed the incipient pleasure she felt at the possibilities of being included in our family. Toys, furniture and appliances shattered into pieces, cabinets lost their doors, clothes their sleeves and pockets. Holes got kicked in walls, pictures, screen doors. The screaming and flailing was like nothing we had ever dealt with before. Her rage demanded limits, trammeled over them, demanded them again, and yet again crashed through the ones we scrambled to supply. For Rana to be "included" it appeared our home and our very family had to come apart.

A primal scene with Rana marked an important turning for me in the notion of the separation between the personal and the professional and between mothering and teaching. I still can think of it only in the present tense. *She is two years and eight months. It's nap time, which is becoming increasingly problematic. I have read her a number of books and now I am leaving her in her crib to wind down into sleep. She is cranky and resistant to my leaving. As I try to give her another hug, she jabs the corner of a book into my eye. I literally see stars. As I back off to cover my watering eye, she throws the book into my face. Without actually knowing how I do it, I am suddenly in the crib with her (in every way imaginable). I am as outraged at her acting out toward me as she is about everything that has happened to her in the almost three years of her life. I'm on all fours, pinning her hands and legs down with mine. "You can't hurt people!" I am shouting into her reddened face. "You hurt me, and you can't do that! Do you hear me?" For an answer she uses the only part of her body I haven't incapacitated and spits upward toward my face as hard as she can. Most of it lands on her own face and she spits more furiously. I stare down hard at her, determined to "win." But as the struggle ensues, I realize what I am doing as I leer over her, supposedly protecting myself from her next attack. I am othering her. She has become all bad, in essence the enemy. And this process of othering is as complicated as it is in any other context. It has to do with the way I am assigning meaning to the various behaviors and personal qualities I am observing in this moment of spectacle. For example, I am projecting everything crazy and unstable from my own childhood onto Rana via her birth mother. It's that crazy woman who accounts for my having to pin Rana's body down. Her crazy white woman birth mother who took up with some Mexican she didn't even know. Now that I've let her birth father into the picture, I realize I am actually racializing the spitting behavior separately as some kind of brute expression of somebody less than (not white, not woman, not "cultured"). And I realize too that I am performing this operation in just the same way that my own mother might have. It is terrible enough that when she did it, she drove a plank between us, but much worse is that when I do it, I am othering not only my own daughter, but dividing me against myself as well.*

Wondering what anybody else coming upon Rana and me in her crib like that might have thought, I crawled out. It had been an intensely personal moment, and indeed it couldn't have happened any other way. But to the extent that motherhood is also a profession (I believe it truly is, and in ways that get evaluated all the time both in private and in public), it was deeply unprofessional. Which is not to say that it was bad, but rather that it was a behavior to be learned from and not repeated. I want to stress that its being personal is not what made the behavior unprofessional. In fact the professional part of the behavior was the most personal moment of all. It was the moment when I had perceived my own racism, classism and sexism in perfect concert, deconstructing my own child. It was at that moment that I became a more competent mother and a more integrated person, someone who might be able to bring her whole self to the teaching of "Women of Color in the U.S." In fact, in the process of mothering Rana, what I—a

mixed-race woman-mother-teacher—was learning about racial identity and the beguiling impossibility of separating it into halves was exactly what I wanted to bring to such a course.

History. The "Women of Color in the U.S." course developed out of workshops for unlearning racism offered by Women's Studies on our campus in the early 1980s. Those workshops were small, with one leader
and twenty or so participants. The emphasis was on process, on how
the participants in the workshops negotiated their own racist attitudes
and discriminatory practices and how, once recognizing the mecha-
nisms of racism, classism, sexism and homophobia among themselves,
the participants might discover ways to think and act differently. Although the course description presently offers, to a much larger enrollment, historical, sociological, cultural and theoretical contexts for
studying the interlocking relations of race, class, gender and sexuality
among four major racial-ethnic groups of women of color in the United
States, the antiracist intent of those earlier workshops has remained
deeply inscribed in its revised curriculum and the students' expectations of it. This legacy, in part, accounts for the volatility and intensity
for which the course is now famous on our campus.

I envisioned my version of the course as an ongoing conversation
about the development of the concept, category and political constitu-
ency of this thing called "women of color." In my months of preparation,
while working at my desk or driving in my car, I would lapse into vivid
fantasies, almost as if they were already memories, of interactions with
students, among students, with the teaching assistants. Together we
would puzzle out the labyrinthine relations between race, class, gender
and sexuality to render those categories ever more dimensional in their
complexity. And with the addition I intended to make, this year, of
mixed-race as a self-deconstructing category in the discourse of women
of color, the relationship among those differences would be rendered
even more rich, more complex. "But then what is a 'woman of color'
anyway?" would get asked at intervals when we would have pushed yet
again on the boundaries of previous definitions. "And why?" I imagined
myself certainly not as an authority in the field, but as someone who,

like some of the students and teaching assistants, would find the construction of identity bound up in these categories as both constraining and liberating and endlessly worth working on together. I imagined, too, the pleasure of introducing the students to the rich variety of readings I was toiling to hone down to a manageable list.

I recognize now that this fantasy, the way I developed and nurtured it even throughout the class itself, had a plot very similar to the one with which I entered into mothering Rana. In both situations, the odds were against a happy outcome. I could name specifically the reasons for that. In each case, I did not minimize the difficulties I knew of only too well, nor did I aggrandize my power to overcome them. But in both situations, I spent inordinate amounts of time and energy detailing the possibilities of the unlikely happier outcome. And as far afield as those fantasies fell from my real experience of mothering and teaching, they informed my every move, especially when I thought I had no moves left.

I have a history with the lecture hall I was assigned. It was the same one in which I had visited friends and colleagues over the preceding seven years when they had taught or TA'd for "Women of Color in the U.S." I have a visceral memory of the rows and seats on the aisle where I sat as, in various visits, students cried, protested, raged, walked out. On the day I entered it to teach the same course, I felt split. My memory still occupied those seats from which I had observed so much tumult. My body, however, took up my position at the front of the room, my arms full of syllabi, books, folders. I assured myself it was okay to feel split. My predisposition to feeling myself always in at least two places at once was something I brought specifically to teaching this class. I reminded myself of the beaded flower Rana had given me that morning. "Show them what I made you, Mommy," she had said, slipping it into my pocket as I left the house. "Okay," I promised, kissing her good-bye. Now I looked out at the graduated rows of seats, filled by women (there were only two men in the class) and I tried to draw around me like a garment the fruitfulness that had filled my fantasies of our interactions. Reality persisted nonetheless: a class list with ninety-something names on it, a large group of latecomers lined up for permission codes, and three teaching assistants I barely knew who ironically had indicated various concerns that the nature of the course and my teaching of it not foster any confusion between the personal and the professional. And indeed I forgot until much later that night about the flower in my pocket.

History is like gravity. It pulls us down. For better or for worse. When I walked into my "Women of Color in the U.S." class on that first day, I was struck, first, by the number of bodies and, second, by race. (It might have been gender in any other situation, but looking out then I saw only women.) What I perceived was a predominantly white enrollment, with perhaps 20 percent women of visible color. Historically, other teachers of this class had struggled to mediate the political effects of that ratio. Some had taught primarily to the women of color, allowing the white women to overhear, but not verbally participate. Others had required that white women monitor themselves to speak no more than 50 percent of the time in the discussion portion of lectures. And although these protocols were in themselves impossible to monitor, they sent a message early on that, unlike any other course on campus, this was a class that privileged women of color. One tradition that had remained through the years, was that the women-of-color students were invited early in the quarter to introduce themselves, for the purpose of knowing, among themselves, how they identified and in what ways they affiliated themselves with their communities. This introduction has always raised a lot of controversy: resentment as to why white students or men of color might not be included; questions as to the color range by which women determine their own placement in the category "of color"; protestations of divisiveness stemming from the inevitable separation that white women and women of color are made to feel from one another during the introductions; affirmations of empowerment in spite of (or even because of) the fallout that occurs as a result of the exercise. There is something compelling and repugnant about this exercise, and I tried to think my way around it for a long time. I wanted to open it up somehow, to do justice to the way that race really is more complicated than skin color, physiognomy and cultural background. I wanted race to take up its appropriate proportion to the countless other ways we identify ourselves, while honoring the fact that race historically has been used to identify us in unforgivable disproportion to the whole persons we long to be.

We finally did the women-of-color introductions during the third class meeting. One thing I did differently. Besides race, I asked them to add anything else to their introductions that felt crucial to who they knew themselves to be (class and sexuality could be included but didn't have to be). The details they revealed mediated their racial identities in countless ways: "I am severely dyslexic," "I am an incest survivor," "My parents were alcoholics," "I was separated from my family at age two," "I am the first person in my family to attend college," "I just placed my baby with an adoptive family," "I'm fatally allergic to bee stings," "I came out last year," "I was an emancipated minor at age fifteen," "My mother is dying of cancer," "I intend to be a lawyer and work for the people in my community." Each detail these women shared helped produce a network of resonances among all of us. The details did not displace racial difference, but they did bridge the differences of race, class and sexuality in a myriad of ways. And that was in part what made it even harder for the white women and men-of-color students to be excluded from speaking, because they shared some of those formative "differences," and wanted to express their consequent sense of connection with the women of color introducing themselves that day. Yet this was an exercise which had historically been used to honor (albeit controversially) the fact that "Women of Color in the U.S." was a course by, for and about women of color. This was the ritual enactment of that honoring. And as much as I wished to problematize race as any kind of fixed category, I also wished to acknowledge its power to designate identity, to contain meanings, to explain our experience.

As a result, and in keeping with other such introductions in previous years, some of the students felt wounded, excluded, frustrated, angry. I was particularly aware of the way some of the mixed-race women had struggled to justify their inclusion or to rationalize their way out of it. In response I wish I could have told them about a moment I had recently in a clinic with Rana. *She has a terrible flu and I can't get her fever down, even with tepid baths and cool cloths and Tylenol and homeopathics. "She's pretty darn sick," the doctor says, "I'll give you that." (I wonder just what he's "giving" me. Approval that I brought her in?*

That I had the good sense to notice that 104 degrees is too hot?) After the routine examination, I explain that even prior to the fever she has been complaining of leg pains, sometimes so severe that she can't fall asleep at night. He looks at her legs, and then at her face. "What race is she?" He asks. The words bump into each other in my mouth, come out jumbled. "Like, umm, she's like me, half, I mean half Latino, and white half." "Well, that's why I asked. Because we see that a lot with Latinos—leg pains. Don't know why. They just seem more prone than other races." "Really?" I say regaining a modicum of composure, "Are you referring to studies, or just empirical evidence, your own experience, what? And . . . ," I don't really wait for an answer, "what would you say if she were just anglo? How would you explain it then?" (The only person I know who remembers having childhood leg pains is my partner's sister, who is decidedly not Latino.) He laughs. "Oh, the same way, 'growing pains.' It's just that Latinos have more of them." So Latinos hurt more as they grow, I think. Well, yes, that's a possibility in this society. But I don't need medical counsel to speculate about the reasons for that. I couldn't tell my Women of Color class this story, however, as a kind of testimonial about the tenacity of race and meaning, because at the time we were doing our introductions, the incident with the doctor hadn't happened yet.

I could have told them, though, about my conversation with a colleague last summer at her graduation for the completion of her doctorate. Sharing with each other our next year's plans, I told her I was preparing to teach "Women of Color in the U.S." "You're kidding!" she exclaimed. "They're letting a white woman teach that course?" Thinking she must have misunderstood me, I said more emphatically, "No, *I'm* teaching it!" In the short silence between us, I wondered if she had actually read any of my work as I believed she had, or if we had ever really talked. Who had we been to each other? And how alienated, and for how long, would I feel about this racial refiguring she had done of me. How much of what we did know about one another would be rendered useless in the face of this racial insensitivity that seemed in the moment so charged?

But I didn't tell this story. I intended that it speak behind the scenes, in the way I responded to their stories. For in the end, it was they who needed to tell their stories to one another in the countless ways a course like this does and does not allow. And it was their stories that would reveal all the complexity anyone could ever ask for in the analysis of the social construction of "differences." In that analysis, I imagined race appearing something like weather—a constant and an intangible, something we endlessly predict and speculate about but that we can only experience indirectly in some combination of its endless rainy, sunny, cold, hot, windy, dry, stormy, sultry, drizzly, humid, etc., manifestations. Because weather, like race, is determined by place and time (How many of us have left a gray rain behind us when we took off in an airplane and reached the altitude of a sunny day?). And the meaning we give to racial identity is similarly determined, changes in differing contexts and historical moments, within individuals and whole societies, too. In any given moment and/or place, race may be utterly meaningful and meaningless, but pervasive, in any event, like the weather we always talk about when all other topics fail. Of course, unlike weather, race is very hard to talk about, unless we are willing to let all kinds of other differences into the conversation as well.

By the middle of the quarter, I found myself longing for some of the drama other incarnations of the course had generated. I was struck, then, and I am still struck by how hard it really was to let difference speak. The complexity of that task overwhelmed the necessity for it throughout most of the quarter. The stultifying predictability of those four words "race, class, gender and sexuality" strung together in their familiar sequence, more often than not thwarted the best of my intentions to endlessly elaborate on their relationship and meanings. We focused on history, sociological data, literature, myths, literary and cultural theory, all of which contribute to the complexity of what it means to be a woman of color in the United States, but we were a huge group of personalities, every one of us sharing various degrees of the teaching assistants' concerns that the professional context of the course keep us safe from having to reveal too much of the personal anguish many of us experience around claiming our racial, class, gender and sexual identities, and particularly in light of the other crucial ways we identify as well.

In the context of the family, of course, myriad identity issues strut about quite nakedly: Rana asks me while I'm drying off after showering if her nipples will "puff up like that" some day; Michael wants to know if we have more or less money than a family that lives nearby; I explain for the hundredth time to Michael's exasperated "why?" that he needs sun block applied more often than his sister because his skin is very light; Rana tells Michael that her penis "is hiding in the dark"; Michael reports at dinner that his buddy's mom told him that what I said is wrong, that men *can't* marry each other; Rana wiggles the skin under her dad's chin and wonders out loud if he's getting old, and when he denies that possibility, she asks, "just fat then?" Inside the family, where relations are personal, intimate, we are all constantly negotiating within, around, between and through categories that identify us to ourselves and each other. The category "mother" has a whole set of its own differentiating features that came to me late in my reproductive life, but that condition every other way I have known myself: my mixed Anglo-Latino background, my laboring class underpinnings, my choice to practice heterosexuality without denying my sexual love for women, my semi-orphaned childhood, my "corrected" left-handedness, my peculiar and enigmatic medical history, my phobia about eating mammals, and so on. In mothering, those endlessly entwining identity differences infuse my every task, like breathing, whether I think about it or not.

But in teaching "Women of Color in the U.S.," where I had imagined my own particular history, knowledge and experience to be similarly engaged and where I had been determined to disavow the sacred separation between the personal and the professional, I proceeded with an increasing sense of my own inadequacy to bring what I knew to bear on what I did. In my attempt to "cover" the promised material, to even gesture toward the topics outlined in my syllabus, I lectured far more often than promoted discussion (an approach that never works in parenting). By the sixth week, going over my class list, I could barely connect twenty names with their persons, and this small accomplishment was only a result of the extended office hours I had implemented in my distress at the sea of faces that remained so troublingly anonymous. In our class meetings, the students' stories, those very ones I had imagined central to getting at the complexity of our subject, had remained guarded and off-limits. More surprising to myself, so had mine. In my anxiety to deliver on the myriad and conflicting promises this course held out, I had fallen back on the most reductive notion of professionalism. I had separated my personal experience from my "material." And it seemed unfathomable at that late date that I might find a way to attend to the real material, the raw material of our lives.

I had never really experienced shame around teaching before. Although I could always think of ways to improve on what I had done in any course, I loved teaching for the very reason that it has always provided me with an arena in which to concentrate my skills and to keep growing. Shame is an experience I have felt, rather, in my parenting. And what I have learned is that it's an insidious and withering state that feeds on itself and requires heroic interventions just in the nick of time. And so it was that in the middle of trying to devise one of my last lectures, a late-night effort riddled by mounting guilt about how thoroughly I had abandoned my family to teach this course, I recognized the need for just such an intervention. The topic was "building alliances and coalitions among women of color." We needed as much of that as we could muster in the short time we had left. Perhaps the shame I was feeling called out the mother, finally. What was it that they really needed, and how could I give it to them? They didn't need a lecture. I put my notes away. They needed to speak to one another with their whole selves, just as I had needed to all quarter. I spent the rest of my preparation devising an open-ended discussion exercise around the readings they had been assigned. It was a classroom experiment entirely out of keeping with our numbers, with our bolted-down seats, and with anything we had done before.

When I told the class we were swapping the next lecture for an exercise on building alliance and coalition, some looked skeptical, some noncommittal, and some of the teaching assistants rolled their eyes. I felt hopeful and light for the first time all quarter. Although at the time I could never have said this to any of the students (except to the few mothers), this class was making me see uncompromisingly what I thought I already knew—that, for me, splitting off mother from teacher is no less diminishing than would be the splitting off of race from gender from sexuality from social class from age from religion from physical and mental health from body type from childhood experiences and on and on.

This experiment turned out to lay crucial groundwork for the final assignment, scheduled on the syllabus for the last week. The assignment required the students to decide in their sections on a presentation pertaining to any aspect of women of color they wished to make to the large lecture class. This presentation had also been somewhat of a tradition in the course, and I was more than curious as to how it would play itself out in our version. After the teaching assistants and I established the parameters of what would count as a presentation (it could be artistic, analytical, literary, culinary, cinemagraphic, musical, dramatic, rhythmical, ritualistic, and so on), the sections—many of them predominantly white women—struggled with how to present something they didn't feel they could authentically own. Could a group of white women read aloud the poetry of women of color for instance? Could African-American women feel any more justified in presenting the work of Asian-American women, Native-American women or Latinas? Should straight women be presenting the words or images of lesbians? Should middle-class women be interpreting the art of *barrio* women? What position could any of them take in order to respect the differences the course had labored to inform them of? What sort of alliances would they have to enter into among themselves to agree on a presentation topic they could all genuinely share? Many of the students alluded to painful, divisive conversations in their sections. Some of them dropped by my office to tell me how counterproductive the assignment was. The teaching assistants' reservations about the assignment were clearly evident. I don't remember hearing a single positive utterance about the prospect of the presentations.

I am not normally someone to persist in the face of such resistance. Usually resistance of that magnitude within a working situation suggests insensitivity, bullheadedness or an unwillingness to include others in a more collaborative process. But this assignment had had some insightful foremothers, and I suspected, from my own experience of actual mothering, that the badmouthing was a productive resistance, a fruitful growing pain. (Many times I considered the possibility that the students and TAs would collectively "just say no.") It was fruitful. In fact, as I reflect on the course now, what most immediately and vividly come to mind are those presentations. They came at the hard questions of identity through a myriad of differences that embraced and exceeded those we had systematically set out to cover. Some were humorous, some poignant, some strident, some fragmented, some combative, some integrative, some deconstructive, some constructive. And even—and especially—the ones that criticized choices I had made in designing the course, choices about what got covered, what got left out, the infamous introductions exercise, and the requirement to make a presentation, yielded understandings and positions that made me feel proud of what we had done together, willingly and unwillingly—very much like my experience of family, though I know this is a dangerous and politically incorrect metaphor to be using in relation to pedagogy ("pedagogy" is itself a term held in low esteem at the University). So I will press on it just a little more to say that during those last few weeks in which I held my ground with my students and my teaching assistants for a developmental outcome I knew only by way of faith and desire, I was drawing deeply and deliberately on my experience of mothering, which is the most integrative and most professional thing I do, besides teaching . . .

Last year Rana went to a preschool that had a mixture of black, brown and white kids. I chose the school over our neighborhood preschool because I liked the teachers and the program there better and because there was racial and cultural diversity. I was especially grateful that a very nurturing, energetic friend of mine was the bilingual aide. I wanted Rana to hear other people besides me speaking Spanish to her, something that is not likely to happen regularly in our neighborhood. She loved the school, the kids, the activities. Now during the first week of summer vacation, we help ease her separation from school by looking at the class picture taken much earlier. She is standing next to Robbie, her nemesis at the time of the picture taking. She points him out a lot and explains that once he used to chase and scare her, but now they are friends (read: She finally figured out how to turn around and chase him, too). She runs her finger along the rows of children naming each one, sometimes elaborating on a detail about one or another of them. At one end of the picture, her finger whizzes by two black-haired twins with the accompanying narrative: "the Spanish girls." "You mean Brenda y Marisa?" I ask. "The Spanish girls!" she says with exaggerated impatience. Brenda and Marisa are the only children in her classroom who spoke no English whatsoever. "They're not Spanish girls," I say softly, "they just speak Spanish. They're American girls, like you are, but in their house, they speak Spanish. In our house we speak mostly English but sometimes Spanish, too." (I guess I am saving the American/U.S. distinction for a later date, a different developmental moment.) "Nuh-uh," she denies, and then with unexpected ferocity she nearly spits out the words, "I hate them. They're stupid."

No matter how many times I am faced with a moment like this, a moment of pure projection (which I take to be the condition of any expression of prejudice), I feel utterly stopped. I think I should be able to intervene more gracefully and effectively with children than with adults, with whom the stakes are higher, the history longer. But in the moment, I am struck dumb. So for the first seconds after Rana's pronouncement, I sit quietly beside her. "Rana," I finally say, kneeling down to eye level, "did you ever play with Brenda or Marisa?" "No!" she exclaims, pulling away from my eyes. "Nobody can play with them. They can only play with each other." I suspect what she has said is true, that is, that the language barrier has been only the most visible and obvious obstacle to negotiating the innumerable differences that separated these children from the rest of the group. Their absent mother, their eccentric threadbare hair ribbons, their constantly runny noses, their quiet acceptance of their own seeming invisibility. Indeed I had never pushed myself to question beyond the most superficial levels their apparent insularity and exaggerated dependence on one another. In my early morning single-minded purpose of dropping off Rana and getting to work, I had never done anything to foster a connection with them for her or myself. I had never started up a conversation with their grandmother, who brought them to school every day and who kept her eyes almost always trained on the floor. I had never tried, past "Buenos días," to break through the insulation of their own downcast eyes, to draw out a response from either girl. How could that have seemed any harder than teaching "Women of Color in the U.S."?

"Rana"—I am still kneeling to meet the eyes that have swung away—"I made a big mistake." The eyes swing back. "What mistake?" I tell her

I realize it must have felt strange to her that Brenda and Marisa could only play with each other, that they were right there in the room with all the other kids, but that she had to pretend they weren't there. "Did that feel bad to you?" I ask. She nods yes. "I realize I should have helped you play with them." She says that it wouldn't have worked. "Maybe," I admit. "The mistake was that I didn't try." She climbs onto my knee then, and her eyes (¡bien oscuros!) are very close to mine. "Mommy, are *you* a Spanish girl?" She wants a simple answer. I know that. "Can mommies who speak Spanish and English be Spanish girls?" I ask. "Yes," she says in her deepest authoritative tone. "Can daughters of mommies like that be Spanish girls too?" "Yes," she says giggling now, her delicious summer-dark arms wrapping themselves around me. "Good."

Mothers Confronting Racism

Transforming the Lives of Our Children and Others

BLANCHE RADFORD CURRY

Mothering Against Racism

Racism has been and continues to be an overwhelming psychological and sociological reality that is destroying American society. When our children are involved, the suffering and injustices that racism places on them are often heavier for mothers to bear than the agony and burdens of racism on ourselves.

Mothers and caregivers of all races can be significant change agents in transforming "race as problematic" into "race as enriching."[1] "Womenfolk," Johnetta B. Cole reminds us, are still our major socializers—the first and principal teachers of our children's values, attitudes and behavior patterns—and as such we can be a "catalyst" for confronting racism.[2] As our children's primary socializers, we can and must confront and challenge racism in their child rearing and their schooling as well as support related efforts like developing political policy that is clearly against racism. We can, as Cole states, socialize our children to respect multiculturalism and diversity, urge our schools to teach an inclusive history of America's many people, and mirror lives which echo the needs of a pluralistic society.[3]

Discovering Their Race as Less Than

As I begin to think about confronting racism, I think of my own daughter's encounters with racism. Given her vivacious and loquacious personality, she is seldom wary of strangers. One day, when traveling through an airport terminal as a toddler, elated over people exchanging smiles and greetings with her, she discovered one white male at our departure gate who refused to reciprocate her greeting. She quickly asked, "Mom what's wrong with him?" I immediately responded, "Oh he's having a bad morning." As my eyes met his, his body language and my sense of his culture indicated his racist wish to deny her existence as a human being. I was pleased to be able to respond so quickly in a way that stunned him and did not further impact my daughter. While we waited for the plane, my daughter got the same reaction from some white girls she wanted to play with. Their white mother whisked her daughters away, and again my daughter asked, "What's wrong, Mom?" Scenes from Toni Morrison's *The Bluest Eye* came to mind, as well as scenarios about white mothers not allowing their children to play with black children.[4] I told her not to worry, that their mother wanted to ready them to board the plane.

Thinking of *The Bluest Eye* reminds me of other occasions when my children experienced racism. At two different schools a couple of my daughter's white classmates had made her feel that her hair and her race meant she was not as pretty as they were. I talked with her about inner and outer beauty and about different styles of physical beauty versus just white people's ideas of beauty. As we continued to talk and to look in the mirror, I emphasized the richness of having inner beauty, and her physical beauty as well, pointing out Queen Cleopatra and other beautiful African-American women, and reminding her of one of her favorite books, *Mufaro's Beautiful Daughters*. We also discussed the advantages of black hair and skin versus white hair and skin. I reminded her that different textures of hair made different hairstyles possible and of the almost daily hair shampooing for whites versus every one to three weeks for blacks. She cherished her daddy's ritual kissing of her forehead and his saying he liked "pigtails" better than "ponytails," she enjoyed wearing "braids" with or without his ritual kissing, and she joyfully commented on Whitney Houston's beauty, giving me a sense of success.

My son has also experienced the sting of racism. The night before his tenth birthday, he shared a painful incident involving racism at his school. [5] As he shared what had happened that day—a white boy's piercing comment that he knew he was white because he didn't stay in the oven as long as my son had, that Africans live in huts, and so on—my son expressed the feeling too often shared by African-American boys. He said he wanted to be white because white people don't like black people, but black people like white people. Why was this, he asked. I fought back my rage and my feeling of failure to fortify him more against such racism. How and when does a mother explain racism to her child? How does she let him know that he will encounter many other experiences of racism, from subtle and not so painful to blatant and very painful? My priority was fulfilling his most immediate needs, making him feel good about himself. I thought quickly about how to build his self-esteem and strengthen his pride in his African-American heritage.

I began by saying that I'm African American, that I like being an African American and that I love having a bright African-American boy like him, that I would not have it any other way. Next, I reminded him of several great contributions to humanity by African Americans such as the gas mask, the almanac, the shoe mold, blood plasma, the horse bridle and so forth. "Remember," I said, "how few of the white students and the teachers knew about these contributions before I spoke at your school? Your unfortunate experience is why it is important for us to donate African-American books in your name to the school library in honor of your birthday—so people like that little white boy can learn that he is wrong." I explained further that too often white people do not know or deliberately overlook the contributions of not only African Americans but also Native Americans, Hispanics, Asian Americans and other people of color. We ended our talk with my singing "Happy Birthday" early, along with the words, "You're my little boy, soon to be my big boy, my little man, my big man—you're my genius, you're my African-American boy and I love you." He smiled happily as he closed his eyes.

While making some progress in rebuilding his self-esteem and in celebrating his African-American heritage, I had not answered his question of why? Is he ready—am I ready—to use the term "racism" in explaining what indeed was an experience of racism? Can knowing the meaning of racism have any transformative significance in confronting racism? In *Sister Outsider*, Audre Lorde defines racism as "the belief in the inherent superiority of one race over all others and thereby the right to dominance."[6] David Theo Goldberg states that "racism is generally considered to be discrimination against others in virtue of their putatively different racial membership."[7] Goldberg also notes that racism can be institutional, which he defines as a characteristic of institutions "whose formative principles incorporate and whose social functions serve to institute and perpetuate the beliefs and acts in question."[8]

Kwame Anthony Appiah[9] and Naomi Zack[10] make a distinction between what I refer to as "transformable racism," involving assumptions and false beliefs, and "pathological racism," meaning the same as Appiah's "cognitive incapacity," a failure to distinguish between the world as it is and how one would like it to be.[11] When we encounter transformable racism, pointing out the facts adequately disputes false beliefs; but no facts are adequate enough for pathological racism. People living pathological racism are not capable of conceptualizing the absurdity of racism as a good reason for opposing it. Given this truth, there is no transformative significance in the meaning of racism to undercut or to undo pathological racism. Mothers must use other options to challenge pathological racism and consider the transformative significance of the meaning of racism as a beginning point for exposing assumptions and false beliefs about different races that serve as the basis of transformable racism. There is encouraging research that transformable racism can be unlearned.[12] It is possible as Spike Lee says, "to do the right thing."

What Else

After my son's experience and our conversation, I discussed the matter with my spouse, pouring out my anger and seeking other options to deal with the situation. My anger was compounded by my husband's immediate response that it would be advantageous to be white. It was his usual philosophy, one of pragmatism wrapped in humor for easier coping. Yes, being white would make all aspects of our lives less problematic. As African-American adults, we understand this philosophy and humor as a means for attaining a greater tolerance of daily racism.[13] However, I was unwilling to trust that our son would understand this strategy as a means of coping with racism rather than deflating his self-esteem.

My husband and I talked about how much harder it is now than it was in our childhoods to instill self-esteem and pride in African-American children. We grew up with two working-class parents. Our children are growing up with two post-college-degreed middle-class parents and experiencing a decent education as well as social and various cultural exposures. Nevertheless, they face the same problems of racism, in varying degrees, that plague all African-American children, whether poor or wealthy, with one parent or both parents. Did desegregation help? As African-American children, my husband and I certainly lacked equal educational facilities and means compared to white children. But we surely had a strong sense of self-esteem. Could it be the media's conveying too many negative images of African Americans? For the most part, there was only one television or no television in our homes with limited viewing allowed.

Neither my husband nor I grew up with substantial daily contact with white people, since we lived in different neighborhoods from whites, shopped in different stores, ate in different restaurants, attended different schools and churches and so on. I concluded earlier that my strong self-esteem and my assertiveness toward white people during my teen and early adult years were somehow related in part to my rearing. Our all-black neighborhoods and schools were mirrors that enhanced our self-esteem and pride in our heritage. Similarly, our limited social worlds further sheltered us from situations in which whites promoted the idea of black inferiority. Of course integration is better than segregation. True integration is the beginning of diversity within unity— bridges to a greater quality of life for all of us. However, I subsequently learned of the overwhelming resistance to true integration in our society. As my social world widened during my early adult years, I discovered that African Americans were *supposed* to be different from whites, not their equals, but relegated to a subordinate position that had unfair consequences for all aspects of African-American people's lives.

Fortifying our children with strong self-esteem is important in confronting racism. Our children's encounters with racism make the fostering of self-esteem an *ongoing process*. The mother of my son's soccer friend recently talked with me about the need to rebuild the self-esteem of her seventeen-year-old son because of police racism directed against him. While driving the family's "nice" Jeep alone, as well as when other African-American teens were with him, the police had followed him and called his mother on three occasions, inquiring whether the Jeep had been stolen and questioning whether she was black when she pointed out that her son had his parents' permission to drive the Jeep and that he was very responsible. Of course, neither the white teenage neighbor who frequently drove his parents' nice Jeep nor his mother had to endure the experience of the African-American family. My friend's son began to lack enthusiasm about being a teenage driver and became reluctant about driving to school, work or on family errands.

This conversation reminded me of too many similar ones shared by other mothers of African-American teenage sons and of what I could expect when my son becomes a teenager. I also recalled how African-American males are sometimes stifled in different ways than African-American females are by racism in our patriarchal society, which models the male as the breadwinner, the hero, the macho one. African-American males have more difficulty achieving these images than do white males because of racism, irrespective of the proven problems with such images.[14]

A tool we mothers can use is collaborative dialogue with each other. Through collaborative dialogue, mothers provide one another with other options in our struggle to resist racism. Just as my son's soccer friend's mother had reminded me that elevating our children's self-esteem is an ongoing process, I shared options for dealing with the police that she had not considered. I began to think about other ways of resisting racism, actions beyond bettering our children's and others' self-esteem via a home richly expressive of their history and culture, by exposure to books, cultural, social and political events reflecting positive images of African Americans and other ethnic groups, by donating books on African-American culture and history to my children's school library, and by making presentations about the incredible contributions of African Americans at our children's and others' schools.

In what other ways can mothers teach antiracism? Many of us can do more sharing about African-American culture and history at schools and elsewhere beyond Kwanzaa and Black History Month. Mothers need to talk more about what does and does not work in their antiracism endeavors. Sharing certain children's books, such as *The Color of My Fur* and *The Best Face of All*, has worked well for me in presentations against racism for both children and adults. We need to encourage open-minded white mothers and other nonblack mothers to speak and act against racism. Their conversations and actions against racism render important psychological dynamics for others who *look* like them, and also for African Americans. In some cases whites will be more receptive to antiracism from persons that look like them than from people of color. Similarly, it is often encouraging to nonwhites to know that there are whites who are willing to confront racism. Too often, white mothers' support of antiracism stops short of action, failing to bridge theory and practice.

Mothers can discuss students' acts of racism with teachers who are likely to address the matter. I recall sharing my observation of an act of racism with a white teacher. She thanked me the next day, relating that the two white girls had been counseled in accordance with school policy about their unacceptable acts toward an African-American male schoolmate of my children. Mothers should challenge school administrators to teach the contributions of different races throughout the year, especially those reflective of their school population. Similarly, mothers should advocate more participation of these students in various school activities and programs that not only elevate their self-esteem but enrich other students as well. We need more mothers to take an active role in the school support structures, in PTAs and as teachers' aids and substitute teachers, providing us more opportunities to teach antiracism to both students and adults.

I remain convinced that the paucity of African-American teachers is not only the result of salary concerns and school violence, but also of institutional resistance to teaching antiracism. Too often white students do not see African-American teachers in the classrooms, especially in more prestigious public or private schools, from primary through postgraduate. During my tenure at one predominantly white institution, one student's evaluation related his total surprise at seeing a black woman with a red Afro teaching philosophy as well as his initial doubts about my abilities. He concluded, however, that my course had been one of the best in his four years of college, evidencing an experience of unlearning racism. On the other hand, another student at the same institution and during the same semester did not grow as much. In his evaluation, he related his enthusiasm over the course, books and what he had learned; however, he never credited me in any way as the person responsible for the development of the course or what he had learned.

At another predominantly white institution, I remember successfully putting out race fires in the classroom as I taught John Hope Franklin's *From Slavery to Freedom*, John Oliver Killens's *Youngblood*, and Alice Walker's *Meridian*. One student said on his course evaluation that he had taken my course to learn more about blacks for himself because he wanted to be able to provide blacks with quality medicine as a future doctor. He expressed much appreciation for what he had learned, relating how one of the readings had been particularly emotional for him. He also related that his grandfather would probably call me a nigger and his father would think it. I believe the experience that taught this student antiracism was one that focused on shared values and humanity rather than racism itself. Seeing common humanity within a racially charged situation helped him to see, and to get beyond, his inheritance of racism. A couple of semesters after graduation, this same polished-looking young man with the racist heritage embraced me in the shopping mall, reminding me of his fruitful experience in my class. I, too, learned antiracism from this experience, for I had concluded from this young man's sparring and questioning during class that he was skeptical of my competence. Over sixteen years of teaching, I have received many evaluations similar to that student's as I continue to attempt to get honest feedback from my students.

More Coping, Fortifying and Confronting

Beyond the absurdity of racism, how are mothers to persevere in confronting racism while balancing the history and continuing presence of racism in America and the world? How can mothers persevere in challenging perpetuating theories and practices of racism? These questions remained steadfast among the many fleeting fiercely through my mind as I pondered my children's discovery of their race as "less than."

When mothers are "tired of being tired," we are reminded by other mothers that we are not alone in our struggle to teach antiracism. Mothers must realize that we cannot afford to count the struggle against racism as one of too many social causes we are too busy to address. Our collaborative dialogues with other mothers provide us with moral support, preventing us from lapsing into a persisting state of rage in our struggle against racism. Some days when I am tired of being tired, I let people know that it is their lucky day, reasoning that I at least confronted their racism in a general way. On other days when I am fighting not to be enraged by the insurmountable realities of racism, I go back to various scholarship on racism which presents acid tests of my belief in humanity and simultaneously re-energizes me to persevere in the urgent need of confronting racism.[15] I also think about Julia A. Boyd's imaginary purse of coins—coins of Hope, Faith, Confidence and Compassion that are always with her. She says, "[W]henever I find myself in a situation that requires me to spend one of my coins, I just pull it out and go for broke. Now over the years I've found that these coins are magic, because they always manage to replace themselves. I think we all have a magic coin when we have hope."[16] At other times, I have found that it is also effective to teach antiracism through unexpected humanizing actions that challenge us all to think beyond our own race. That act may be leaving behind my children's placemat coloring along with brown and black crayons for the restaurant manager, suggesting the need for these colors.[17] Or it may be yielding to white persons who sometimes take note of my "Color Me Human" car tag that challenges all of us to expand our limiting assumptions of race.

This is a challenge reflective of multiculturalism, a principle that provides encouraging theory and practice for confronting racism. It balances tension between the one and the many within a pluralistic society and strengthens the political movement for a truly inclusive democratic society. Multiculturalism offers compelling reasons for not conceiving differences as inferior, Other or threatening—conceptions that lead to racism—but instead seeing differences as sources of strength. Mothers can gain strength for antiracist work through reading and discussing works of multicultural theory[18] and contribute invaluably to its realization by discovering ways of practicing it.[19] Within the last five years, I have used multicultural theory to teach antiracism during my Black History Month presentations. Black History Month seems to be an opportune time to address African-American culture and history, as well as to examine other ethnic groups in the spirit of unity within diversity—dispelling the fear and ignorance that perpetuate racism. It is mothers' work, more so than academicians', that will transform racism so that all children will value diversity and know their own preciousness.

Notes

1. The use of "caregiver" here refers to both women and men as well as to feminists of both genders. Also, while I write here as an African-American feminist mother, I acknowledge that some of my experiences are shared to different degrees by some men.

2. Johnetta B. Cole, "What If We Made Racism a Woman's Issue…" *McCall's* (October 1990): 39.

3. Ibid.

4. For instance, see Elizabeth Hood, "Black Women, White Women: Separate Paths to Liberation," in *Black Scholar* (April 1978): 45-56, and Audre Lorde, *Sister Outsider* (Freedom, CA: The Crossing Press, 1984).

5. I have found that racism occurs in the lives of African-American boys more frequently than in the lives of African-American girls; hence my focus here on boys rather than girls. This situation is partly attributable to American patriarchal society seeing African-American boys as more of a threat than African-American girls, in competing for jobs, wielding power, and having influence. I do not, however, intend to minimize girls' experiences with racism.

6. Lorde, *Sister Outsider*, 115.

7. David Theo Goldberg, "The Social Formation of Racist Discourse," in *Anatomy of Racism*, ed. David Theo Goldberg (Minneapolis: University of Minnesota Press, 1990), 295.

8. Ibid., 296.

9. Kwame Anthony Appiah, "Racisms," in *Anatomy of Racism*, ed. David Theo Goldberg (Minneapolis: University of Minnesota Press, 1990). The distinctions Appiah makes are extrinisc and intrinsic racism. He states that "[E]xtrinisc racism [is] discrimination between people [based on people's] belief that members of different races differ in respects that *warrant* differential treatment, respects—such as honesty or courage or intelligence—that are uncontroversially held. . . . [I]ntrinsic racism [is defined as] differentiat[ing] morally between members of different races because [one] believe[s] that each race has a different moral status, quite independent of the moral characteristics entailed by its racial essence. [B]eing of the same race is a reason for preferring one person to another." In the case of extrinsic racism, Appiah points out that awareness of facts will suffice to counter false doctrine. In the case of intrinsic racism, no amount of facts will suffice to counter false beliefs (5-6).

10. Naomi Zack, *Race and Mixed Race* (Philadelphia: Temple University Press, 1993). Zack draws a distinction between intentional racism, which involves conscious preference for one race over another, and unintentional racism. The former involves awareness and resistance to the idea that there are not differences between races, while the latter involves unexamined assumptions (26).

11. Appiah, "Racisms," 5.

12. See Nancy P. Greenman, et al., "Institutional Inertia to Achieving Diversity: Transforming Resistance into Celebration," in *Educational Foundations* 6, 2 (1992).

13. The appreciation of such humor is apparent in work like Daryl Cumber Dance's *Shuckin' and Jivin': Folklore from Contemporary Black Americans* (Bloomington: Indiana University Press, 1978).

14. Given this reality of racism, one understands the notable sociological case of a little black boy placing his feet on top of his desk daily without comment. He responded to his teacher's inquiry about his behavior by saying he was "playing white man."

15. Works like: Frantz Fanon's "The Fact of Blackness" (1990), Cornel West's *Race Matters* (1993), W.E.B. DuBois *Souls of Black Folk* (1903), Maude White Katz's "End Racism in Education: A Concerned Parent Speaks" (1968), Patricia J. Williams's *The Alchemy of Race and Rights* (1991), Gertrude Ezorsky's *Racism and Justice: The Case for Affirmative Action*

(1991), Ernest J. Gaines's *A Lesson Before Dying*, (1993), Jacqueline Jones's *Labor of Love, Labor of Sorrow*, (1985), Bill E. Lawson's *The Underclass Question*, (1992), John Oliver Killens's *Youngblood* (1954) were acid tests for me as I contemplated the focus of this essay.

16. Julia A. Boyd, *Girlfriend to Girlfriend: Everyday Wisdom and Affirmations from the Sister Circle* (New York: Dutton, 1995). This is one of many affirmations for getting through daily obstacles presented in the book.

17. This effort reminds me of a mother who colored one of the Charmin tissue babies brown in the sixties for her baby's self-esteem. Of course the company, as well as others, does this today. However, restaurants don't seem to have followed suit.

18. Our tendency to resist "differences" is related to the belief that to recognize differences is to order them hierarchically, with someone's (mine or theirs) family, community or values (spiritual, educational, social and political) inferior. Shelley M. Park and Michelle A. LaRocque suggested in a paper presented at the South Eastern Women's Studies Association Conference in 1992 that multiculturalism is a synthesis of unity and diversity—*shared* community that maintains the integrity of the different groups that comprise it.

19. Peter McLaren, in "A Dialogue on Multiculturalism and Democratic Culture" with Kelly Estrada in *Educational Researcher* 22, 3 (1993), explains that multiculturalism teaches us to displace dominant knowledges that oppress, tyrannize, and infantalize. It encourages us to imagine possible worlds, to create new languages and to design new institutional and social practices. He also explains the need for positive, affirmative discourses on race, ethnic identity, multiculturalism and gender. The definition of American culture needs to be expanded and understood not as negating a national identity, but as addressing the reality of diversity and a new pluralism. See also the works in the bibliography by Ronald Takaki and Vincent G. Harding for exceptional discussions of multiculturalism, Boyce Rensberger for the anthropology of race, and Taylor and Wolf for diversity and a new pluralism.

Lessons in Failure

Narrative of a Puertorrican Mother

EILEEN DE LOS REYES

> *Beloved sister,*
> *woman of scars and solstices*
> *friend of beggars*
> *eternal companion of the tortured*
> *come, help me at the break of dawn.*
> *In your skirts that washed the bitter,*
> *inundated grief of the despair,*
> *let me place a dream.*
> — Marjorie Agosin, *Circle of Madness:*
> *Mothers of the Plaza de Mayo*

The plane ride from Puerto Rico to the United States is very strange, almost magical. While in Puerto Rico I enjoy class and "white" privilege; once I land in the United States I become a "person of color." This unintentional transformation determines in large measure who I have become.

I started my undergraduate education in the United States when I was twenty-five and raising two boys. I spent the next eleven years in elite institutions and cloistered libraries with their wonderful books. Like bell hooks, who left her world behind and "entered the strange world of a predominantly white elitist university,"[1] I struggled to remain grounded in my culture and balanced enough to understand where I was and what was expected of me. During that time I, as a Puertorrican woman, engaged in a struggle against the "founding fathers" to reclaim my history and to understand the colonial status of Puerto Rico.

After eleven years of individualistic training, I felt prepared to compete and win. With time I learned, however, that that very training would be my biggest handicap in achieving what I wanted—namely, an academic career, which I defined in the Caribbean, Central American, and South American tradition: transforming words into actions that supported one's political beliefs. Embarking on a new journey with this internal contradiction, I began to observe the difference between being a sheltered student and re-entering academia as an administrator and a faculty member. Thus began my "real" education in racism. What I had not been able to see because of the pressures of family and studies became very clear and painful when I started working with students.

My experiences as an administrator and now as a faculty member taught me the fierceness of racism and the never-ending emotional violence against those that are defined as "others" or persons of color. To be a professor of color means that in addition to teaching a full load and publishing, one must work on grants to support "minority programs" while simultaneously translating the students of color for the administration and faculty. To this definition of what it means to be a faculty or administrator of color, one must add the experiences that characterize daily life. These include being invisible in meetings and being subjected to countless stereotypes, from being told that Latinos need smaller furniture because we are short people, to having people scream at you because they believe that since you have an accent you must also be deaf, to being told that Puerto Ricans come to the United States to get more welfare. This steady stream of ignorance and abuse slowly consumes one's strength, creating an internal tension between anger and fear, pride and humiliation, resistance and capitulation.

Were this my own private experience, it would not be as devastating. After all, I come from a long line of very strong Puertorrican women who know how to resist and struggle. But racism is a disease that is contagious, and it extends to the treatment my children receive. They understand the fierceness of racism and know that "spics" who go out with white girls will be punished and beaten, that the police may stop and search them because they cannot possibly own the car they drive, and that violating the mainstream dress code results in discrimination and retaliation. They know that if they go with their African-American friends to look for work, all of them will be turned down, but if they go alone, they stand a better chance. Looking for summer employment, a routine activity for teenagers, transforms itself into a test of loyalty, friendship and principles. Together with their friends they test the system each day with the same results: They are feared, unwanted, expendable.

I have also seen firsthand the neglect of and violence against students of color in schools and universities. To be a student of color means that in most school systems you are considered to be automatically "at risk" and a candidate for all kinds of remediation programs. As a student of color you know you are spoken about and discussed in all meetings dealing with retention and drop-out problems, but seldom in meetings about academic excellence, college courses or accelerated programs. It also means that you are identified by principals and teachers, from the first day of school, as a potential gang member, as if this were a genetic trait, a remnant from *West Side Story*. Everyone knows that the "flood" of these students with all their "inherent" problems has lowered the standards of the institutions and depleted much-needed funds. Every day you are aware that whatever the problems in education are, you are the cause; you are the problem. Finally, to be Latina or Latino in the United States means being asked in utter exasperation: What is it that you people want? Why are you here? When are you leaving?

Like many in our position, my family and I have been forced to choose sides. We could possibly try to be upper-middle-class white Latinos who are part of the American dream and who exemplify the innumerable opportunities available for those able to melt in the so-called melting pot. But at what price? Being "white" to the eye and palatable to the tastes of those in the mainstream allows one to listen to the language of hatred for those "spics" who excel only at stealing hubcaps and cheating the welfare system, "spics" who, like blacks, Chicanos and others, are destroying the nation and making it a "third world" country, corrupting the American dream and the institutions and culture that support it.

In my mind, there is no choice: We can only be Puertorricans, which in this country means being part of those who are oppressed and in conflict with those who are in power. In choosing to remain Puertorrican, one discovers that to be a person of color means to be in the extraordinary company of the courageous people who suffer the violence and their allies. To be a person of color means that one is in the struggle for the duration and that one must fight to remain healthy both physically and spiritually while retaining one's dignity. Struggle, health and dignity are what will determine whether we survive or collapse. These experiences and observations inform my politics and my actions.

I have tried to explain what it means to be a Latina mother to colleagues and students from the United States with little success. More often than not the stereotypes that describe women of the "third world" include submissiveness, docility and underdevelopment. These stereotypes not only distort reality but also prevent us from learning important lessons of courage and determination from the women of Central and South America and the Caribbean. Latinas who struggled against horrifyingly repressive regimes in their countries during the 1970s offered me clarity in the midst of confusion and pointed to a life of committed struggle against racism and all other forms of oppression targeting my children and all those that become part of my family, in the tradition of Las Madres, the mothers of the Plaza de Mayo in Buenas Aires, and the Chilean mothers during the Pinochet years.

In the book *Don't Be Afraid, Gringo: A Honduran Woman Speaks from the Heart*, Elvia Alvarado captures the frustration and sadness of continuous struggle and also the courage and the conviction essential to succeed.

I must admit that sometimes I get so overwhelmed by the odds against us that I break down and cry. I see our children dying of hunger, and the ones that live have no jobs, no education, no future. I see the military getting more and more repressive. I see us being persecuted, jailed, tortured. I get exhausted by all internal problems between the campesino organizations. And I see Central America going up in flames.

I start to wonder if it's worth it. I start to think maybe I should stay home and make tortillas.

But whenever I have these doubts, whenever I start to cry, I put my hands into fists and say to myself, "Make your tears turn into anger, make your tears turn into strength." As soon as I stop crying, I feel the sense of power go through my body. And I get back to work with even more enthusiasm, with more conviction than ever.[2]

Women like Alvarado persevered and resisted, and, as a result, their countries—and in some instances the world—had to listen. Instead of submissive and docile women, what emerges upon close examination are models of quiet resistance where necessary, and determined action where required. This approach, coupled with a firm commitment to community and cooperation focusing on long-term grassroots mobilization, defines a clear philosophy and a political agenda for these women and for those of us who learn from them. I am indebted to these women for showing me a path and guiding me after I experienced a professional failure that also had serious repercussions for those who worked for me. Yet this experience taught me very valuable lessons.

After receiving my Ph.D., I accepted the position of project director of a learning center, a grant-funded program dedicated to working with students of color who had been rejected by the college but who were allowed to take college courses provided that they participated in tutoring and counseling sessions at the learning center. After two years of successful participation in the program, they would be accepted as regular students and could continue taking college courses without the support of the tutoring sessions.

I arrived at the learning center with the certainty that my training would allow me to make a contribution to the transformation of an organization that clearly needed leadership. This frame of mind proved to be the most serious mistake I could make. I focused constantly on what I could do to revamp the center and neglected to focus on the painstaking process of building a community of people committed to a shared agenda of change. That fundamental mistake led to others.

In hindsight, there were problems with the mission of the learning center that I should have anticipated. For example, everyone I spoke with during my initial interview articulated the urgent need for leadership and change and pointed out that the relation between the college and the center was problematic. I could have asked questions such as, How are the students of color seen by the college if everyone knows that they were initially rejected by the college? Or, How does the faculty feel about teaching these students when it could be argued that they are not prepared to be in college? However, the possibility of working with three hundred students of color, a staff of eleven professionals and what seemed to be a reasonable budget was very attractive to me, and so I chose to ignore these problems.

The belief that as an individual I could change the organization led to an error in strategy. My plan was to identify the problems, implement changes and begin transforming the organization very quickly. My assumption was that since everyone had articulated the need for leadership and change, I would have to prove that I could do both in rapid succession. I worked endless hours trying to define the problems and identify the solutions.

After determining that the learning center lacked credibility as an organization committed to academic excellence, I visited all department chairs and asked for a window of opportunity. Given that I was the project director and that we were in the process of transforming the organization, could they help us by giving us an opportunity to prove the depth of the transformation? They all agreed, since they wanted to put a stop to the learning center's practice of choosing "easy" professors for the students and, consequently, putting large numbers of learning center students in those professors' courses. My mission was to work with the departments in choosing courses taught by faculty who felt confident that their philosophy and methodology were particularly effective with our students. For example, I recommended that all of our students register for writing-intensive courses where they could hone their skills in critical thinking and research. I also recommended courses that emphasized group work and discussions because those methods allowed the students to be visible, express their opinions and perfect their skills in public speaking.

The faculty had other issues of concern regarding the learning center. For example, they objected to the practice of placing large groups of five to ten learning center students in one class because they felt these students required additional support. My commitment to the departments was to explain our choices and to meet regularly to resolve any issues the faculty might have. In other words, at no point would the faculty be surprised by any of our decisions. My hope was to engage the faculty in a discussion about the learning center. By beginning this discussion, I wanted to address both the needs of the faculty and those of our students. In a very short period of time I created a feeling of hope about the possibility of change at the learning center. I believed this meant I was being successful.

I was completely oblivious, however, to certain structural problems that defined the discussion about the learning center. For example, that the center was a grant-funded organization had serious repercussions. I have learned with time and experience that "minority programs" are usually supported by outside funding. Regarded as peripheral to the institution and defined as temporary problems, these students are seen as the responsibility of someone else and not of the institution. Even as demographic changes suggest that "minority" students will someday be the majority in our colleges and universities, they are still relegated to the fringes of the college budgets.

External funding generates several problems: First, the institution may feel it does not have the responsibility to tackle the problems of the grant-funded organization or of the students participating in grant-funded programs. This generates the second problem: lack of accountability—both for the college that does not engage in discussions and problem-solving with the grant-funded organization, and for the grant-funded organization which begins to see itself as autonomous yet relegated to the periphery of the institution and in constant risk of disappearing when the funding stops.

The staff at the learning center, for example, did not have any medical or retirement benefits, was not part of the union, and could not use faculty or administrative parking. Most important, the staff was not part of any college committees, such as those dealing with academic policies and curriculum, thus eliminating the possibility of engaging in any meaningful discussion about the learning center that included the college community. And, clearly, we were not part of the structure of academic or administrative discussion and decision-making. In retrospect, I was busy paying attention to what I considered to be the important issues, but neglected the structural problems that, by definition, limited the range of things I could do.

I was surprised that the learning center participated in its own isolation. It seemed that there were some benefits in being so neglected: The learning center could establish its own rules, define its own priorities and set the timetables. My insistence that we had to establish a relationship with the college as equals and that to do this we had to begin speaking the language of academic excellence broke the silence and the isolation. My carelessness in not paying attention to structural problems and my determination to change what had been in place for more than a decade in a short period of time resulted in an environment of tension and conflict that affected my staff and the students at the learning center. I also neglected to ask the most fundamental question: Why was the isolation of the learning center accepted as a way of life by both the center and the college? Even if I had not been prepared to answer this question, it would have eventually led me to a structural problem that had to be resolved.

Coupled with this series of mistakes was what I consider to be the most painful problem I faced. The learning center was dedicated to students of color and as such served African-American, Latino/Latina and some Asian-American students. For a more experienced observer, the tensions that characterize the relationship between African Americans and Latinos were evident. I refused to acknowledge that my presence was seen as very threatening to the definition of the center, which was directed by an African American. Within this definition, the Latinos were relegated to the periphery of the periphery. Comments such as "Now that you are here, we will have more Hispanics than African Americans" should have alerted me to the problem. Another clear indication was that even though most of the Latinos at the learning center were English-as-a-second-language (ESL) students, appropriate support for them was nonexistent. Once more, had I known what to look for, I could have identified this problem not only at the learning center but also at the college at large, where the racial problems were defined as being between Anglo Americans and African Americans; Latinos were seen only as an ESL "problem." I continued to insist that I was the project director of a learning center dedicated to all students and that these divisions would destroy the center. This argument could not be accepted since it threatened a hierarchy that defined racial problems in a way that was tolerated by both the college and the center.

The tensions between the so-called minority groups are seldom discussed openly. Instead, they are often interpreted as personal problems between two "minorities" or as a nuisance to be addressed quickly and effectively. A white student, exasperated by a discussion between Chicanos and African Americans in class, might comment, "I don't want to participate in this game of seeing who is more oppressed; we must continue with the discussion." Or an administrator complains, "Why don't the African Americans and the Latinos speak and resolve their issues and get it together!" These reactions, which acknowledge that tension exists but define it as a minor conflict that could be resolved easily if we "got it together," reveal a lack of understanding of the history of both communities and the struggle to survive with some measure of dignity in a society that creates and nurtures the idea that "minority groups" get whatever is left after taking care of the "regular" students or the "mainstream" society. In turn, many African Americans and Latinos fall into the trap of seeing each other as competitors for scarce goods and, once more, neglect to ask the important question about the structure of power: Why are we in this condition? What must be done to transform the struggle? Would recognizing the struggle between African Americans and Latinos as an attempt, in many instances successful, by those in power to divide those who together could be a significant force for change, provide us with an assessment that would lead us toward a more effective path?

Throughout this conflict, the administration chose to position itself as a spectator, waiting for the two "minorities" to resolve the situation.

Time provides wisdom, but I have to admit that while I was working at the learning center I defined what was happening as a personal struggle that involved two individuals. A deeper understanding would have led me in a different direction, one that should have included serious conversations and discussions with the African-American community at the college.

Throughout this very painful experience, I was supported and guided by a senior faculty member at the college. She became my "enlightened" witness, reassuring me that what was happening was not my fault; as she explained it, the situation was the result of internal and external dynamics that I had not anticipated. She gave me advice and support and taught me in one year what it takes others a lifetime to learn. Her role as union president, her experience fighting and winning salary equity for women in the state colleges, and her role in founding the Women's Studies Program at the college provided me with a wealth of information and guidance. She not only provided the support I needed to understand what was happening, but also began speaking about other opportunities for me outside of the learning center.

Pressure escalated to a point where I was forced to resign and accept the most devastating defeat I had ever suffered. Five staff members resigned within the next six months. For the staff and the students this represented a period of fear in which they had to make very difficult choices. The tension created health problems for some and for others a situation both humiliating and destructive. I was very fortunate that the senior faculty member also guided me after this experience.

To make sense of a very confusing and painful experience, I began to study the work of activist mothers in South and Central America. Instinctively I knew I needed role models to whom I could relate and who could provide me with the necessary guidance to move forward. These women spoke about patience, determination and courage, all of which I needed in order to understand my condition and create a path I could follow. Interestingly, as a result of these readings and conversations with Marjorie Agosin, who has written extensively about the mothers of the Plaza de Mayo and the Chilean women, who fought against the military governments that disappeared their children, I was able to transform my personal search into a course on women, children and human rights in Latin America, sharing with my students what had become for me a path of hope.[3] What follow are the lessons I have learned.

First, as a strategy for transforming our and our students' condition as people of color, the model of individual competition and achievement results in systematic failure. Inherently, individualism is a conservative approach that accepts that one's mission is to compete and win within the system. Instead, change and transformation come as a result of grassroots work in which one focuses on the community, which must function as the center of our lives. For those that need to shine and be recognized as individual contributors, this approach is impossible. I, who had been so carefully trained and who had accepted and adopted this model wholeheartedly, had to learn that there was an inherent contradiction between who I was and what I wanted to do. Resolving this contradiction has become a long-term journey, the result of which is that I now walk in the opposite direction of where I started after graduation. My focus is not on what I can do, but on how I can work with others to transform our communities.

I also learned firsthand why Paulo Freire argues for the necessity of action preceded and followed by careful reflection.[4] I engaged in action that escalated to *re*action without stopping to reflect on the external and internal dynamics of the institution and the political nature of the discussion. I forgot my political core or that system of beliefs and values that holds my life together and guides me in my work. For example, by not analyzing the politics of institutional racism, so prevalent in most of the institutions where we work, I missed the foundation of the problem, without which I could not possibly succeed.

The ability to reflect assumes the ability to be patient and to understand the importance of long-term struggle. The Latina mothers who fight for the "disappeared" in Central and South America and those Latinas who struggle in countless towns and cities in the United States have a deep understanding of the communities in which they live and work. Yet they take the time to begin the process of understanding fully the conditions that oppress them, and this has allowed them to remain engaged and visible, in the case of the mothers from Argentina and Chile for more than twenty years. I finally learned what the women in Latin America understand so well: that transformation is a slow process requiring patience and endurance. By moving so fast, I neglected the essential step of observing, learning and reflecting before making decisions.

Although I was very successful with the faculty and administrators in presenting an alternative vision for the learning center and, in many instances, delivered the results I had promised, the transformation could not possibly be sustained since it threatened the informal and unarticulated arrangements between the learning center and the college. These arrangements included accepting that the students were second-class citizens who did not fulfill the necessary conditions for admission to the college. This resulted in stigmatization for the duration of the college experience of the students of color at the learning center and, by default, of all students of color at the institution. This arrangement also included accepting the second-class citizenship of the staff of the learning center, who did not receive the benefits of full participation in the college community. Needless to say, the definition of the staff and the students as mediocre had the most serious repercussions both for the individuals and for the college community in general. Clearly, I could not reach this deep understanding of the learning center in two months.

One of the most difficult issues I faced at the learning center was the tension between many African Americans and Latinos/Latinas. I remain firm in my position: As a teacher and a mother I refuse to choose a side and fear and struggle against the other. Instead, the principle that supports my actions is the commitment to justice and dignity for all of our children. I also incorporate the principle used by those mothers in Latin America who, coming from all classes and races, recognized the need to fight not only for their children but for all children who had been the victims of repression. This principle not only is morally right, but also reflects the reality that the individual struggle of one mother can be quickly destroyed, while that of a large community of determined women will endure the most difficult challenges.

One of the critical questions I have learned to ask is, Why is this organization supported by a grant? Many of us have accepted that for new programs to exist, we must find grant money. Furthermore, we accept as a fact of life that when the money is gone so is the program. I have learned to argue for a rethinking of the allocation of money to address the needs of a growing number of students of color in colleges and universities. Accepting the "grant mentality" for students of color reflects our acceptance of neglect and invisibility for both our students and ourselves. For those working in grant-funded minority programs, the question we must ask is: What price do we pay for accepting a position in the periphery of the institution supported by money that is renewed every three years? In 1996, we face a more urgent question: What will we do when the grants are gone?

Painful lessons entail lessons of hope. The most important lesson I learned was the need to identify those people who share one's political vision and system of beliefs and values and to nurture those relations. The activist mothers in Latin America and throughout the United States understand the value of creating and nurturing communities committed to long-term struggle and change. In my case, that a senior faculty member became my advocate turned a negative experience into a positive one and laid the foundation for a long-term relation of collaboration and friendship. I have learned that if I do not find at least one person in an organization who can become an ally, I must recognize and accept the futility of any attempt at being successful. From a core group of two, one can move to organize a community that includes those who are committed to a shared political agenda. This in turn increases the possibility of long-term success in transforming our workplaces and communities.

Elvia Alvarado speaks of sadness and joy, of weakness and strength. These extremes represent the nature of our struggle against racism and other forms of oppression. Who among us has not sat down and cried or vowed to stop fighting; to give up? And yet, when we think of our children, when we become angry, we feel as Alvarado does, "the sense of power go[ing] through my body," and we start again. This power is to be found in communities, for in our days of weakness, they come to our rescue. Together in those communities we reflect and understand the problems in depth. We ask the fundamental questions and avoid the superficial ones. Finally, we sustain each other in what we must understand is a long-term commitment to recover our children and together with them create communities in which justice, honor and dignity are valued and nurtured.

Notes

1. bell hooks, *Sisters of the Yam: Black Women and Self-Recovery* (Boston: South End Press, 1993), 9.

2. Elvia Alvarado, *Don't Be Afraid, Gringo: A Honduran Woman Speaks from the Heart*, trans. and ed. Medea Benjamin (New York: HarperPerennial/ Harper & Row, 1989), 142-143.

3. Marjorie Agosin, ed., *Surviving Beyond Fear: Women, Children, and Human Rights in Latin America* (Fredonia, NY: White Pine Press, 1992).

4. Paulo Freire, *Pedagogy of the Oppressed* (New York: Continuum, 1993), 33.

Teaching the (Bi)Racial Space That Has No Name

Reflections of a Black Male Feminist Teacher

GARY LEMONS

> We believe that although we are oppressed because of our color, we are privileged because of our sex and must therefore take responsibility for ending that privilege.
>
> —Black Men for the Eradication of Sexism

> . . . you addressed feminism in a way that opened my eyes to how 'white' my idea of feminism really was.
>
> —a student response

As a black male college professor committed to the belief that the struggles against sexual oppression must be waged as powerfully as the battle against white supremacy, I have crafted an antiracist-feminist teaching strategy that enables students to take an oppositional stance to white skin privilege and to the power that all men hold because we are men. Thinking about what it means to be a feminist teacher who is black and male, I am led to reflect upon the complex interconnection between my race and my gender as they influence the feminist stand-point from which I teach African-American literature. This essay aims to show the effectiveness of a feminist teaching strategy crafted for first-year college students in which literary texts by black authors serve to challenge white supremacist thinking.

Before making a case for an antiracist, "male" feminist teaching strategy, certain fundamental issues must be addressed concerning the relation of men to feminism. The very notion of a man declaring himself a feminist necessarily raises questions. In a patriarchal culture where men are conditioned to believe themselves superior to women and therefore possess the right to sexually oppress, objectify and brutalize women, is it any wonder that many feminst women view the idea of a "feminist man" with great suspicion? Yet progressive feminist women have supported including pro-feminist men in the movement to end sexual oppression. As an advocate of feminist education, I believe that the liberation of all women will be fully achieved when children and adults of both sexes are educated about the dehumanizing effects of sexism and its relation to racism. Males in our society—particularly black boys and men, who must confront racial oppression—need to know that understanding the interconnected nature of sex and race oppression is crucial to achieving liberation, not only for black people but for all people.

Toward an Antiracist-Feminist Pedagogy

Asserting that men can be feminists contests the notion that feminism is only about women. Bell hooks has argued that women's struggle against sexual oppression requires including men in feminist movement. Asserting that black men can be feminists opposes the opinion that black liberation struggle is only about racism. Black male teachers advocating joint struggle against racism and sexism can make the classroom a space for critical consciousness. In that space, students seriously work toward a radical revisioning of race and gender oppression within a politic of coalition struggle that recognizes the interrelated nature of domination.

Those of us in literary studies can call on the art of storytelling to teach students an oppositional view that exposes the interrelation of white supremacy and male supremacy. For me, feminism rooted in the critique of racism offers a liberatory strategy for antiracist movement. Placed in the service of antiracist pedagogy, black fictional and auto-biographical narratives about racism in the United States employ the classroom as a liberatory space where, as hooks says, education takes place as the practice of freedom. This classroom empowers students, helping them to understand how to cope in a nation still besieged by racial strife and under the burden of a legacy of racism nearly four hundred years old.

This essay posits the idea that African-American literature studied in the classroom can be a powerful site for antiracist-feminist work. By employing black literary texts to show the interrelation of racial oppression with other forms of domination, teachers committed to the politics of coalition struggle make a powerful move in the classroom against racism. From the slave narrative to the liberation stories of contemporary women, black writers have recreated with unparalleled skill the complexity of American race relations—the atrocities, the pain, the suffering born of white supremacy. Teaching black literature against racism is a transgressive act, involving tremendous risk-taking for both teacher and student. Despite its transformative possibilities for progressive antiracist education, teaching narratives of racial oppression often requires that teachers (black teachers in particular) bear the burden of the emotional fallout from students. Even white students claiming to be antiracist exhibit anger, fear, guilt and resentment toward us and toward students of color when required to read stories of black people victimized by acts of white supremacy. On the other hand, students of color (and black students in particular), experiencing some of the same emotions, display resentment toward white students, all white people, and teachers (especially if we are not black) for opening up the wounds of racism. But taking risks lies at the heart of transgressive pedagogies. Feminist critiques of racism and sexism defy the premise that the classroom ought to be a "safe" space for learning.

Contesting accepted ideas of white supremacy and patriarchy poses a threat to what many students hold sacred. Pedagogy in critical opposition to racism and male supremacy necessarily (en)genders pain, especially when students have to confront their own race and/or gender. I engage antiracist feminism in a course I call "The Whiteness of

Blackness, the Blackness of Whiteness: The Novel of Passing."[1] Students learn that being antiracist lays the groundwork for critical opposition to the dehumanizing effects of sexism, classism and homophobia as the major interrelated systems of oppression at the root of nearly all forms of domination in the United States.

My first-year students embark upon a radical study of African-American literature focused on an analysis and critique of U.S. race relations around the subject of miscegenation. The context is white supremacy. We examine the problems of biraciality, racial passing and "colorism." I hope to facilitate students' understanding of the mechanics of racism, perhaps toward a vision of a multiracial society and an end to the painful legacy all Americans bear as a result of white supremacist thinking.

Teaching "The Whiteness of Blackness" Against White Supremacy

> Through studying bi-raciality I have come to realize . . . the irony of the possibility that all "whites" may in fact be passing for "white" (according to racial laws still on the books in certain states that adhere to the "one drop of blood" theory). Thus, there may be few "Caucasians in the great republic who can trace their ancestry back ten generations and confidently assert that there are no Black leaves, twigs or branches on their family trees." —George Schuyler (author of *Black No More*)
>
> —a student response

I have taught "The Whiteness of Blackness" for several years, once each semester at a small interdisciplinary liberal arts college in New York City. A year ago as a final take-home exam, I asked the thirteen students in the course—eleven women (three women of color) and one man—to write about the impact the class had had on them. I wanted to determine beyond the standard questions on the course evaluation form whether a study of African-American fiction based on a feminist critique of racism could persuade students to adopt an antiracist standpoint.

As the moment to hand in the exams approached, I sat in the empty classroom with trepidation, wondering what their responses would bring. I could not be completely sure of the success or failure of the course, since this particular one had represented my first *active* attempt to link antiracist pedagogy to a critique of sexism. As I watched students hand in their exams and leave, that moment called up all the other times I had observed them leaving the classroom, wondering what each one was taking from it. As personal reactions to the course, the students' exams provide telling narratives of attitudes, opinions, reflections and revelations about the complex interplay of racial issues arising in and outside the classroom.

Reflecting on the first writing assignment from the beginning of the semester, in which students were to explain why they enrolled in the course, one student wrote on her final exam,

> I distinctly remember the response that I carefully composed: 'I was tired of talking about race issues in clinched-revolutionary terms with Blackfolk or in politically correct safe-zones with whites.' I'm not tired anymore; I'm fatigued and weary. I can't get over, under, around or by the feeling that I'm saying the same thing over and over and no one's listening . . . [S]omeone needs to tell the truth: we ain't moved and things ain't changing and we sure ain't saying nothing new.

This student, expressing her desire for a truly liberatory discussion of racial problems without falling into traps of dogma and clichés, voiced a common sentiment among students first entering the course. Each time I have taught "The Whiteness of Blackness," confronting student cynicism about the chances of race relations improving in the nation has made me more urgently aware that a radical pedagogy of race is needed not only in the classroom, but in the country. To combat the increasingly pessimistic feeling many students voice that no one's listening, things haven't changed, no one's saying anything new about a solution to the problem, I have challenged myself to take more risks pedagogically, to be more vocal in the classroom about the necessity for student commitment to coalition struggle against racism.

Teaching "the novel of passing" is a transgressive act against white supremacy, essentialist ideas of racial purity and the fallacy of racial categorizing. Advocating student responsibility to antiracist thinking, I position an analysis of the (mis)treatment of mixed-race persons in the "biracial" novel as a crucial strategy for both white students and students of color to begin divesting themselves of white supremacist ideology. Developing critical consciousness in the classroom means that students must reject an essentialist racial politic (based on oversimplified, fixed dichotomizing of people into "either-or," black-white categories of race), which only serves to reinforce the hegemony of whiteness as the symbol of racial purity/supremacy and blackness as the sign of racial inferiority.

As a subversive narrative contesting racial purity (that is, white supremacy), the novel of passing representing (bi)racial characters moving across racial categories not only works to destabilize racial distinctions but also calls into question the entire concept of race itself as a natural phenomenon. When boundaries of race break down at the level of skin color—complicated by gender, class and sexuality—the fallacy of white power is exposed. I insist that for student critiques of racism to be most effective, they must illustrate the effect of white supremacy on the biracial figure in terms of the interrelation of oppression. Students learn to decipher the profoundly pervasive and systematic ways racism operates in racially mixed space. And framing class discussions and writing assignments that help students actively erase the line between fact and fiction, between the world of the text and the "real" world they inhabit, empowers them to talk and write more openly about the influence of racism on them, across race, gender, class, sexual and ethnic borders.

Creating an arena for students to participate imaginatively in the lives of biracial characters is another means of achieving a form of sympathetic identification. When this happens, students experience a sense of freedom to let down guards, to let go of fear, anger, resentment. At this moment a process of healing can begin. To make this happen, I ask students to write a paper, in any form or style they choose, in which they assume the persona of a mixed-race character from one of the novels we have read. This exercise draws them into the narrative, getting them to feel, see, taste, hear and touch the effects of racism on the biracial body.

In "Passing"—Does a Pedagogy of (Bi)Raciality Make A Difference in Students' Lives?

One female student, writing about the particularities of her mixed-race background, had this to say:

> When you asked the first day of class who considered themselves "white," I hesitated raising my hand for the fact that I am not just white yet I look it . . . I must cling to my color—because of my pale skin and my facial features . . . I look in the mirror sometimes and . . . I see my Irish grandmother's pale skin and my Korean heritage in the slant of my eyes, my African blood in the weight and texture of my unconditioned hair, yet I am "White."

Another white female talked about the nonracialized view of whiteness she had before taking the class and the impact critical consciousness about race and racial inequality had on her interaction with other people outside the classroom:

> It is true that I never considered myself a (part of a) race. I really only took the identities I was oppressed by, such as gender and class. I never considered "white" a race. I always have said I wasn't a racist; therefore, I thought I didn't need to examine "whiteness" . . . Discussions about this extended beyond the walls of the classroom. My roommates and I have gotten in bitter arguments about race, which was amazing to me because these arguments were not about being racist but how to deal with racial inequality. I often left class confused about where I should fit into this discussion: whether I had a right to an opinion or not; whether I was a stupid little white girl who thought she could save the world or a concerned *woman* who knew the actions of her race affect her, too. I grappled with this during the semester.

I maintain that the complex representation of biracial experience in black literature (re)presents a strategic platform on which to build a case against racism and white supremacy. To help students understand the fallibility of race, the hegemony of "whiteness," and the ways racist thinking dehumanizes all people, I ask them to traverse the border of the racial identity they inhabit, to experience the ambiguity of an identity formed between two (or more) races. In negotiating the unstable, shifting boundaries of "bi" racial space, students in "The Whiteness of Blackness" bear witness to the dehumanizing effects of racism on the body, mind and spirit of the mixed-race person we read about. Affirming my belief that biracialism provides a radical space in which to argue against white supremacy (at the intersection of sexism and homophobia), a white female student wrote:

> Biraciality as the course's theme helped me come to the conclusion [that] [t]he application of gender . . . sexuality . . . and class (in the texts studied) seemed to create a space for a white person to actively critique white supremacist ideology. If this biracial person can exist, serving as a go-between in the discussion of equality, then certainly a white person could also add to the discussion.

When white students come to understand that racism is the most salient feature of American life today, they comprehend the pervasive ways it operates in every aspect of all our lives, across divisions of race, gender, class, sexuality and every other line of separation we configure. But while exploring racial tensions in the narrative space enlivens our discussions, those same tensions charged the classroom space, creating an air of distrust, contempt, disillusionment and despair. Intervening against the emotional roller-coaster to which students frequently feel I strap them, I encourage them to meet the emotional demands the course, texts and their peers require of them.

During the term, one black woman student persistently doubted the relationship of the biracial text to the reality of her daily life and the liberation struggle of black people. She wrote passionately on her final exam about her feelings of frustration regarding race and class injustice, as they affect the lives of poor black women and men. She opened with a question about life in the real world:

> Were those Blackgirls in that free clinic I passed or was everyone wearing a mask? Did I just hear that white boy say he only pays $1500 a

month for rent or did someone slip me an acid tab and I didn't know it? . . . What, exactly, have we accomplished? There are unemployed or illegally employed Blackmen on my corner from sun up to sun down . . . And when I pass making my rounds—"Whatup Dex? Hey Keith. How you feelin' Blackman?"—and they ask me what I learned in school today, what do I tell them? That we-talked-about-how-fucked-up-shit-is-and-how-it-got-that-way-and-isn't-it-terrible-simply-horrible-and-we-can't-let-stuff-like-that-go-on-any-longer-cuz-it-ain't-right-it-just-ain't-right-goddamit. No, I smile and say, "Racism and shit like that." They smile back knowing that—I'm not fooling them or myself—somebody's paying for me to sit up in a class and talk about what they already know and live.

Remarking on the economic and gender politics in the language of the neighbor"hood" where she lives, this student spoke pointedly about her way of justifying her own privileged position as a black woman enrolled in a course on race at a private university to a group of black men living out the frustration of racial inequality that she feels. Reading her reaction made me wonder, as she had, What exactly had we accomplished? In what way(s) could antiracist feminism intervene in the situation she described? Placing her commentary back into the context of the classroom, it strikes me that students talking about and listening to their own experiences with racism offer a moment of critical intervention in which the activist teacher can initiate dialogue about education practice committed to teaching social responsibility. Had we been able to talk again, I would have liked to tell this student that her frustration—and guilt perhaps for attending an expensive private school—could become the catalyst for thinking about ways to politicize her feelings through social activism. Not having had this conversation with her left me feeling exasperated, realizing the limits of the classroom.

Yet the course had produced moments of personal liberation for some students. An outspoken white female wrote about her personal struggle to contest the borders of race, as she claimed a racially "bicultural" identity:

I can pass or more likely get along in either (black or white) society, yet I will never fully fit into either one . . . am cursing those who say I do not belong in the places I go because I'm white. I grew up in the arms of black society—let go from a white womb—raised in a sea of blackness. I was raised as a "sistah" even though you will never see me as one, outside my old neighborhood. Color does not always tell the truth . . . [T]his class has forced me to deal with a lot of deep-rooted issues that have been inside me for a while.

Even the most culturally liberatory moments in the classroom cannot guarantee that students will apply what they have learned there outside the classroom walls. The same black female student who had written the sobering passage about "life on the street" also wrote about what she perceived as a breakdown between theory and practice in our class. She noted her experience in another class with a white woman student from the course:

One day in another class that I share with one of the girls in our class, we were having a discussion about the politically correct terminology for Latinos. I commented that there is a reasoning behind the demand to be called Latino. This girl said, 'Well, I don't care what the reasoning is. I'm just going to call them Latinos. Who has time to learn the history behind all of those words?' She shrugged cutely and went on discussing eyebrow pencils. I had to grab a wall for support: Wasn't this the same girl who was talking about how wrong things are for the marginalized classes in America? So much for budding intellectuals . . . There are so many Black story lines and I'm afraid that for many of my white classmates our study of the novel of passing was just that, another Black story.

The same black woman questioned the success of the course's objective, measuring by a sense of failed expectation. "The Whiteness of Blackness"—one class on racism predominated by "liberal white kids from who-knows-where trying to understand" the immense problem of race in America against an enormous history of racism in America—simply could not have borne the sole responsibility for coming up with the solution for ending racism, as this student pointed out. I will always remember the outspoken way she took on me and her classmates, insisting that our racial optimism washed cold, frozen in theory, void of practice. I will remember her certainly not because this view affirmed my "liberatory" vision of race, but because the reality of the pessimism she bore made me realize the limitations of my work in the classroom.

The words she wrote followed me from the classroom. They speak poignantly to all progressive educators who believe the classroom can serve as a liberatory site, whether they employ feminist thinking to critique racism or not:

> Many a time, while reading the text or looking around the room at my white classmates, I would be floored by how out of hand and absolutely absurd racialization in this society has become. (People get paid a whole lot to talk and talk and talk about race!) Here I am sitting in a class with a whole bunch of liberal white kids from who-knows-where "trying to understand" a phenomenon that didn't come to us by way of a classroom and won't be leaving that way either. What's wrong with this picture? Is it just me; am I imagining white kids living life "as usual" once they walk out the classroom?

Like this black woman student, I have asked myself the same questions as a black professor, teaching mostly white students over the course of seventeen years, wondering whether white students in my "race classes" leave them to live life "as usual." "What is wrong with this picture?" she asks. Perhaps a partial answer may be found in the exam response of a white woman student who was not so sure how much transgressive ground we had covered in class by the end:

> The stories of the struggles of biracial individuals or black men and women who could pass serve to bring to light the dichotomy of white and black, but they do not carry us any closer to a resolution. I walk away from this class wondering if there is a resolution. What positive outcome can result from a recognition of racial difference? . . . Even in a [post]modern context, when "diversity" is all the rage and difference appears to be valued, such value does not feel truly honest . . . [A]n end [to racism] seems desperately far beyond the scope of my own imaginings.

Teaching in the Spirit of Black (Male) Feminism

Resisting my own intense feelings of pessimism when reflecting upon the present state of race relations in the United States, I imagine Frederick Douglass and W.E.B. Du Bois waging war against both racism and sexism. Remembering their struggle as antiracist feminists reaffirms my vision of the classroom as a site for social transformation. And for one student leaving "The Whiteness of Blackness," the course had made a difference in her struggle to make a connection between racial and sexual oppression:

> That I am a woman who has been grappling with growing up in a sexist world . . . I can almost see racism. Almost. And so I have viewed with feminist eyes the arbitrary privileging of "white" and light-skin in the novel of passing and have come out of this course . . . with the hope that my voice, that so often gets caught trying to climb over my teeth, will serve me better than it has in the past.

Her words confirmed my conviction that the practice of education ought to compel students toward critical consciousness. This consciousness is the first step in a commitment to progressive antiracist politics founded on a belief in the liberation of all people, across the borders of race, gender, class and sexuality.

In a course where so many complex issues, problems and questions around how to strategize an end to racial oppression remained unattended, in the end a vision of antiracist feminism survived.

—I would like to thank the following students in the fall 1994 session of "The Whiteness of Blackness" for their commitment to the seminar and for permission to reproduce in this essay excerpts from some of their final exams in the class—Peggy Bennett, Megan Chase, Tara Crichlow, Carolyn Egazarian, Ann Fuller, Wubnesh Hylton, Elaine Mejia, Hannah Miller, Carla Montoya, Rachel Weiss, and Brooke Willmes.

Notes

1. "The novel of passing" constitutes a genre in African-American literature begun in the slave narrative and reaching its most representative form during the Harlem Renaissance. I selected seven novels for study in the course: *Our Nig* (Harriet Wilson), *Clotel, or the President's Daughter* (William Wells Brown), *The Autobiography of an Ex-Colored Man* (James Weldon Johnson), *Quicksand* and *Passing* (Nella Larsen), *Plum Bun* (Jessie Fauset), and *Black No More* (George Schuyler).

Connections

The First Lesson, and Many More

MARGUERITE GUZMAN BOUVARD

It is the height of World War II, and I am five years old, trying to understand the adults around me, adults who do not share their thoughts. I do not have names for all I see, but I am learning one of the most important lessons in my life, that nationalities and races are capable of destroying each other because of their differences. My mother is not given to words, so I examine her face for clues. She stands between me and the world, making me feel safe, but her expression is always somber and drawn. Letters keep arriving from Trieste, letters that she takes into the bathroom to read in private. When she comes out, I know she has been crying. My parents, my sister and I have come to New York City from Trieste, Italy, but the rest of our large family has stayed behind. I know my mother is terribly worried about them. When we take walks along Fort Tryon Park, the Hudson River has a darkness about it. "What is death?" I ask. "It's a long sleep," she answers. I am disappointed with this reply and when I go to bed at night, I am afraid to fall asleep. I may not wake up.

The war is my mother's face, coupons for food, shoes that fall apart in the snow and radio messages that both puzzle and amuse me. The radio bombards us with, "Whistle while you work, Hitler is a jerk, Mussolini is a meany and the Japs are even worse." I don't know what it means, but I repeat the jingle with my friends. There are two young German girls, Lisel and Trudy, who play in the park with us on the weekends. One afternoon a group of kids starts to taunt them for being German. I think it is a game, and I join in until I see tears in Lisel's eyes. I turn away, terribly ashamed.

One day, my mother comes to fetch me at school. I know it is something important because she works and is never free during the day. Also the nuns have told us that we can never leave school except for doctor's appointments or family emergencies. My mother is taking me to the movies, a very rare treat since we are poor, but she doesn't tell me about the movie or how she managed to take me out of school. The title of the film is *Mr. Emmanuel* (1944). For what seems like an endless afternoon, I watch an elderly man being dragged off by soldiers and put in prison. I can hardly bear it as his fists bang against the cell doors and he screams, "Open, open, let me out!" I am in that cell with him screaming, and I don't know why anyone would want to harm an old man.

With the Sisters of the Sacred Heart, 1943
In the park, the roses offer me / their reds and pinks. / I am learning the names of colors. / But across the highway the river / flows silently by. / I want to know where it brings its cargo, / and my mother, holding my hand, / tells me that "death is a long sleep."/ She steers me through the city / with its cacophony of streets / but nights in my room / the river hums beside my bed.

It is wartime but the war / is distant as Tibet. / It is a blimp seen from the classroom, / waiting in line for shoes. / Then my mother fetches me / at school. Something important / but I do not ask.

In the movie theater / we watch the corridors of prison, / two guards dragging a white-haired man. / Mr. Emmanuel is locked inside / banging his fists against the door. / He is alone / and I am locked in beside him.

My mother never told me why she took me to that film, which I later understood unmasked the genocide of the Jews occurring in Europe. That memory took root; even when it vanished from my consciousness, it floated like water below ice, waiting to be released. Taking me to witness suffering taking place across the world and to different people because of racism was the first of my mother's many lessons. When our circumstances improved, and we were able to leave our small apartment, our house became like Noah's ark, filled with people who needed a place to stay for a period of time.

My mother also brought me up to honor my Triestine heritage, and when my grandmother joined us after the war, I listened to them converse in Italian, French and German. I knew they also spoke a little Slovene and that multilingualism was typical of that part of the world. From the time I was able to read, my mother provided me with Turkish, Russian, Chinese, French and Irish fairy tales and stories, and therefore I felt at home with and attracted to different cultures. I continue to read authors from around the world and have introduced them in my international relations class as a way of helping my students connect to what often seem like distant cultures.

Throughout our life together, my mother remained a book without words. She was a woman of action—working at her career as a dress designer, sewing, repairing things around the house, perpetually in motion. Despite her schedule she always managed to take time for people who were down on their luck as if it were the most natural thing in the world. Even though she died many years ago, I continue to learn from her example. Like her, I see and act with my heart, often in a risky manner and sometimes without pondering the consequences. It is my motor in life even though it causes me to make mistakes. When I had my own family and a profession, I began volunteering: hosting inner-city children for the summer and giving high-school equivalency classes after work. But it was the memory of Mr. Emmanuel that stirred me into action during the Vietnam War. At the time, Martin Luther King, Jr., kept insisting that this conflict was racially motivated, and I concurred with this assessment. Outraged at the senseless destruction of an ancient culture, I became active in antiwar protests.

Sometimes this led to dilemmas. My children were in middle school at the time and one day my son brought home a book about the war containing a picture of a Vietnamese man with the caption, "Who is the man in the funny hat?" I stormed into the school library, demanding to know how an educational institution could circulate material that inspired hatred. In response to my outrage, the librarian replied that I wanted to curtail freedom of speech. She had a point—I imagined self-righteous members of the extreme right invading libraries. I resolved the issue by never returning the book and using it as an example of propaganda and racism in the international relations class I taught.

If the relentless bombing and napalming of Southeast Asian countries had filled me with shame and grief, the aftermath of the Vietnam War seemed equally painful, as frail boats loaded with families headed out to sea to escape repressive regimes. One day, no longer able to bear the photographs crying out to me from the front pages of the *New York Times*, I called the newspaper and asked them to put me in touch with social agencies bringing Southeast Asians into the United States. I contacted one agency and discovered that I could sponsor a family, though it would involve finding housing and providing language instruction, health care and job training. Despite this daunting list of obligations, I gave the agency my name and address. One afternoon months later, when my French in-laws were sitting in our living room celebrating my son's high-school graduation, I received a phone call from the *Times*, in response to my initial call, "Your family of boat people is ready to be adopted. You will receive a monthly stipend to help pay for their upkeep." I was stunned and replied that I wasn't ready for this responsibility. My heart had leaped forward without considering the limits of my personal resources.

However, an answer to my yearning to help came only weeks later when I saw a notice in my local newspaper, the *Wellesley Townsman*. People interested in finding ways to help the boat people were meeting at St. Andrew's Episcopal Church in town. About twelve of us gathered one summer evening, and that was the beginning of the Friends of Southeast Asian Refugees, a nonpolitical interdenominational group. We agreed that a group was better equipped than one person to handle the financial responsibility and extended commitment of bringing over a family.

Within a few weeks our numbers grew, and we developed an

organizational structure that could ensure a smooth entry of the families into American society. It meant finding housing and arranging for ongoing health care for people who suffered from malnutrition and the health problems associated with life in refugee camps: skin ailments, parasites and dental problems. It also involved arranging for English lessons for the adults and schooling for the children, and above all raising money. We decided to help our family without accepting any government funding, feeling there would be strings attached. We also looked for housing in an area that would shelter the family from possible racist acts. With the optimism of the inexperienced, we estimated that all this could be accomplished within six months, little suspecting that we were entering into a five-year commitment.

One of the members of our group found a house in nearby Needham temporarily donated by a person who had heard of the Friends of Southeast Asian Refugees. A few of us painted the rooms a glowing white, while others found furnishings and equipment. The group also kept in close touch with a Laotian community in Rhode Island who educated us about their culture and customs. Among other things, we learned about revering the aged and greeting people with a bow, as well as the kinds of food Laotians preferred. Some of us started to learn a few words of Laotian but were unprepared for bridging both a language and a cultural barrier. At the time, we also had little understanding of the psychological and emotional burdens that most refugees carry and which would surface after the families had been settled into their new homes.

By early November the group was at the airport waiting for Thaivin and Veo Vonvienkam and their four children, Daovin, Sinkam, Kamkeo and Pankam. It was an emotional moment for us, and we clapped as they stepped off the plane, tired, happy and bewildered. One year before, Thaivin, who was pregnant at the time, had crossed the Mekong in a small boat with her three children while Veo swam beside them. They braved the dangers of pirates and drowning for life in a Thai camp filled with refugees from the communist regimes in Cambodia and Laos. When his English improved, Veo told us about the single loudspeaker in the camp through which announcements of sponsors for families and individuals were called out day and night. If a family was asleep and missed the announcement, they could miss a chance for freedom, so Veo and Thaivin took turns sleeping for the entire year.

The Friends of Southeast Asian Refugees split up into small groups for health care, education, food, housing and contacts with the U.S. Immigration Department. We decided that one of us would always accompany the family to protect them from racial incidents; luckily over a period of years, only a single incident occurred: a child threw a rock at Kamkeo, knocking him off of his bicycle. We knew that racial tensions existed in the Boston area, and the families we were sponsoring would be the first Southeast Asian arrivals in a community that had experienced a furor over school busing in the early 1970s and continuing tension between ethnic groups. Therefore, we deliberately looked for a home in a neighborhood we hoped would be hospitable to minorities. Because we were afraid of the resentment our financial support of the new arrivals might spark among disadvantaged groups, we decided to help Veo find a job as soon as possible and to ensure that the family would stay off welfare.

One of our members, Lynn Finn, quit her nursing job and spent most of her days taking care of the Vonvienkams' considerable health needs. I opted for the responsibility of taking the family shopping in both an American supermarket and an Asian market where they could find sticky rice. I also introduced them to American cooking. We got around the major language barrier by using posters my daughter made for me with different foods pictured on them.

However, language was not the only hurdle to overcome. I took Thaivin and her children out for lunch a few weeks after their arrival to introduce them to New England cuisine. The children enjoyed themselves hugely, but then Pankam threw up all over the table. I learned the hard way that people who have suffered from malnutrition for long periods of time should return to a full diet very gradually. As we mopped up the mess, I was irritated with myself for my ignorance and insensitivity.

I spent many hours visiting with Thaivin and her children. The children were immediately drawn to television and American games, but Thaivin harbored a sadness that was hidden behind her gentle smile. When I looked at her, I imagined she was still seeing her own landscape, knowing she would never return to it. We had few words in common. Once, in desperation, I brought a coloring book and crayons, and Thaivin and I colored landscapes together. After all, my mother had taught me that one can communicate by acts when language fails.

The time passed so quickly for all of us that soon it was December and we were introducing the Vonvienkams to an American Christmas. My son Pierre, who had a career as a magician while in high school, gave a magic show at a Christmas party for the family's children. He was an important part of this experience, and when he was home, spent hours entertaining the younger Laotian children.

By 1980, the Friends of Southeast Asian Refugees were ready for a second family, the Vongsys and their four children. Shortly afterwards the third family arrived, and they were able to benefit from the resources of a growing Laotian community that served as translators and counselors for the new arrivals. By that time, our numbers had grown to almost fifty people, and members of the Congregational Church within our group decided that their numbers warranted splitting up and sponsoring a family on their own.

I took on the task of teaching English to the Vongsys. I tried to learn Laotian while teaching them English, but I had difficulties with the tonal language, and my clumsy efforts sparked much amusement among the family. The Vongsys were a peasant family and had great difficulty adjusting to an urban setting. Unlike Veo Vonvienkam, who arrived with the advantages of a profession and a smattering of English and who was eager to become part of American society, Mr. Vongsy refused to work or take part in any of our activities to ease his family's entry. He would sit at home brooding and seemed very uncomfortable in his new setting. Through the contacts of one of our members, we ultimately found a new sponsor for the Vongsys in Vermont, where several communities were welcoming Southeast Asian families and where we hoped they would feel more at ease, but our hopes that life in a rural setting would inspire Mr. Vongsy to begin work were dashed. Although the children responded to their new home with enthusiasm, Mr. Vongsy still refused to work. We discovered that not all the people who had made the heroic journey to the United States could adapt to a strange environment. Behind Mr. Vongsy's seeming inertia might have been grief at the loss of his country, fatigue from the turmoils of war and life as a refugee, or simply the desire to be taken care of. Given the language barrier, we would never find out.

Bounthavy Vongsy in Needham, Massachusetts

Arms folded, / you lean in the doorway / of your new house / light / as a cluster of leaves. / In your eyes / is more time / than I will ever know / though I chase it / with scissors. / Beside you / the four-year-old child / with an infant's body / the transparency / of the very old. / You do not complain, / you greet me with a bow / palms joined / above the forehead. / I bend towards you / stiff-waisted. / I know now, / the forehead is sacred, / hears God / in syllables of rain, / the slow unfolding / of fields. / I want to reach over. / But across the Mekong / is yet another river.

By 1982, we had several families in the area, and we shared celebrations and visited each other on a regular basis. We were learning almost as fast as our Laotian friends, discovering "survivors' guilt" as we tried to help Veo cope with his nightmares and his bouts of depression. In our eagerness to help, we had hoped that freedom and security would bring him happiness, overlooking that though he had fled a repressive regime, he had left behind a life and many loved ones. We were awed by the strength of family and community ties within Laotian culture. Our Laotian friends gave unstintingly to each other, and we discovered that the clothes and supplies we gave them were being shipped back home to Laos. Everyone participated in childcare—aunts, uncles, and friends—and they took equally tender care of the few elderly people we were able to bring over (the government had imposed an age limit on refugees at the time). Yet, in helping these brave people adjust to the United States, we were also instrumental in unraveling those supportive ties. Years later, Daovin married and moved, breaking a tradition of several generations living in the same home. While Daovin was happy to start a new life, Veo was saddened and felt as if the family was breaking up.

We also learned about differing concepts of time. A Laotian gathering was a leisurely affair, with the hosts often leaving to shop for food after guests had arrived for a meal. They cherished just being together, and it was a considerable adjustment for those of us, including myself, who were juggling jobs, child-rearing and household chores. At the time, I found it unnerving, but years later, saw the inherent wisdom and pleasure in that mode of life. I am certain that Laotian families had to make painful adjustments to the hectic rhythm of life in the United States.

It was during one of our many celebrations, when we were having a meal of sticky rice as well as Uncle Ben's at the Vonvienkams' apartment, that I met Vanhkham Singname. On the other side of a room crowded and noisy with festive adults and giggling children dodging in and out stood Vanhkham, exquisitely beautiful, yet an image of sadness. We looked at each other, and without thinking, I went over to her and put my arms around her. We wound up going upstairs, where she sobbed in my arms. It took many months to unravel the causes of her grief: the abortion she had given herself in refugee camp, the sweetheart she had left behind, the faked marriage to be able to enter the United States, a marriage that had ended in abuse. However, from the moment I held her in my arms, she became my daughter. When I first met her at the party, she was helping out the Vonvienkams and staying with a family in Newton where she was very unhappy. Because she seemed to need someone to take care of her, I wanted her to move in with us, and this sparked numerous arguments with my husband. He won out, but she remained a very big part of my life.

A year later Vanhkham married an older American who I knew would take advantage of her. Because her culture revered the aged, she was unable to understand that he might not have the best of intentions and would use her as a maid and nanny for his two obstreperous children. When she moved to Connecticut with her new husband, we remained in constant touch, and thus I lived through a stormy and difficult marriage with her. Once I was summoned to a family conclave as the "elder." When I arrived at Vanhkham's home, her sisters and numerous cousins were seated around Vanhkahm and her husband, Joe, expecting me to arbitrate. "What do you want out of this relationship?" I asked Vanhkham. To my astonishment, she answered, "More power." Joe listened without responding, knowing he would continue as before, holding the purse strings while profiting from a maze of slum apartments he rented to refugees and collecting disability for a supposedly damaged knee. A few years later, I helped her get a divorce.

Shortly after her marriage, Vanhkham sponsored her two sisters, Kak and Joy, who came to this country with no knowledge of English and yet managed to finish high school in two years with the assistance of a devoted Catholic priest. I helped them get into Salve Regina College under a scholarship and proudly attended their graduation. But it was Vanhkham who always tugged at my heart and with whom I had a tender relationship. I was touched that she made it through her high school equivalency at my urging even though I knew she was content with her job in a factory and welcomed the quiet after the turbulence of her life in the refugee camps. I was equally moved by her spirit, her defiance and tempestuous nature so like my own daughter's. Once after her divorce, when her sisters asked me to call her up and intervene because she was dating a particularly unsavory character, she hung up on me. Later she sent me a letter, which I keep in a special folder with my children's cards: *Dearest Mother. I apologized about that day, that I did hang the phone on you, and I did not call you back. Mother, I'm very truly sorry. I don't know what to do. It's so confuse. from myself mother. Vanhkham.* In short, we were like any other mother and daughter. Two years ago, Vanhkham married a Laotian man, and last year she had a little daughter. "Now I must grow up!" she exclaimed. She did and no longer needs me. I miss her.

It is ironic how much easier it is to heal the ills beyond our front doors while we founder in our own families. It is only now, after many years have passed and the pain has been transformed into acceptance, that I can write about my niece, Mia. My sister and brother-in-law adopted Mia from Korea when she was only three years old. When she first arrived in her new home in Northfield, Illinois, she would spend hours in deep concentration, eating a piece of bread. She was quiet and shy, totally unprepared for the turbulent life that awaited her when some years later, my sister and brother-in-law divorced and remarried, my sister moving to France with her new husband, and Mia remaining in Chicago with her father, a new stepmother and new siblings.

Before my mother died in 1976, she had asked me to ensure that Mia would get a good education in an eastern university. She felt that Mia had had such a difficult life that she needed a solid education to prepare her for independence. Mia was my son's age, and I was intent on carrying out my mother's wishes for her and seeing them both off to a good start. Mia came to visit me while she was in high school preparing her college applications, and we developed a very close and affectionate relationship, spending many hours talking in my study. But Mia fit uneasily in all of her worlds. Her skin was very dark, and when we would walk down the street, I felt the stares of passersby at the sight of two such different looking people exchanging affectionate banter. Once when we were waiting on the platform of a subway station in Boston, someone came up to her to ask where Chinatown was. Even some of our friends made tactless inquiries when they met her for the first time, asking if Mia was "really" my niece with looks of utter shock on their faces as they stared at her. Among those who registered surprise were very close and old friends of ours who were from France and whom we visited at their cottage in Maine every summer. They were like grandparents to our children, but when we brought Mia to Maine with us one summer, their behavior was hurtful and shocking. They barely spoke to Mia and kept whispering to me about her without bothering to wait until she was out of sight. I immediately sent Mia on a walk along the beach with my son, but the damage had been done: We left for Boston shortly afterwards in gloomy silence.

Mia had grown up in the United States and felt American. But for most strangers, she was still a foreigner and, worse, while she was in Paris visiting her mother, the French considered her Korean, not American. To make matters even more difficult for her, my sister had converted to the Bahai religion from Catholicism, and Mia's stepmother was Jewish. I know Mia was confused and felt like an outsider wherever she went.

When Mia was ready to apply for college, I suggested that she look over some top-notch schools and then choose whichever appealed to her. However, after she applied and was accepted at Bryn Mawr, her decision caused us some misgivings. Before she left for her first year that September, we spent time together, perusing the list of freshmen.

My heart sank as I read their names and addresses: All of the young women seemed to come from expensive upper-class suburbs while Mia had been living in a multicultural area of Chicago. I feared she would feel out of place. She was indeed nervous about starting at Bryn Mawr, though for different reasons, and hugged me with some desperation before leaving for her flight to Philadelphia.

I visited her that first year, and we kept in close touch. By her sophomore year, however, it was clear to me that she was unhappy in that setting and also beginning to wonder about her roots and the details of her adoption. I suggested she transfer to Boston University, which was close to our home and had a large Asian student population. Mia seemed to like being back in an urban setting when she visited the university; she immediately applied and was accepted for her junior year.

The dormitories at Boston University seemed unsafe and made Mia nervous, so my husband and I found a small apartment for her in Kenmore Square within walking distance of her classes. My husband painted the walls and laid down linoleum, and together we furnished it for her. She seemed pleased although I know she missed having a roommate.

That first semester seemed to go well. She had met an Asian boy, and though she was terribly shy with men, I think they were dating. Meanwhile, I had started reading voraciously about postwar Korea and was finding Korean novels and short stories I intended to pass on to Mia. I told her that when she graduated, we would visit the country of her birth.

She spent Christmas with us as usual the December of her junior year and appeared happy. After the New Year, Pierre drove her back to her apartment, and as I waved to them, I never suspected it would be the last time I would see her. In mid-January, shortly after beginning the new semester, she called me on the telephone and unleashed a torrent of anger, telling me she really didn't want to be in college and that I had forced it upon her. I was stunned and unable to reply. That was the last time we spoke.

When she didn't answer my calls after that exchange, I contacted the psychology department where she was a major. They refused to give me any information because "I wasn't immediate family." I responded that they should check with the financial office to see who was paying her bills. Eventually, a student secretary took pity on me and said she would drop off a note in Mia's box. The next communication I had was a call from her landlord. He told us that Mia had left, that the apartment still contained her furniture, and that since we had co-signed the lease with her, we owed him rent for the rest of the semester. I didn't have the heart to pick up the furniture or even check to see if she had left the quilt I made for her behind. We paid the rent, and I spent the next months in utter anguish, worrying about Mia and wondering what had happened.

At first, I hid my grief beneath anger that she had turned against the one adult member of the family who really cared deeply about her. Couldn't she have left before I dished out the semester's heavy fee, I wondered. I did find out from her sister that Mia was well, but I didn't know where she was. I felt I had failed miserably. Years later, I discovered she was living not far from Boston, in Somerville, and that she purposely remained without a phone because she didn't wish to communicate with her family.

The anger continued, coupled with a sense of rejection and failure, until much time had passed and I was alone at an artists' retreat writing poetry. I then realized that I was avoiding my grief and was able to release my hurt. I read Ian McEwan's novel, *The Child in Time*, about a child who is kidnapped while his parents are shopping, finding a strange parallel to my own situation. Like a kidnapped child, Mia remains forever frozen at the age I last saw her, a young woman of twenty in a pair of shabby jeans with shiny black hair.

For a long time, in my sorrow, I thought I had learned nothing from this experience. However, eventually, I began to understand. Mia had undergone too many searing ordeals, had been uprooted much too often and had felt rejected at home. I came to realize that no matter how much attention I had lavished on her, I couldn't erase those traumas. I learned a sense of the limits of life: There were many situations I couldn't heal, many times when I had to simply let go.

Elegy

I have removed your picture from / my office. I cannot bear / to look at it, / your moon face like wind-riffled / water when you smile, / or solemn, a still pool. / Always I see you sitting / on the couch, your hands resting / on your lap, / staring straight ahead or dreaming, / a bush giving off fragrance. / I remember the letter / from the orphanage, / "She sits quietly in a corner / but responds to kindness." /

You were ashamed of your small / Korean feet, thick waist. / You didn't see the landscape / in your mirror, gentle fields / misted over, splayed petals / of wild rose, / what is secret, and must be found. / I see you waiting for me / at the train station, / rumpled jeans and sandals, / an old shirt, you, / who wanted to travel lightly.

Through their close ties with their grandmother and their experiences while growing up, my children have learned that living with racial and national diversity can be more than a challenge and often provides a great richness of being. My daughter Laurence, who lives in England, is fluent in seven European languages and is currently studying Hebrew and Chinese. She tells me she can understand much about a culture from syntax. As an actress, she has played an Italian nun in an Israeli movie, the Puerto Rican wife of Buddy Holly, and a French girl on a television series. She feels at home in many different countries and has found that learning about languages and cultures is also discovering oneself in a very profound way. My mother and grandmother would be as proud of her as I am.

From the time he was a young child, my son Pierre always had room in his heart for whoever needed help, walking around with a gaggle of neighborhood kids tagging after him. He takes after my mother. It is not surprising because they were as close as he and I are, and often I see her in the way he tilts his head to one side and in the mischievous gleam in his eyes. He and I look at the world in the same way, reveling in its diversity and especially in its young people. He has a special way with them. Although a busy executive in the radio industry, he has spent his summer vacations for the past four years caring for HIV positive youngsters at the Birch Camp. I have photos of him with children of all races and ethnic groups in his arms. They are snatching moments of happiness together from what often seems like a cruel and indifferent world—

knowing that such times have their own immensity.

The lessons my mother taught me by the values she upheld in her daily life became part of me and have assumed new dimensions in the lives of my children. If anything, they reveal the importance of example and how powerful individual gestures can be in bringing different people together across what may seem like impassable gulfs.

Passing Over*

JANE LAZARRE

I am sitting in a large circle of friends who for nearly twenty years have together attended an annual Seder, the ritual meal and story telling that celebrates the Jewish holiday of Passover marking the liberation of the Jews from slavery in Egypt. Rachel, the hostess and leader of the Seder, grew up Protestant in New England, converted to Judaism in her thirties and went on to become a rabbi, so she knows something about belonging and something about being a stranger; something about the slow pace of real change. On this night, she begins with the traditional words: *Once we were slaves in Egypt, but now we are free.* Slavery is a "narrow place," she tells us, a way of being that constrains, holds a person back or down; a heavy burdensome place where choice, individuality and safety are obliterated, where the only possibilities are to labor, to obey and to endure. The opposite of slavery, of course, is freedom, and we are invited to tell personal stories from the past year which illustrate either state.

---

* This essay is excerpted from the author's memoir *Beyond the Whiteness of Whiteness: Memoir of a White Mother of Black Sons.*

A young woman talks about her workshops on family violence with high school students, the enslavement of gender definitions still dominant in American life. A mother tells the story of her son who has just come out as a gay man, and she describes the narrow space of people's reactions to him, even her own struggles with disapproval until the invisibility of his life opened her eyes and expanded the space around her. Rachel, who is recently widowed, describes blinding grief over the year since her husband's death, then the slow widening of vision that begins to suggest possible recovery.

Soon our personal stories broaden—because that is the requirement of the ritual of Seder—into talk of more collective enslavements and liberations. This is the year of the Gulf War and the widespread approval by the American people of the bombing of Iraq; it is a year which has seen the continuation of the steady disintegration into poverty and fear of our own neighborhood streets.

As the ritual Seder plate is passed around and we dip our bitter herbs into the salt water meant to represent tears, I remember accompanying Rachel to a sermon she gave in a Westchester temple. I listened along with an audience of Jews as this blond-haired rabbi described the idea of the Stranger in Jewish law, a concept which, in the Seder, is symbolized by the welcoming of Elijah; he is the uninvited guest who comes to the opened door to share in the drinking of the wine and the telling of the liberation story. He is the wanderer whom we must wait and provide for, without whom our ritual of remembrance and redemption is incomplete, because there is always a stranger, always someone new or forgotten knocking at the door. At a certain point in the ritual storytelling which accompanies the eating of symbolic foods, a child is asked to go to the door to welcome Elijah, and all watch the cup of wine set for him in the middle of the table, wait for him to drink.

When I was a child, attending a traditional Seder among my grandmother's siblings in Brooklyn, the story was told in Hebrew with partial and occasional translations on the side for the awestruck and mystified children. But when Elijah approached our table, I always thought I saw the level of wine in the goblet decrease.

As Rachel spoke from the platform of that wealthy Westchester synagogue, I heard whispers behind me. *Some Jew,* a woman murmured nastily. *A shikse (non-Jewish woman) if I ever saw one.* And connected by years of friendship to Rachel, having learned through her to understand something of the best spirit of Judaism, I knew that in the world of religion I would always be the Stranger in a way.

I had never questioned my Jewishness which is as thick and real as the food smells, the language of Yiddish, the musical rhythmns and psychological patterns I grew up surrounded by. But now I remembered another temple where recently, inspired by the strong cultural identification which had released the spirits of so many people I knew, I attended a Yom Kippur service. In that temple on the Day of Atonement, although I was moved by the symbolic meaning of the holiday (the relationship between atonement and cleansing, between forgiveness of others and forgiveness of the self), the emotional experience evident on the faces of others was elusive for me. I felt only that I wanted to go home, which meant four rooms in a building several blocks away.

I suppose it was because I found cultural belonging to be so attractive and yet eternally problematic that at Rachel's Seder, where I was surrounded by old friends, I wanted to tell some of the story of American Blackness I was learning to understand as Adam and Khary began to grow into men. Where better to tell this story of liberations, of broadening visions? But I was reticent, afraid too many would misunderstand. They would think it was only because of love for my children, but the reality is the children are the cause of a change in myself. The fortunate accident of loving a Black man and becoming a mother of Black children has enabled me to see the world more truthfully.

The sentence I have just written seems simple—a straightforward idea, uncomplicated words. But it has taken a long time to construct it so directly. A conversion, as Rachel might remind me, with its requirement for reassessment, study and change, can take many years.

During that year's Passover, no one in my family speaks. I wait, hoping one of them will talk about being Black, about racism, but when I look around the room with their eyes and see that everyone is white, I realize they will not speak, and most likely no one else here will speak of racism escalating in our country because race is not often the first thing on white people's minds.

Spirited back to a much earlier Seder, I hear Adam's ten-year-old voice. We have reached the part of the narrative that describes the Jews in their escape to freedom coming to the Red Sea which is parted by God so Moses and the Israelites can pass over safely to the other side. When their Egyptian pursuers enter the space between the parting of the waters, the sea closes over them and all of them are drowned.

"What do they do with the people who are half Jewish and half Egyptian?" I hear Adam say, a look of anxiety knitting his dark brows.

I sit among friends at the Seder and listen to the story of slavery and freedom, about the long journey from one to the other through the wilderness of exile and doubt, and I am not able to retrieve into words the story of narrowness or renewed life I am beginning to comprehend. Its shape is still forming in my imagination. Embedded in contrary feelings and undigested realizations, I am nowhere near the end of the wilderness and often I feel it is not possible, nor even desirable, to speak.

Around this time, the summer of 1992, Khary needs arthroscopic surgery, a minor operation on the knee. Although I try to discuss any fears he might have about the operation, Khary is a young man of eighteen, and even sensitive young men do not easily confess fears to their mothers, or even, perhaps, to themselves. "There is nothing to worry about," he insists. "It's a minor operation; everything is under control." His annoyance with my questions silences me quickly, and I force myself to believe in the casualness of his anticipation as much as he does himself.

After a ten-minute procedure performed by a famous white surgeon, Douglas and I, waiting anxiously in the hallway, are told Khary will be out of anaesthesia in minutes and we can see him then. We stand outside the recovery room while minutes become an hour, and still there is no word. Maternal terrors fill my head, and I begin desperately asking the nurses what is going on. I am told he is still not out of surgery, that he is "having trouble" coming out of the anaesthesia. In a panic, I nevertheless go into action, calling the famous doctor who by now is back in his office, shouting and threatening (encouraged by the nurses who are obviously furious that they do not know any more than we do, and who are nearly all Black). The doctor is back within minutes, genuinely worried and also, no doubt, afraid of suit. After going back in to see Khary, he emerges to tell us the following story.

Khary has repeatedly come out of the anaesthesia violently, thrashing and flailing about. With most young people Khary's age, the doctor tells us, there would be no problem; the doctors and nurses would gently but firmly hold him down. With our son, however, who is "so large and powerful," they are worried that he might injure himself or the medical personnel, and therefore they have to keep sending him back under rather than simply restraining him with their hands.

This happens to be the summer following the acquittal of the Los Angeles police officers in the beating of Rodney King. The repeated descriptions of my eighteen-year-old son, who admittedly is six feet tall and athletic but no body builder, as "enormous and powerful" resonate with descriptions of Rodney King as an "inhumanly powerful animal" and back to the nurse in the delivery room calling my crying, six pound baby a "militant Black Panther."

We insist upon seeing Khary immediately and are suddenly told we can go into the recovery room where we can see for ourselves that "nothing is wrong."

He is obviously agitated, floating in and out of consciousness, turning over onto his stomach and covering his head with his arms, a movement which threatens to dislodge the IV. Seeing he is afraid, not angry or violent, Douglas and I lean over him, whispering gently, stroking his head and shoulders, and soon he begins to calm down. As soon as he does, the doctors begin to stroke his head too, to whisper gently, *calm down, it's all right.* And I am convinced that in the operating room, they were too rough, holding him down in a way that could only have increased his fear. I watch them closely as they lean over him now, their gentle words and gestures ringing slightly false, as if they are copying our gestures and words, and I would swear they are ashamed, that they see what I have seen—that they handled the situation badly, with fear instead of tenderness.

Later, when he is in his own bed, drowsy and relaxed, I ask Khary again about his thoughts before the operation. He tells me he remembered movies he has seen about patients dying or disappearing after some minor operation, about the blind trust we put in strangers just because they are doctors. He thought about all this as he watched the anaesthesiologist inject the chemicals into his IV.

Now it is clear that he was frightened when he went under and frightened when he began to wake up. Being a boy, in some ways already a man, he had learned to manage fear with stolid denial, a conscious bravery which contains anxiety but which can also become fragile when consciousness is suspended for a time. Being Black, white doctors were no symbol of security and superior knowledge for him. Rather, their skins must have triggered many stories of terror, their faces looming over him as he tried to resist sinking into unconsciousness and loss of control.

After about an hour of lying in his own bed, he falls asleep again, turning onto his stomach as always, and I notice large bruises on his shoulders and neck.

Last year, as always, Rachel called us to the Seder. This time only Douglas and I are there from our family, Adam and Khary in different cities unable to come home, and Douglas is the only Black person in the room. "Once we were slaves in Egypt," Rachel tells us, "and now we are free." And then the question, once again: What is slavery? We are invited to describe that narrow place.

People of serious moral consciousness, some of them our oldest friends, begin to talk about the Jews in Russia, the Muslims in Bosnia, the war in Somalia, the Kurds in Iraq and, because these are people who are committed to fairness and against domination and war, about the suffering of the Palestinian people on the West Bank.

When it is Douglas's turn, I can see he has decided to speak out once again, to resist the combination of exhaustion and anger which often makes Black people choose silence instead of yet another instructional speech to an all-white group. He speaks briefly but intensely about the dangers to young Black men on the streets of our city, in the classrooms of our schools. When it is my turn, I continue the story, telling about how often Khary is stopped and asked to present his identification card at the New England college he attends; how several weeks before his friend was presumed to be a thief and arrested for riding his own bike at night; how frightened and angry I am. I tell of these dangers some of our sons are living with every day. I talk about a generation of Black children in American schools, sacrificed by neglect and the great pathology of racism to the destruction of guns and drugs; about the recently reported statistic that by the year 2000 one out of three young Black men will be in American prisons. I speak with Khary's voice in my head: *If this were happening to white American boys, would no one care? Would they talk only of building more prisons and killing people in the electric chair?* I hear a man's voice, a boy's voice, and I hear, like notes from a musical instrument slightly out of tune, the high and low tones mixing and alternating during the months when his voice changed from a boy's into a man's.

Feeling like some weird, modern, female version of the ancient mariner, I have been recounting this story whenever I can, trying to convey some of the alarm I feel all around me. We cannot continue to ignore all that we ignore, I say. There is the requirement to remember, which also means to see, and in seeing to act. Silently, I retrieve fragments of Jewish tradition to keep back the fear that I might be thought of as intrusive by some, speaking irrelevancies. I think of the Stranger in Jewish law as Rachel described it in that sermon years before and of Rachel, the rabbi, being treated like a stranger herself; of Elijah's place at the table; of the tradition of the Jewish storyteller, like my father, who when asked a philosophical or moral question would often begin—*Let me tell you a story.*

After the blindness of whiteness is gone, the time of passing over begins. Blackness is. There is no escape in a world which everywhere has made color a sign of caste. But skin which is various shades of brown is still only skin which is various shades of brown. Imagine the grace of that ordinary enlightenment ending the great evil of color and culture remade into race. I think of Adam and Khary as children, before they knew the difference; of my white niece, Gabrielle, who when she was seven years old and told that Douglas and I were an "interracial" couple, asked, Which one is white? I think of Douglas's childhood, and of his mother Lois's, centrally constructed around the need to fight off injustice and create a sense of pride. Every single day, again and again and again.

But I am thinking also of all I have learned from Black literature and from my family about survival and resistance, about the long haul of internal liberation, about the need for many voices and memories working together to narrate the past, a story Black writers have told with exquisite precision, a finely tuned perfection that has been necessary in order to survive. Paying the price of the ticket and understanding the meaning of the blues. In my long journey of escape from the whiteness of whiteness, I have come upon a piece of understanding of the blackness of Blackness after all.

As I speak at that recent Seder, I look over at Douglas and see the tears I am just barely resisting filling his eyes. I think of the story of the biblical Ruth who became part of the Jews through love of her mother-in-law, and who at the moment of her decision spoke words I might say to my sons, Douglas and his family, the community and history to which they belong: *Entreat me not to leave thee or to return from following after thee: for whither thou goest, I will go, whither thou lodgest, I will lodge: thy people shall be my people, and thy God my God.*

Words that suggest a myth that might change the world.

Between Exiles

JULIA EPSTEIN

Commentators on the "baby boom"—my population cohort—have coined the phrase "sandwich generation" to describe a late-twentieth-century phenomenon: Many of us who were born in the decade after World War II became first-time parents later than was once the statistical norm, and we now find ourselves confronting the work of managing young children and aging parents at the same time, a set of family circumstances that used to occur serially rather than simultaneously. Born in the middle of the boom, in 1951, I became a parent by international adoption in 1987, at the age of thirty-six, and adopted a second child in 1991, shortly before my fortieth birthday. As I write, my children are ten and six and a half, and my parents, whose health is beginning to affect how they live, are in their mid-seventies. For me, this in-between position has more than just generational significance. It also bears on ideologies of family, race, and identity.

My approach to race prejudice as a white parent of nonwhite children derives in large measure from my experience growing up as the daughter of an immigrant mother who survived the Nazi onslaught against European Jews. My mother and my daughters are immigrants to the United States, naturalized citizens born in countries in which their families lived under menacing personal and political circumstances. I am the only U.S. citizen by birth in the female lineage from my mother to me to my children, and the appellation "unnaturalized" feels all too descriptive. I am supposed to be the all-American girl, a category I would resolutely resist even if—as a Jewish lesbian living in a transracial family—I had any prayer of being taken to belong to it.

My mother is a Hungarian Jew. The disruption in her already difficult life circumstances occurred most radically in May of 1944, when she was deported to Auschwitz after an unsuccessful escape attempt. My older daughter was born in Guatemala, where my partner and I adopted her when she was eighteen months old. My younger daughter is Peruvian, and we adopted her when she was twenty-one months old. All three of these lives contain a moment of radical change such that there will always be an incommensurability, an unbridgeable gap, between the before, with its set of what ifs that never played out, and the after. Their identities—as Jews, as Indians, as immigrants, as survivors of malnutrition and of the exigencies of human evil and human impoverishment—do not preclude the usual forms of narration ("I was born . . . ") so much as render those forms inadequate, even obsolete. Because these identities are more entangling than most as well as because I have no right to violate their privacy or the privacy of their families of origin, I have changed my children's names in this essay, and use only my mother's given name.

The moment of radical rupture from before to after in the lives of my mother and my daughters defines their experiences of Otherness and alienation, at least to the extent that their lives take definition from the anti-Semitism and skin-color and class prejudices of the twentieth century, a century critic Shoshana Felman calls "the post-traumatic century,"[1] writer Eva Hoffman calls "a post-tragic condition,"[2] and theorist Geoffrey Hartman refers to as "post-humanist."[3] Even for me, my mother's daughter and my children's mother, there is no way to cross that divide or to join them in inhabiting it. This circumstance underlies every encounter my family has with forms of racism current in the United States.

My mother was born in Sátoraljaujhely, Hungary, in 1923, and was deported in a cattle car, never to return to her hometown, in May 1944. After the British liberated Bergen-Belsen in 1945, she was taken to a tuberculosis sanitarium in Sweden, where she stayed for over a year before coming to live with relatives in Cleveland. My older daughter, Rosa, born in a small city on Guatemala's coastal plain, was brought by her birth mother to an attorney for adoption when she was a few days shy of her first birthday. Rosa spent her first year in a one-room dwelling with a dirt floor in which two of her siblings died of diseases North Americans pretend no longer exist as killers: measles and malnutrition. My daughter, Gabriela, born in a village at 14,000 feet of altitude in the Andes near Lake Titicaca and the Bolivian border of Peru, came into foster care when she was sixteen months old. Both children were malnourished, and both spent about half a year in foster care during their adoption processes. Although their foster families spoke Spanish, Gabriela's first language was Aymara, and Rosa's first language may also have been one of the more than two dozen Indian dialects spoken by the surviving Maya, the indigenous people of Guatemala.

This essay is an attempt to untangle a family history that moves from the apocalyptic devastation of Nazi racial ideologies in mid-century Europe to the ongoing oppression of the indigenous peoples of Guatemala and Peru. My mother and all her family were forced from their homes; in a very different sense, my children also left their homes involuntarily. Both mother and daughters have lost their birth names, their families of origin, their languages of origin and their countries of origin. Have I caused, or at least participated in, my children's repetition of some of the structures of my mother's history? To what extent did my mother's past lead me to a life that includes raising children of a race and culture different from my own?

Disruption and incommensurability are the twin abstractions that define racism for my family. My mother, Rosa and Gabriela each experienced a radical rupture that can never be adequately narrated, a biographical break that is foundational because it dictates the axiomatic paradox of the twentieth century: Far from being a haven of safety and love, a home is something you must struggle to keep, something you can lose at any moment. Roots are ephemeral.

The chancy status of home means that for many people the home cannot provide ballast for a stable identity. Identities of race and class may shift and multiply within the home itself. When I was growing up, my mother presided over a loving household of relative privilege and comfort, yet she had only the political precariousness of her past to turn to for a model. My brother and I were insulated and overprotected within an inherited context that clashed with the circumstances of our time and place in the North America of the 1950s and 1960s. My mother never spoke about her past—she told us her family had been killed in the war, and we did not ask for details until our early teens.

What became clear then was that our mother utterly disapproved of survivors who regaled their children with horror stories or who held forth publicly about their experiences: She called these people "professional survivors" and wanted above all to spare her children. In many ways, her circumspection did mitigate the effects of her past on us. Nevertheless, in an ineluctable way a European identity of the beleaguered, wandering Jew became a part of who we were to become. Despite the geocultural distance between our working- and middle-class, mostly Catholic neighborhood in suburban Pittsburgh, and the Jewish ghetto of Sátoraljaujhely, Hungary, we too grew up in an unnamable atmosphere of danger, of potentially impending catastrophe.

My children are growing up in a racially mixed though still white-majority middle-class environment, an environment in which their particular racial identity differs from that of their parents and finds reflections most often when we interact with other families with internationally adopted children. The efforts we make to connect them with their cultural heritages—through music, art, books, festivals and the stories and photographs of their adoptions—inevitably remain largely intellectual efforts of projection because we cannot recapture their birth ethnicity. We have become friendly with a few families from Guatemala and El Salvador. Nevertheless, for Rosa and Gabriela, the world of the *campesino* has been lost just as thoroughly as the world of the Jewish communities of eastern Europe has been lost for postwar European émigrés of my mother's generation, more so, because Rosa and Gabriela were too young to have retained their languages of origin or to have stored adequate memories. My mother can talk about her transition from Irén to Irene, but my daughters feel no resonance with the names bestowed upon them at their births. Their pasts are as speculative as their futures, and they have no one to ask. They belong to what Russian critic Mikhail Bakhtin called a "chronotope"—a particular time-place— yet they have scant access to it.[4]

I live inside my originary chronotope, but my mother, Rosa and Gabriela have been *diasporized*, a condition most closely connected to patterns of Jewish and Black Atlantic history.[5] Native Americans in the western hemisphere represent those who came first, those who were there before and thus whose alleged "primitivism" must be conquered, converted and displaced. Whereas Jews did not predate Magyars in the Carpathian basin, they also came to represent the alien element that needed to be "ethnically cleansed": the neoeuphemism for genocide in our own time. Both Jews and Native Americans have been the targets of mass, systematic genocide the goal of which is to erase history and origin. Jews and Indians have served as the foundational Other against which white, Christian Europeans defined and made dominant their notion of a collective identity of political hegemony and social power. No new empire can be built without degrading and supplanting what came before. As ethnographer Jonathan Boyarin writes in a discussion he titles "Europe's Indian, America's Jew," the "Other, dead or alive, is an almost inexhaustible symbolic resource."[6] From this perspective, it is not surprising that we are witnessing a wave of anti-immigration sentiment across the United States as well as in western Europe. Now that white Europeans "own" the United States and have redefined primacy and rewritten history to include the "discovery" of the Americas, ranks are closing to prevent the cycle of newcomers, upon whom most progress in this country has depended, from continuing.

The 1990s term "identity politics" refers to a cultural phenomenon Eva Hoffman, who came to the United States from Poland as a teenager, analyzes as "the number-one national problem" in the United States.[7] North Americans police our identities on a daily basis: Are they becoming slippery? Are they multiplying? Can we reinvent ourselves? For immigrants, especially when they are also refugees, a large portion of identity derives from nostalgia and absence, from the unrecoverable past preserved in untrustworthy memory. "Memory can perform retrospective maneuvers to compensate for fate," Hoffman remarks. "Loss is a magical preservative," she goes on, yet she also calls herself "pregnant" with nostalgia: "[T]he largest presence within me is the welling up of absence, of what I have lost."[8]

There is another kind of nostalgia, not for the details of a perhaps idealized personal past but for a collective memory that may shape moral consciousness. Families and ethnic groups need stories to pass on, to paraphrase the character Sethe of Toni Morrison's *Beloved*, but what kind of stories can be fashioned from historical calamity? What meaning emerges on the other side of catastrophic loss? This is the subject of Morrison's fierce and seductive novel, in which memory becomes not a sacred place but the place of the scar and the "disremembered," the "disremembering" working actively to bury and move on from the past. It is also the subject of another recent novel that depicts the private effects of public terror, Isabel Allende's Chilean family epic, *The House of the Spirits.* Morrison's and Allende's fictions take part in a movement to restore the legacy of calamitous memory. Discussing the kind of public and collective memory these novelists tap, Geoffrey Hartman cites Caribbean poet Derek Walcott, who writes of the need to reconstruct "this shipwreck of fragments, these echoes, these shards of a huge tribal vocabulary, these partially remembered customs."[9]

Many "Holocaust" memoirs have been published,[10] and most of them recount a relatively coherent narrative, a movement of lives from ordinariness to unspeakability and back almost to a returning ordinariness, but always with a dark center. This by now well-known trajectory has achieved for these stories their own kind of horrifying normalcy in the narrative conventions of autobiography. As memoirist Patricia Hampl puts it in a review of a book by the Latvian-born writer Agate Nesaule called *A Woman in Amber: Healing the Trauma of War and Exile*, "the survival stories keep coming as if they were breaking news."[11] Such memoirs often urge, as Nesaule's title suggests, the possibility of redemption or salvation in the act of testimony itself. I am not convinced of that possibility. In this essay, I can only explore some fragments of my family's history as it has been transmitted from mother to children to grandchildren. My mother experienced a cataclysmic event in a terrible personal way and at the same time witnessed that event as the professional historian she was later to become. To gauge the ways in which her history shapes my response to the racism encountered by my daughters requires an analysis of the memory of that history, the ways it returns and remains and never becomes fully part of the past.

Memories do not come in coherent wholes, as stories with beginnings, middles and ends. Nor do lives as they are lived, although of course it is possible in hindsight or from a distance to see a life as an apparently straightforward movement from birth through various predictable or not so predictable rites of passage to eventual death. The incursion of the death camps into the lives of Jews and others in Europe labeled "undesirable" in the middle of this century was not only not predictable or even imaginable to those to whom it happened, it continues to be unimaginable in some ways even in memory despite the memoirs, the histories and the films. The terror of those years returns in fragments, in moments, in images, in dreams.

And it can only be transmitted to others, to the extent that such transmission is thinkable at all, in metaphorical shards of glass, painful to hold. My own life story has been deeply affected by this legacy, the passing on of personal, family and cultural memory. Its bits and scraps, its remains, belong finally to the children and the grandchildren who try to make sense of them in order to understand their mother and grandmother, and in order finally to understand themselves as survivors, as people who bear witness, whether they wish to or not, to the worst of which the human condition is capable. My children may not connect their complicated origins and hybrid ethnicities with their grandmother's past—they will find their own analogies and their own metaphors—but I cannot interpret my family history in any other way.

How does any of this intersect with the daily grind of racism, prejudice and stereotyping experienced by people whose identities embrace difference? For us, these encounters live as mere shadows, ghostly reminders of a catastrophic history that disowns that very history. A few vignettes will have to take the place of a chronological story.

"Don't get too close to those nigger girls," a childish voice chirps. I look up. Two young children, white to be sure, were playing with their sand toys on the beach of a pond on Cape Cod. Maybe nine and six. My daughters, Rosa and Gabriela, five and two, gorgeous in the way their brightly colored bathing suits flash against their deep brown skin, paddle in the shallows, oblivious to the insult they have just been thrown. The children's mother sits nearby and must have heard what they said. She does not even look up. I don't think my daughters heard the remark. Even if they had, they would not have recognized the word "nigger"—it is not (yet) in their vocabulary. What should I do? The truth is, I teem with so much anger I know that if I try to speak at all I will become incoherent with rage, with the kind of fierce maternal surge that overpowers with its very uselessness. The same rage that stops me from speaking to either the children or their mother also prevents me from trying to explain this incident to my daughters, although my partner and I go over it at length.

A friend from India is visiting during the summer. Everywhere we go, people assume she is the children's mother, and, if they see me at all, that I am just along for the ride. This happens even when we converse and they hear my friend's unmistakable Anglo-Indian accent, proving that skin color blinds people to every other cultural or identity marker. I have become invisible in my whiteness. We do converse about this apparently more benign form of racial assumption; race trumps all other cues, it seems. And the cues, like our speech patterns, aren't subtle: If she is their mother, why are they tugging on *my* arm and calling *me* "Mommy"? But they share skin color; they're brown and I'm white, and my daughters bond with my friend over this similarity they share, manifested in their concerned participation in slathering me with sunblock.

Rosa, Gabriela and I are in the pharmacy, filling a prescription. The clerk looks at Gabriela's hair and says, "It's *so* black, it's almost blue," reminding me of something my uncle said when he first met my daughters: "I can't get over how black their hair is." The clerk is being friendly, apparently, even doling out a compliment, but something about the line feels odd—she's really saying, "Oh, how exotic and interesting!" She adds, "Some people would die to have hair that color," an addition that doesn't help. Die/dye: The idea is that the hair is artificial, unnatural, strange. She doesn't say foreign; she doesn't ask where they're from, yet the question hangs in the air. Am I stiffening because I remember the thin, scraggly, chestnut-colored hair Gabriela had when I first met her, the hair that is now so thick that washing it is a major chore? Do I fear being questioned about my right to mother these girls? The way the pharmacy clerk says all this—well-meaning, in the sense of unconsciously thoughtless, that last word meant literally rather than judgmentally, though of course I'm judging—conveys that these children are alien objects to her rather than neighborhood people.

Should I explain all this to the enthusiastic woman at the local pharmacy where we fill our prescriptions? Am I obligated to educate people to think about the way they talk about children? My children miss the nuances I hear, and politely smile and say "thank you." Should I discuss with them the ways in which I think this woman is unconsciously objectifying them? Would I want them to behave in any other way toward her? I leave it alone. This is, I know, a form of covert, even inadvertent, racism. Racial difference becomes exotic, which turns into a commodified cuteness: Where did you get those? as though they were performing pets. A white friend whose husband is Chinese reports the time a woman came rushing up to her in a mall—my friend's then-infant son in his carrier—to ask, breathlessly, "Where did you get the baby?" as though perhaps there were a sale on she might miss if she didn't hurry. Another white friend reports a question posed to her in front of the produce bins at our local food co-op concerning her toddler from Honduras: "Is she yours, or is she adopted?" "She's mine, and she was adopted," our friend replied, and the woman had the grace to apologize. We continue to treat children as property.

The clerk in the pharmacy, the women at the mall and in the food co-op, are not snarling with distaste, or refusing to serve us: Latinos and Asian Americans (at least in the northeastern United States) do not as often have to confront the bone-jarring refusals that make African Americans justifiably sizzle with resentment. But African Americans, I know, also experience these quieter forms of racism—most distressing precisely because they are so often well-intentioned and you have to decide on the spot what is and is not racist. Whites coo over white

children—babies especially, of course—and surely this is just as objectifying. But for nonwhites, it is never possible to distinguish the cultural
"thing"ness of the bodies of pregnant women and babies from covert
racism. Should we ignore it because it is often unmeaning? Along this
line, there is also a special variety of public remark that comes to the
white parents of nonwhite children: Strangers feel free to tell us how
"good" we are and how "lucky" our children are to have been "saved," a
set of assumptions so skewed and ignorant as to defy correction.

My attempts to think about the forms of racism my daughters have
so far encountered in their young lives must of necessity remain partial, speculative and profoundly selfish in the most literal sense of the
word. I am all too aware that the racism they face takes nuanced forms;
it is rarely manifested by in-your-face brutality. My dark-skinned daughters are occasionally taken as black, as they were on the beach; more
often, they represent a kind of difference almost for its own sake, since
in the urban northeastern quadrant of the United States, Central and
South Americans Indians do not throng the streets in great numbers. Or
they melt into an undifferentiated brownness in which national and
ethnic identities from Guatemala, Peru and South Asia merge into one
generic idea of "Third World," as they did when our Indian friend visited. Our experiences would be different if we lived in the Southwest,
where my daughters' ethnicity would be recognizable. Here, we are often asked if the girls are Chinese, or simply, stunningly, asked, "What
are they?" To this one, I have found an answer: "They're children," I try
to make myself reply.

I'm in junior high school, on a shopping expedition. My mother and I
approach the counter with our purchases, and my mother converses
with the clerk, who asks her, "Where are you from?" I feel her freeze
and go pale. She hates this question. "I'm Hungarian," she replies, apolo-
getically but also rather curtly, a curtness only I hear; the idea is to
discourage further questions, a noninvitation that carries an unintended
yet necessary aura of the haughty. The clerk, not taking the hint, continues to barrage her with questions about her life while she bags the
items we have paid for. As we leave the store in our Indiana hometown,

she tells me, "I'm never going to shop there again."

My mother has hated to be asked where she's from for as long as I can remember. There is nothing of shame in this distaste; indeed, her European identity contrasts with American openness, pragmatism, surface emotions, and obsessions with the new and improved in lieu of the venerable and the wise in ways she wants very much to retain and celebrate. Rather, she objects to the presumption to intimacy of the question, the notion that identity and origin are external attributes to which any stranger can have access simply by initiating a public conversation, that these are questions that have easy one-word answers. Where is she from, indeed? Her self-consciousness—in the basic sense of self-definition, of place in the world—dates from before, before the war and the horror. It derives from a deep sense of privacy that recoils from inappropriate boundary-crossing by democratic-American-we-familiarize-everything attitudes. This is a reticence she identifies as European and dignified, the way people ought to behave. In addition, the world in which my mother grew up was one in which such questions were not just rude, rather than friendly, but flatly dangerous. No doubt the tension she experiences when someone poses this question also reflects a politically protective reflex, a defensive response to the fear and violation of an official "Papers, please?" request. She has already paid much too steep a price for having been born a Jew in Hungary.

United by history, survival and forced emigration, grandmother and granddaughters share a complex past that will always haunt them, a past I have inherited and taken on but can never own for myself. To build this family we have crossed borders of race, of language, of national identity, of ethnicity, of religion. My mother survived a set of unthinkable but all-too-real atrocities that destroyed her family of origin and whose memory never leaves her; my daughters survived poverty, malnutrition, illness and finally abandonment.

Every survival entails a loss. To survive is to inherit an entire realm of loss, to live with loss as a possession that cannot be shed or sold or given away. When my partner and I adopted Rosa, my mother's intense identification with this toddler from a place she had never been and a culture she knew very little about took me by surprise. As it has turned out, the line from grandmother to granddaughters has remained thoroughly uncanny and yet also become thoroughly *heimlich*, an untranslatable German word that literally means "homey" but conveys something more like familiar.

Rosa carries a particular burden from the difficulties of her past; malnutrition or perhaps an encephalitis from measles may be the reason she now has to struggle with a language-based learning disability, and for reasons we can only surmise, she is a more anxious and fearful child than her younger sister. I persist in seeing some of the classic signs of post-traumatic stress in both my mother and my older daughter, and I share many of their symptoms by way of a kind of bequeathed empathic mimicry. Indeed, Rosa could not have fit more into this family had she been born into it genetically. She brought to us something we already had and understood in abundance: a legacy of ruined memory, of trauma, of loss.

A sense of violation participates in the production of the form of shyness—reticence and self-protection—that my mother and Rosa share. They crave anonymity, the erasure of external markers of difference. When as a teenager I wanted to get my ears pierced, my mother announced that ear-piercing is "barbaric." Her own ears were pierced when she was an infant, as was the tradition for Hungarian infant girls. When she emigrated to the United States from Sweden in 1946, wanting to start over and fit in, the holes in her ears were yet another sign, along with the numbers on her arm and her accent, that set her apart. These were marks that were, precisely, (re)markable signals of Otherness.

When my mother lived in Cleveland after the war, she went to nursing school so she could continue to work in hospitals, as she had done in the Jewish hospital of Sátoraljaujhely, and to acquire a paying vocation so that she would not be a financial burden on her relatives. As a student nurse at Mt. Sinai Hospital, she met my father, then a graduate student in clinical audiology. Student nurses wore short-sleeved uniforms, and many of the Jewish doctors commented about her tattoo, "You know, that can be removed, you should have it removed." About to marry an American, and wanting to erase the past as much as possible by building a new family, she agreed, and in 1949 a surgeon at Mt. Sinai excised the numbers from her left forearm. Those numbers engraved by the Germans—A23575—represented an imposed anonymity and a constant reminder that for nearly a year her basic humanity had been under siege. The surgical wound did not heal in the usual way. An abnormal keloid scar developed, raised and reddened, and did not begin to subside for several years.

My mother describes this scar as a symbol of what she calls "my failed attempt to become an American" and her failure to erase history. For several years, she wore long sleeves, or self-consciously turned her left arm away from others, until the scar began to diminish in prominence in the early 1950s. Growing up, it never occurred to me to ask about it, or maybe I did and was told that she had hurt herself when she was young. My father has a similarly oval-shaped forearm scar, a place where his otherwise hairy arm was smooth, from a childhood accident, and I crazily thought it was rather sweet that my parents had these more-or-less matching marks. For my mother, this scar represents an ineradicable past. The place where the numbers were is now virtually unnoticeable, completely flattened out and the same skin tone as the rest of her arm. Over time, the past becomes invisible, yet it never goes away.

Rosa's closest friends have always been African-American children. She picks them; they pick her—that part is unclear. But whereas she talks only rarely about her sense of race, that's where she identifies herself. Like my mother, she has a strong idea of how she is perceived from the outside—the accent, the scar on her arm, the skin, the face, and, in Rosa's case, her height, as she is shorter than many children her age. Not that these things define the inner self, but that people nevertheless make judgments based upon them. My mother's situation as a foreigner, a misplaced/displaced person, is "readable" as soon as she speaks, and she seems to feel it as a sort of continual outing of what she would rather keep private. Her story—even the mere statement that she was born in Hungary—cannot help but be a war story. Rosa's choice of friends and homes where she feels most comfortable also reflects a sense that she needs to enclose herself in her racial identity rather than to stand out as different.

Unlike Rosa, Gabriela has little self-consciousness about her race, though she frequently brings it up in conversation as one of her attributes. I took her to a birthday party held at a synagogue a year ago. She was the only child of color, and when Rosa and I came to pick her up, we felt distinctly visible, while Gabriela seemed quite oblivious. Rosa was eight then, and Gabriela only five, and surely Rosa's greater maturity explained some of the differences in their responses. In addition, of course, these children were Gabriela's classmates, and she felt comfortable with them. Yet Gabriela simply accepts difference, and her own brown skin, as part of the fascinating diversity of the world and continues to seem more comfortable with it than her older sister, who is more inclined to notice when she is the only dark-skinned person in a room. I was especially tense because the setting—a synagogue—is one in which I am supposed to feel at home but where I also stand ready to bristle at the conservative political opinions and racial stereotypes I have come, rightly or not, to find intertwined with upscale suburban American Judaism. It is this discomfort I associate with my family's mixed racial identity.

So far, we have been lucky enough to avoid major confrontations with bigotry, either about our children's race or about our family's structure. If the girls faced a direct challenge that was racially motivated, it would be clearer how to fight back. But the more subtle remarks people send our way leave me thinking that it might be better to remain silent. Would a mother whose skin was as dark as her children's have sat quietly seething on that beach on Cape Cod? I can't know the answer to that, and isn't the question also racist? Why should I think all people of color would have some standard reaction that I cannot know because I am white? I've asked my friends of color what they would have done, and the consensus seems to be that the most effective move is to speak directly with the children (the mother being written off as already a lost cause, the children still redeemable), explaining that first, the word they used is hurtful and rude, and second, they have it wrong anyway.

We have talked about lesbianism with our daughters, about what it does and does not mean to have two moms and the best ways of answering questions about their family. We have explained homophobia, pointedly telling the children that they might get teased because of what some people think about their mothers and their family Recently, we were able to finalize a second-parent adoption, so that both of us are now legally Rosa's and Gabriela's parents, a political near-miracle in this neoconservative period. These discussions have become more intense as Rosa, in particular, grows more self-conscious and worried about being different and begins to hear homophobic jokes at school. Last year, she came up with a solution. Hedging her suggestion with many apologies and assertions that she didn't want to hurt anyone's feelings, she proposed that the two of us jointly marry a gay male couple who are close friends and of whom the girls are fond. She had even figured out the pairings (based on height and religion). All of us could then live together—since she didn't want these couples who she knew loved each other to have to separate—but both she and her sister would acquire fathers in the deal. She was quite triumphant about the brilliance of her resolution of the prejudice problem. Gabriela, on the other hand, saw right away that four parents might prove to be *de trop*, but the idea generated long dinner-table conversations.

We also talk about race prejudice, but in the most general way—it's wrong and stupid and unfair. We have been reticent to talk about racial identity itself. Why? Nice liberal white parents tell their white children that skin color doesn't matter, we are all the same, and so on. Good line if you're all white. But from moment to moment color blindness is not a very useful skill for a child trying to forge her own sense of who she is. Not when she's not white. We are stymied in part by the complexities of race categories for Latinos in the United States: The catchall term "Hispanic" is imperialist and racist in itself, not to mention artificial, and it bears little relation to racial identity as well as erasing Indian, Arabic and African ethnicities in the Spanish-speaking world.

If we indeed live in a "post-traumatic," "post-tragic," "post-humanist" time, how *accidental* are anyone's life circumstances?[12] More bluntly, how intimately related are rescue and genocide? I think about this especially when people remark that my partner and I have "saved" our daughters from lives of poverty. This is one of the forms of subtle racism we encounter frequently. It suggests that we deserve praise for rescuing these poor children from their unfortunate birth circumstances, when indeed this "rescue" has inevitably entailed a deprivation of their origins. We hope, of course, that we have given our daughters a loving and secure family, yet we know at the same time that we have been complicit in taking away their original identities, beginning with their very names.

Has history itself—a trajectory I come more and more to see as a continuous series of atrocities—become pathological? Can we only experience history—and the complex tribal filiations it tracks—as a set of symptoms?[13] "In the face of life's horror," Elias Canetti wrote, "there is only one comfort: its alignment with the horror experienced by previous witnesses."[14] My mother and Rosa and Gabriela have lived beyond the histories of their origins, even to an extent abandoned history. How does the world into which they have survived assimilate the past it incorporates? Boundaries of time and place can be crossed, yet the need to make meaning from other times and places—and most notably from the haunting question of what if?—never goes away. Charlotte Delbo, a French writer who outlived Auschwitz and has written eloquently about it, describes this form of survival as an evasion of one's fate, a state of living *en sursis*, under reprieve.[15]

The challenge for my mother and for my daughters is to integrate who they were before their arrival in the United States with the realities of the lives they now lead. My mother has struggled with this for nearly fifty years, and it remains a daily battle despite the groundedness of her established American credentials and family life. Rosa and Gabriela, too, must assimilate into their current lives the pieces they can gather of their beginnings, and the knowledge that they are not living in the world in which they were born, and that no return to that world will be possible. My mother raised children in the bourgeois age of hula hoops and transistor radios, a world far removed from eastern Hungary but still one she came to own. Rosa and Gabriela are being raised in a postmodern world of two-career families, divorce and remarriage, sexual and racial diversity and competitive birthday parties. They are comfortable in their world. One of my parenting jobs is to see that they can be proud of the world that produced them and led them here, that the past is never fully erased or forgotten.

Notes

1. Shoshana Felman, "Education and Crisis, or the Vicissitudes of Teaching," in *Trauma: Explorations in Memory*, ed. Cathy Caruth (Baltimore: Johns Hopkins University Press, 1995), 13.

2. Eva Hoffman, *Lost in Translation: A Life in a New Language* (New York: Penguin Books, 1989), 248.

3. Geoffrey Hartman, "Public Memory and Its Discontents," *Raritan* 8, 4 (1994), 24.

4. Mikhail Bakhtin, *The Dialogic Imagination*, ed. Michael Holquist, trans. Michael Holquist and Caryl Emerson (Austin: University of Texas Press, 1981), 84.

5. Jonathan Boyarin, *Storm from Paradise: The Politics of Jewish Memory* (Minneapolis: University of Minnesota Press, 1992), 3.

6. Ibid., 21.

7. Hoffman, *Lost in Translation*, 262.

8. Ibid., 115.

9. Hartman, "Public Memory and Its Discontents," 40.

10. I use the term "Holocaust" in quotation marks because I dislike it. I do see the Nazi "Final Solution" for the "Jewish problem" to be unique among historical genocides because of its industrialized and premeditated nature. But that does not make it necessarily the "worst" horror of world history, and competition among atrocities seems to me to be a form of obscenity. I prefer to call this historical moment by the quoted Nazi term for it—the "Final Solution"—or by the Hebrew term *Shoah*, which has a linguistic particularity.

11. Patricia Hampl, "The Tenacity of Ruin," *New York Times Book Review*, 14 January 1996, 14.

12. Cathy Caruth, ed., *Trauma: Explorations in Memory* (Baltimore: Johns Hopkins University Press, 1995), 13.

13. Ibid., 5.

14. Felman, "Education and Crisis," 14.

15. Lawrence L. Langer, *Admitting the Holocaust: Collected Essays* (New York: Oxford University Press, 1995), 22.

Voices from the Deep South

LINDA H. SOUTHWARD AND PHYLLIS GRAY-RAY

Editor's note: The voices in the dialogue that follows belong to two university professors from the deep South, Phyllis Gray-Ray (who is black) and Linda H. Southward (who is white). They are also mothers and mentors. Together, they invented questions to help them reflect upon the personal and professional experiences that shaped their perspectives on racism and sexism.

Q: When and how did you first become aware of racism's role in your life?

Phyllis: School desegregation was my first introduction to racism. Desegregation came so suddenly and forcefully to our community that most of us children did not know what hit us, but our parents were in an uproar. I remember my mother's anxiety when we left for and returned from school. In "our" world, my mother was a very domineering woman who never seemed to fear anything. Once her fear was evident, I knew something bad would happen. Her reactions made me more fearful than the actual interaction with whites at school. During desegregation, I interacted with white children. It was through this interaction that I came face to face with racism. Ironically, it was also this interaction that later shaped my interest in race relations.

I was never aware of any violence that resulted from school desegregation, but I was fully aware of whites' resistance to it. Although blacks resisted it, too, our resistance was mostly from fear for our lives, in contrast to whites' resistance, which was simply racism. I remember the school buses picking up white children first, then picking us up. This guaranteed the white children always had seats. We rarely had seats, and even if seats were available with the whites, we still stood. The white children were mean and intimidating. Desegregation was a frightening experience for me. I remember the lumps in my throat as I became fully aware of racism; worse, was the abrupt introduction to this horrible reality, one that would haunt me for the rest of my life.

Linda: My awareness of racism also centered around school desegregation. Twenty-five years ago, during Christmas vacation of 1970, I became acutely aware of the discrimination that existed in the deep South. Although the United States Supreme Court's decision in Brown v. Board of Education of Topeka, Kansas occurred in 1954—two years before I was born—it wasn't until sixteen years later that school desegregation actually became a reality in Mississippi and throughout the South. It was this experience, more than any other, that heightened my awareness of the injustices encountered by African Americans. While I remember many symbols of racial discrimination, such as different waiting rooms and bathrooms for African Americans and European Americans—often marked "colored" and "white"—it was the desegregation of schools that brought together the fears, injustices and prejudices of these two worlds in ways that were unknown prior to the 1970s.

Prior to 1970, two schools existed in the predominantly blue-collar rural county of fewer than ten thousand people in which I grew up, one black and one white, each serving grades one through twelve. The decision had been made that the formerly black school would house all students in grades one through six, and the formerly white school would house all students in grades seven through twelve. Since I was in the eighth grade, I did not have the experience of actually changing school buildings, but that seemed to be the only thing that did not change. In fact, this event literally changed my life forever. The county was typical of most counties in the deep South in that social events centered around the school and the church, and throughout my life, these events had been totally segregated. Without a doubt, the world I had known for my first thirteen years was on the verge of changing forever.

Q: How did you learn to confront and work against racism?

Phyllis: My mother never talked much about racism, and sexism was blended into tradition in our community. Blacks and women always knew their place and seemed content with what was expected of them. As a black female, you're socialized at an early age, in very subtle ways, and sometimes without words, to know you're treated differently. As a result, I am constantly fighting this double bind of racism and sexism, and they are interwoven into my psyche and interactions with others. Since these two ills have been ever-present, I cannot recall exactly how I learned to act against them. They are a given in my life and affect every aspect of it. Professionally, I teach courses on the subject of racism and sexism. Thus, I am continuously thinking, acting and working against them.

Linda: My thinking about racism was greatly influenced by both my family and my church, but in different ways. My family's influence was very positive regarding antiracism, while my church's influence was extremely negative. Let me explain.

Throughout many areas of the South, new private academies sprung up as the direct result of public school desegregation. That many had the word "Christian" in their names was the height of hypocrisy to me. To be sure, prejudicial attitudes and behaviors underscored the founding of the "Christian" academy movement throughout the deep South.

The behavior of many of the white religious leaders and church congregations of my county was totally inconsistent with Judeo-Christian values. In the church in which I grew up, this inconsistency between what was preached and what was practiced was evident: the minister of the church was also the principal of the "Christian" academy in the county, and our congregation generously supported foreign mission work while simultaneously the majority of its members supported the "Christian" academies to avoid interaction with anyone different from themselves. Reflecting upon these experiences, I wonder if these members were attempting to compensate for any guilt they felt or if they simply could not or would not see the inconsistencies.

I have vivid memories of my parents sitting down with my brothers and me to explain the changes in the school system. Our parents gave each of us the choice of where we would like to go to school, even though we knew that our mother's intention was to continue her teaching in public schools. Our unanimous choice was to continue in public schools, though many of our friends and relatives had chosen otherwise.

I have often reflected on that family dialogue and our parents' demonstration of trust in us to make the right decision—to stay in public schools. While I am confident they must have known what we would decide, given our upbringing and their example, it was their trust in us that empowered us to rise above the "emotional fallout" of making a choice different from that of many of our friends and family.

In the South, the phrase "falling out" was very common in those days. It meant some dispute or disagreement had resulted, literally, in a parting of ways. Sometimes this parting of ways would be for a day, sometimes weeks, and some had been known to last for generations. Well, the "emotional falling out" was quite real for me during that time. Families and churches split, and many relationships became tenuous, resulting in a lack of trust among peers. For some, the primary social-psychological developmental task of adolescence—acceptance by one's peers—became impossible.

While much has been written about the prejudices experienced by blacks during this time, there is less documentation of whites' experiences of prejudices. The primary discriminators against whites were other whites, and I was called names and treated differently by my former classmates simply because I continued in public school. I knew, though, that the amount of prejudice black students endured was monumental compared to what I experienced. For example, black students did not have any nonpublic school choices. Ostensibly, the phrase "freedom of choice" was used by whites to promote more equity in busing; in reality, it was often just another strategy to delay or circumvent desegregation.

As I got to know my new classmates, I quickly realized that more similarities than differences existed between the two groups. For example, black students generally did not want to leave their school and come to the former all-white school. And parents of both black and white children were fearful about the interaction between these two student groups.

At the time, I was unaware of how these experiences and events during the early 1970s would eventually influence my career path as a social worker. But, in retrospect, I see that the values of social work—fostering and supporting respect, dignity and self-determination for all individuals—were being formed on a daily basis. My experiences promoted a keen interest in learning more about how prejudices evolve so that I could teach others to be aware of and to overcome them.

Q: What do antiracism and antisexism mean to you? In what ways and to what people have you tried to teach antiracism and antisexism?

Phyllis: I have tried to teach antiracism and antisexism whenever the opportunity arises. I feel all mothers should begin talking to their children about gender and race issues at a very early age—even before their children can understand. There are two benefits to this strategy: (1) The mother gets into the habit of mothering this way. (2) The child gets into the habit of receiving this type of mothering and therefore may internalize these thoughts.

All mothers should first acknowledge that children are not born with racist or sexist attitudes and should make an early attempt to ensure children do not develop these attitudes. Mothers themselves must come to grips with the wrongness of racism and sexism and must take active roles in shaping behaviors of all children. Often white women are not as aware of racism as they are of sexism and may appear insensitive to racism. This causes some women of color not to have as much faith and trust in white women. And women of color often feel used by white women who only want to parade them to give more credibility to their (white women's) own agenda. All women should become aware of and sensitive to social inequities. Women account for a large percentage of all racial groups in the United States, and if we put our racial and ethnic differences aside, we can work together to alleviate such ills as racism and sexism, and effective mothering will come naturally

Other strategies mothers can use to end racism and sexism include the following:

- Never put children on the defensive. They feel more comfortable and more open to differences when they can experience a non-threatening exchange of ideas.

- Reach out to each other; invite a family of a different makeup and cultural background to spend a day with you. This provides an opportunity for interaction among children of all races and both genders.

- Resocialize men to the role of the "new woman." Some black males, though fully aware of racism, may tend to be insensitive to sexism. Socialize young boys as well as adults to appreciate women's strengths and contributions. Mothers can be very instrumental in this socialization.

- Take a stand to ensure the legal system acts on the ideal of blind justice instead of focusing on extralegal factors when dealing with diverse groups.

- Demand that educational curricula be revised to provide all children with a well-rounded, culturally diverse and culturally appropriate education, as early as preschool.

- Support affirmative action. If it is dismantled, then work to put in place some other means to help achieve economic equality. Racism and sexism still persist in every major institution in the United States, and we must continue to combat them.

Linda: As a social worker in the deep South, I have often described myself as an eternal optimist, but I must also acknowledge the realities of many other people whose everyday lives are affected by discriminatory behaviors and practices based on gender or race.

For positive changes to occur, however, we cannot just acknowledge that prejudice and discrimination exist, but—as mothers and educators—must act upon our convictions of promoting social and economic justice. In addition, we must encourage others to be involved. That involvement may come in many forms; two social work options would be examining changes needed in systems to make services equitable and advocating for legislation and policies in all size systems to level the playing field for all, especially those who are most vulnerable.

It is also important that our children, our students, our coworkers and all with whom we come in contact understand our convictions by our role modeling. I agree that education about antiracism and antisexism should begin at home, with all children, at a very young age. As we know, children develop a sense of fairness early on, so we need to be consistent in our actions.

Q: When and how did you first become aware of racism's and sexism's roles in your children's lives?

Phyllis: When I was pregnant I often hoped that my child would not have to experience life the way I did. I hated the thought that he would be part of a racist society that had judged his worth before he was even born. That seemed so unfair to my innocent child, and there was nothing I could do about it until he was old enough to understand.

Fortunately, my four-year-old son cannot distinguish racist or sexist behavior or prejudicial attitudes from any other attitudes or behaviors. However, he has been exposed to racial issues in his daycare. One night he told me that he was brown and his friends and teacher were white. His assessment was accurate, as he is the only black child in his class, although there are others at the school. I often talk to him about racial issues, which, at this time, do not seem to have an impact on him one way or another. He does not understand it now, but I want to develop the habit of communicating with him about racism. Although he has not, to my knowledge, experienced individual racism, it is definitely lurking and waiting to introduce itself to him. And when it does, I hope to have him mentally ready for his rude awakening. I also talk to my son about respecting women. I tell him that everyone is created equal and should be treated fairly regardless of race or gender. I stress these points now so that he can internalize them.

Linda: Although today's children will not experience massive desegregation and busing, the emotional fallout from past generations still exists. While many of the academies no longer exist in the deep South and those that do have dropped the "Christian" in their names, I believe many racist attitudes and barriers to antiracism still exist, though they may be more subtle.

I wish my eleven-year-old child did not have to ask the same questions regarding racism that I asked as an adolescent almost three decades ago. For example: Why do people go to the academy? Do we go to a private church? Why are so many African Americans poor? While I am troubled that these conditions still exist, I do believe that my experiences coupled with the values and beliefs taught by my parents have made my answers and actions more credible to my child and other children.

Q: How have the dynamics of racism and sexism manifested themselves in your life?

Phyllis: I first encountered the double bind of being a black woman in America in graduate school. The school I attended was predominantly white, in a predominantly white town, in a predominantly white state. I experienced the biggest culture shock of my life. I was so far away from home, no blackness anywhere. Even the radio stations were white-oriented. However, once the initial shock wore off, I was headed for the next phase of reality.

In graduate school I confronted racism, which I thought I knew how to deal with, but something was different about this racism—it was usually very subtle, hard to detect and therefore went unnoticed until after the fact. It was institutionalized racism, and it was worse than the individual racism I had faced as a child.

Along with this "new" racism came an unwarranted foe, sexism. I never thought my gender would be a handicap for me, but it was during graduate school. I chose to specialize in criminology at the doctoral level, which is an area that females are not commonly mentored to pursue. Sociology itself is basically a white, male-dominated discipline. I experienced discrimination mainly from my classmates, who thought that women should specialize in the family and sex roles, and that blacks should specialize in race relations. Apparently, criminology was reserved for white, research-oriented males.

Despite racism and sexism, I earned my Ph.D. and thought life would start to improve since I had proven myself as someone worthy of making a significant contribution to society. I thought I would get the same respect as every other Ph.D. I left graduate school with these thoughts and with new hopes.

My first job was ideal, and just as I thought I had won the racism-sexism battle after earning my Ph.D., I was faced with another battle, tenure and promotion. However, I had more baggage this time: racism, sexism and motherhood. They lingered and melded into one as I approached and achieved tenure and promotion. Today, they are ever present.

Linda: Having been raised in the deep South, where white males dominate decision-making in most avenues of life, it should not have been surprising to me the first time I was denied a promotion. When the directorship was open within the social service agency where I had been employed, I applied, but a white male was given the job. My credentials and experience on every count were superior to his, yet I was denied the job. This was my first experience of job-related discrimination. Not only was I female, I was also an "outsider," for though I am native to the state, I was not reared in the community in which I work. In the deep South, it is said that, in small towns, you are a stranger for just one day, but a newcomer for the next fifty years. Since my family of origin is not "from there," I have never really been considered "one of them." I persevered, however, and did get the promotion the next time the job was open.

This dialogue suggests that an awareness of and action against racism and sexism in our own lives and the lives of our children is a beginning step in ending discrimination. Since we know that discrimination often occurs because of fears and lack of understanding, it is incumbent on all of us to educate and to be effective role models for our children, our students, our families, our colleagues and our communities.*

---

* During the final editing of this dialogue, one of my "other" mothers, Mrs. Ella Ruth Oglesby, died after a ten-year battle with leukemia. She was the first social worker I ever knew. She demonstrated the consistencies that I was looking for as an adolescent, and these consistencies continued throughout her life. This is the type of "community" mothering that is so vital to us today. Therefore, I would like to dedicate this dialogue to her.

—L.H.S.

Mothering Across Racial and Cultural Boundaries

SHELLEY PARK

As a white feminist who is the adoptive mother of a child of Guyanese-American heritage, I think about race and racism frequently. I think about the current atmosphere of identity politics and wonder how my daughter will go about constructing her own racial and ethnic identity and how I might best prepare her to do so. I think about how to provide her with the coping skills to survive and thrive amidst racism, ethnocentrism and nationalism. I think about what I can do to change these social conditions. And I think about what I need to change in myself, attempting to monitor my own "whiteness" and exorcise the racism within.

Many of the issues I grapple with are specific to being the adoptive parent of a child of color. When whites adopt children of color, they are eyed suspiciously by both the white community and communities of color. In some instances, the children they have adopted may likewise come to view them with suspicion. Such suspicions are often warranted and, if taken seriously, highlight the ways in which transracial adoption is both politically and personally problematic. While these problems are not insurmountable, they do challenge feminists—like myself—to rethink and reform traditional adoption practices.

On October 13, 1992, my husband and I joyfully adopted a four-and-a-half-month-old baby girl who had lived with us since her third day of life. After the court proceedings, we took numerous photos of ourselves, baby in arms, and celebrated. Tomi, a beautiful brown-eyed, ebony-haired, olive-complexioned infant, was now finally *ours*.

Tomi's birth mother was not present at the proceedings that day, nor had we previously met her. Indeed, at that time, we knew little about Tomi's birth mother save that she was quite beautiful (we'd been shown a photo), was twenty-one years old, had no known medical difficulties and was of Guyanese heritage (we'd been provided with her medical history, which contained this minimal personal information). We were equally uninformed concerning the specific circumstances that led her to relinquish Tomi into our care, knowing only that she was single, had no continuing relationship with the birth father and hoped to go to college.

I cannot honestly say that any of this bothered us at the time—we were entirely focused on *our* baby. However, in retrospect, the entire situation seems odd, and I am, frankly, embarrassed that I made no attempt to alter it. My retrospections were greatly sharpened by unexpectedly becoming a biological mother myself fifteen months after adopting Tomi. While I'd like to think the reflections here would have occurred independently of this event, I suspect my firsthand experience of ill-timed and unintended pregnancy and childbirth made me more sensitive to the emotional complexity and difficulty that must attend a birth mother's decision to allow another to mother her child. At any rate, I now wish I had attempted to meet Tomi's birth mother at the hospital (she was only down the hall from the room into which we were discreetly ushered to meet "our" new baby) or at some other time prior to legalizing the adoption. I also wish I and my spouse had involved Tomi's birth mother in the naming process. I'm very pleased with the full name we carefully chose for Tomi (a nickname I'm using here for simplicity and some degree of privacy). In addition to being melodious and rhythmic, it signifies our daughter's dual maternal lineage. Yet, this does not alter the problematic fact that *we chose a birth name for a child birthed by another.*

According to birth mothers critical of contemporary adoption processes, we did not adopt our daughter, so much as "kidnap" her. One birth mother sums up her feelings about contemporary adoption practices as follows:

> Closed adoption is legalized kidnapping and has nothing to do with "feminism" and everything to do with the patriarchy. Closed adoption is child abuse. It's violence against women and children . . . Let's [do] away with the word "adoption" and tell it like it is: i.e., not, "I adopted a baby," but "I am responsible for violently separating an infant from its natural mother and pretending like she doesn't exist, like it's no big deal."[1]

This woman's anguish and anger is unmistakable and should, I think, be taken seriously. Although feminists have sometimes portrayed adoption as a path to the emancipation of women from compulsory reproduction and the attendant exploitation of women's bodies,[2] this view of adoption makes sense only from the perspective of potential or actual adoptive mothers—typically, like myself, white and middle-class. From the perspective of birth mothers who have faced relinquishing *their* children—often women of color and/or women of meager financial means—adoption may seem far from emancipatory. Once this second perspective is taken into account, adoption (like most other reproductive alternatives) becomes problematic.

Further problematizing adoption is the recent trend toward transracial and transcultural adoptions. While transracial adoption encompasses all people who adopt children from racial groups different from their own, transracial adoption—like adoption itself—has been largely the prerogative of white parents. Similarly, transcultural adoption is predominantly a Euro-American phenomenon in which advantaged (white, middle- to upper-class) members of privileged countries adopt children of color from war or poverty-stricken nations.

Viewed in this context, interracial families—or "rainbow families" as these are often referred to in adoption circles—appear as a microcosm of racial hierarchy, economic imperialism and cultural colonialism. Indeed, this has been the consistent position of the National Association of Black Social Workers who, in 1972, publicly denounced the adoption of black children by white families as a form of "racial genocide."[3] Similar critiques of transracial adoption have been voiced by other racial and ethnic groups, including Native American Councils,[4] as well as by the adult children of transracial adoptions. In the words of one adult adoptee:

> Racism is made real to me by the Europeans in my family and in my life when they *choose to adopt* me into their world, either literally or figuratively. I have been officially "adopted" as the daughter of a European patriarch and made "legitimate" under his name.[5]

The anger of adopted children, like the anger of their birth mothers, is often dismissed by adoptive parents but should be taken seriously. Transracially adoptive parents would be well served, for example, by examining their motives in light of the following questions raised by another adult child of color:

> Are they exoticizing their own children? Are they trying to make some statement about race? Is it their naive ideal that racial mixing eliminates racism? Is this their answer to some Black ex-lover's accusation of racism? "How could I be racist? My own child is Black!"[6]

Although liberals may view transracial adoption as a way of achieving a racially integrated and color-blind society, this view of transracial adoption embodies the perspective of white adoptive parents. For people of color, transracial adoption may appear as simply the most recent in a long series of attempts to destabilize minority families and assimilate minority cultures into the white, Eurocentric mainstream.[7]

As Lois Melina notes, it is "easy for white adoptive parents to minimize the importance of race, since race matters less if you are part of the majority."[8] Being color-blind is one of the many everyday (often unnoticed) privileges enjoyed by those in the dominant group.[9] White privilege also extends to the ability to choose when, where and how to fight racism and who to "invite" into the struggle.

In contrast, people of color cannot afford to, nor are they permitted to, ignore color. This is so even when (perhaps especially when) a person of color is adopted by white parents. No parents, including white parents, can protect minority children from the racial prejudice, discrimination and oppression that exists outside of the family unit. And white parents, unlike parents who share their child's racial identity, risk perpetuating racism and ethnocentrism within the family itself. On the one hand, if white adoptive parents practice color-blindness, they will fail to acknowledge, respect and preserve their child's racial and ethnic identity. On the other hand, if they strive to preserve the child's racial and ethnic identity, they risk exoticizing the child as "other."

In response to the above concerns about adoption, one might elect not to adopt transracially or, perhaps, not to adopt at all. This may be a sound decision even for women who would like to participate in child rearing, but cannot or do not wish to procreate. After all, as bell hooks reminds us, childcare is a responsibility that can be shared by people who do not live with children.[10] Certainly sharing time, money, talents and love with children does not necessitate biologically, legally, physically or emotionally "appropriating" them.[11]

But what of those who (like myself) have adopted transracially? How can we (can we?) practice antiracist parenting? Some obvious forms of praxis for white parents of children of color include familiarizing ourselves with the history, politics, literature, art, music, dress, food, language and religion of our child's culture(s) of origin, as well as that of other cultures; purchasing or creating posters, greeting cards, books, puzzles, dolls, toys and children's magazines that feature people of our child's race and families of diverse racial composition; living in an integrated neighborhood; and cultivating friendships, professional relationships and political alliances with people of a variety of races, religions, classes, ages and lifestyles.[12]

Many of the above strategies for antiracist parenting could be used by non-adoptive parents and uniracial families. It is important, for example, for all parents to become culturally literate and to expand their social circle to include people of diverse cultures. These issues take on a special significance, however, in the interracial family formed by adoption. Adopted children often experience a sense of "genealogical bewilderment,"[13] and this confusion is exacerbated when racial differences exist between the adopted child and adoptive parents. Such bewilderment may be alleviated, in part, by providing the adopted child of color with information about her culture and relationships with people of similar genealogical descent. But, ultimately, these are only partial solutions to the child's confusion and to the more general dilemmas posed by transracial adoption. The best way to provide the adopted child of color with a sense of personal as well as racial and ethnic identity is to provide her with the opportunity to know her birth parents. This is also the best way to exemplify respect for and build sisterhood with the birth mother.

On May 1, 1992, prior to going to the hospital to get "our" newborn daughter, my husband and I went to the adoption agency to complete paperwork. Among the documents we signed that day was an "agreement for exchange of information." This committed us to providing the birth mother (the birth father was unknown) with pictures and letters describing the child and our feelings about and plans for the child at regular intervals. According to the contract, we would utilize the agency as the mediator for such correspondence and were, in fact, prohibited from "sharing last names, addresses, places of employment or other identifying information."

We were not required to sign this document, but simply invited to participate in a "new experiment" the agency was trying. Since we saw nothing threatening in this agreement (all information "exchange" was unidirectional—from us to the birth mother—and indirect), we agreed. At the time, we had no vocabulary for describing this experiment, but we now know that what we had agreed to that day was a "semi-open" adoption.

For the past seventy-five years, closed adoption has been the norm in the United States.[14] In a closed adoption, birth parents surrender their parental rights to the state or a private adoption agency, which subsequently transfers legal guardianship to adoptive parents screened and approved by their "experts." Birth parents are expected to forget the child. Even the pregnancy is erased as a fictional birth certificate records the adoptive parents as the child's biological parents. All court records that might undermine this biological fiction are sealed, and the parents of record raise the child "as if" he were their own flesh and blood.[15]

The emerging trend toward openness in adoption has resulted, in large part, from adoption reform movements led by adult adoptees and birth parents seeking reunion. Many adoptive parents feel threatened by this movement, but in most cases of open adoption, as in our own, all members of the adoption triangle—birth parents, child and adoptive parents—benefit.[16] This is especially true in cases of transracial adoption.

Birth parents, especially birth mothers, benefit in some obvious ways. As Judith Modell describes: "Open adoption accords the birthparent a lasting identity as parent, a status the birthparent loses in a closed adoption. With openness, too, a birthparent 'makes a plan for' rather than surrenders her child."[17] In a fully open adoption, the birth mother meets the prospective adoptive parents prior to delivering the baby and may even invite the parents she selects to share the birth experience with her. In a semi-open adoption, such as our own, the birth mother may choose one of several families previously approved by a social worker mediating the arrangement. In either case, "the birthparent can feel less the victim of circumstances—or coercion—and more the actor in a course of events" than she would in a closed adoption arrangement.[18] Because of this, combined with ongoing communication with the adoptive parents, a birth mother is less likely to suppress her past or fantasize about her child. Thus, she suffers less grief, guilt and loss and is better able to build an integrated life for herself—a life in which her past, present and future are connected.

Similar benefits accrue to the adopted child. Children of closed adoptions may have difficulty developing a positive and realistic self-concept. Not only do they lack information concerning their genealogical descent, but they may also feel shame and guilt at being "rejected" by their birth parents and fantasize about being reunited with their "real" mother and father. Open adoption, in contrast, provides adoptees with a sense of life continuity, personal history and self-worth. Children of open adoption know where they come from, who they look like and why they were adopted.

Since it would be clearly ludicrous for white parents to pretend that a child of color was their own genetic offspring, the transracial adoptee typically grows up knowing that she was adopted. In a closed adoption, however, the adopted child often learns of this by recitations of the "chosen-child story." Parents wishing to impress upon a child how much they wanted and loved her will recall that "she has been chosen, specially picked out, and is a special child." In addition to exoticizing the child, this narrative fails to mention the parents who had to relinquish the child and thus leaves out a crucial piece of the child's identity: "An adoptee has been given away by one and taken in by another parent."[19]

In open adoption this "fact of life" is neither erased nor fantasized about. By having access to accurate information about her birth parents and the circumstances of her relinquishment, the adoptee is able to form positive, yet realistic images of her birth parents as persons who cared for her and thoughtfully transferred primary parenting. Ideally, her birth parents will continue to be an ongoing part of her life and family. Under such circumstances, the child is less likely to suffer genealogical bewilderment. She is also less likely to feel abandoned by or snatched away from her biological parents or cultural group.[20]

Many adoptive parents are nonetheless fearful of opening their adoptive arrangements. Indeed, I must admit to being apprehensive about our first face-to-face meeting with Tomi's birth mother. In particular, adoptive parents fear that the birth parent(s) may attempt to reclaim their adopted children—physically, legally and/or emotionally. This concern is largely foundationless. Birth parents who are informed of their child's whereabouts and well-being are less, rather than more, likely to think about reclaiming their child. And the emotional bond between adopted children and adoptive parents may be strengthened, rather than weakened, by openness in the adoptive arrangements.[21] Those who adopt openly have less opportunity to deny infertility by fictionalizing their child's origins. We also have an enhanced ability to communicate accurate information regarding our child's personal, medical and cultural background and heritage.[22] These factors, together with the friendship that often develops between birth parents and adoptive parents, enable adoptive parents to build honest and enduring relationships with their adopted children and their children's birth parents—relationships that exemplify honesty, compassion, trust, integrity and respect for individual and group differences.

In the past three years, Tomi's birth mother and I have begun to develop a friendship as our adoptive arrangements have evolved toward greater openness. I continue to send Tomi's birth mom letters describing Tomi's growth, development and activities, in addition to photos and samples of Tomi's art work. She sends Tomi cards and gifts on special occasions including Tomi's birthday. We have exchanged names, addresses and phone numbers in addition to other information about ourselves and no longer use the agency as an intermediary for our communications. We chat on the phone occasionally and meet for lunch about once a year. I have a photo of Tomi's birth mom holding her at our first meeting about eight months after Tomi's birth. I treasure this photo and have included it along with cards and notes in Tomi's photo album. Although our busy schedules and the distance between our respective cities make it difficult for us to meet frequently, I hope that our relationship will continue to evolve toward even greater mutual openness and that someday I will have earned the privilege of calling Tomi's birth mom "sister."

In recent decades, white feminists have critiqued the family as a primary site of patriarchal oppression, which isolates women from one another and appropriates their labor in the interests of capitalism.[23] As such feminists urged abandoning the family as a biological imperative, people of color, however, have attempted to uphold genealogical bonds as a source of racial identity and cultural pride. From the former perspective, relinquishing children may appear to emancipate women from the yoke of motherhood, and adopting children (especially children of color born to poverty) may seem an altruistic, politically correct practice. Indeed, this view is not far from my original feminist perspective on adoption. From the latter perspective, adoption (especially transracial adoption) appears as an imperialist assault on the family of color, and surrendering children (especially to white families) denotes an inability to withstand this assault. Indeed, I suspect that some members of Tomi's birth family feel this way about her birth mother's decision to relinquish. Here, as elsewhere, the demands of white feminists seem to conflict with the needs and desires of people of color. Here, as elsewhere, however, this tension is not inescapable. Closer attention to different types of families and alternative forms of adoption practices dissolves the apparent dilemmas.

By focusing on the appropriation of individual women's productive and reproductive labor in small, isolated nuclear families, feminist criticisms of the family have largely ignored the ways in which families can and have been formed in opposition to sexual, racial and economic oppressions. In particular, they have overlooked the ways in which families of color—typically characterized by extended kinship networks participating in collective domestic labor—have often been sites of political survival and cultural resistance.[24] Similarly, criticisms of adoption by people of color have focused on the appropriation of children of color by small, isolated, nuclear white families, overlooking the ways in which adoptive families—like my own—can and are being reformed to resist sexism, classism and racism.

Certainly the oppressive aspects of adoption should be recognized, not minimized. Many white adoptive parents attempt to appropriate children of color in ways that would be laughable, were they not so harmful. I recall, for example, listening to one white mother (an experiential "expert" on a panel concerning transracial adoption!) recount telling her black son that "he tanned well" when he questioned their different skin colors. This sort of erasure of a child's racial heritage and identity is clearly problematic as was indicated by the angry grimace of her then-adolescent adoptee. Also problematic is the sort of exoticization of children that exaggerates or overemphasizes differences. The children of one large interracial family, for example, routinely compare their various hues. While curiosity about difference is natural, I could not help but wonder why they seemed obsessed with comparison.

Moreover, even if individual parents are well intentioned and well educated, traditional (closed) transracial adoption remains structurally problematic. In such adoptions, institutional bureaucracies impose their (white, European and typically Christian) conceptions of a "good family"—and more specifically a "good mother"—on birth parents and adoptive parents alike, reserving for themselves the power to "take" children from some (young, single, gay, poor, working class, nonwhite, non-English-speaking) parents and "award" them to (more mature, married, financially stable, professional, white, English-speaking) others. In closed adoptions, birth mothers and adoptive mothers are, thus, defined in opposition to one another and kept physically, legally and emotionally—as well as ideologically—separated. There is little opportunity here for personal or political solidarity across racial, ethnic or class lines and a substantial risk that the child of color "placed" in a white, nuclear family will be dispossessed of her personal past and cultural inheritance. Yet, as Mina Davis Caulfield urges, we "must look not only at the ways in which the colonizer acts to *break down* family solidarity, but also [at] the ways in which the colonized—women, men and children—act to *maintain, consolidate, and build anew* the basic units in which children can grow and be encultured in the values and relationships that are independent of and in opposition to the imperial culture."[25]

Tomi's birth mother and I have slowly begun to knit together an extended family for our daughter. Although we are still negotiating our own relationship, we have begun the process of sharing our connection with, and thus extending it to include, others. Tomi's birth mother has slowly disclosed her situation to various members of her family and has shared the photos I send her with her mother and grandmother. She has also shared pictures of her siblings, parents and grandparents with me. Tomi's birth grandmother has sent birthday gifts to Tomi, and I have been able to speak with her on the phone on a couple of occasions. I have slowly accustomed my siblings, parents and grandparents to the idea of meeting Tomi's birth mother and I hope that some of them may be able to meet her on Tomi's next birthday.

While the adoption reform movement has, thus far, been largely conservative, led by individuals (birth mothers, adoptees, social workers) and groups seeking to maintain fairly traditional family ideologies and structures,[26] the ramifications of open adoption are quite revolutionary. Open adoption resists conservative ideologies and embodies feminist and antiracist principles in several ways. First, open, interracial families visibly depict a motherhood that is socially (re)constructed, rather than biologically given and, thus, a kinship that is "contrived," rather than "natural." Second, in open adoption this contrived kinship *begins with* and is sustained by the alliance between birth parent(s) and adoptive parents (and especially between birth mothers and adoptive mothers) forbidden by closed adoption. This link "eliminates the sharp evaluative differentiation between a birth and adoptive parent, between a person who 'just has' a child . . . and a person who is 'qualified' to be a parent."[27] Third, the connection, rather than separation, of birth parents and adoptive parents transforms the exchange relation that characterizes adoption from a calculated, *commercial* transfer *of* a child to a *gift* (of parents) given *to* a child (by another set of parents). In the words of one birth mother, writing to her birth son before his birth:

> I have chosen Mark and Eleanor to be your parents. I have been with them for two months now . . . I think they are very loving, understanding, giving, sincere people. I'm not giving you up, Jason. *I'm not giving you to them. I'm giving them to you.* I love them.[28]

Finally, as the above remarks suggest, open adoption transgresses the notion that a child can have only *one* "real" mother and thereby urges cooperative parenting that focuses on the needs of children, rather than the rights of parents. Transracially adopted children have, as adoption rhetoric implies, "special needs." In particular, they need to be empowered to live in and identify with (at least) two different cultures. The best way to enable a child to do this is to provide him with an extended kinship network that includes multiple parents. Ideally, in such an extended, blended family, each parent brings unique abilities and personal and cultural information to the child-rearing task, and all parents collectively model the possibility of cross-cultural kinship.

While there are no maps for successfully building multiparent, interracial families through adoption, our families resemble (albeit imperfectly and often unconsciously) the extended kinship networks found in other sites of cultural resistance. Like the reconstituted African families found on and across southern plantations under slavery in the United States or the *compadrazgo* (godparenting) system in Mexico during the American period (post-1848), for example, our families struggle to preserve and transmit a cultural inheritance to another generation while situated within the parameters of (legal, political, economic and educational) institutional structures designed to annihilate those cultural values and traditions. And like Chinese sojourner families, our families struggle to preserve their integrity while dispersed across cities, countries and continents.[29] Because we will need to adapt to, as well as resist, the circumstances in which we find ourselves embedded, we will need to emphasize resourcefulness, flexibility and creativity. Even then, we will make (and I have made) mistakes. I do not mean to imply that openness in adoptive relations inevitably or irrevocably makes the transracial family nonoppressive. But I do hope to suggest that future analyses of interracial adoptive families need to go beyond the assumption that our families can *only* be agents of racial or other forms of oppression.

Notes

1. Randa Phillips, "Closed Adoption Is Child Abuse," in *Sojourner* 20 (May 1995): 5.

2. Jeffner Allen, "Motherhood: The Annihilation of Women," in *Feminist Frameworks: Alternative Theoretical Accounts of the Relations Between Women and Men*, 3d ed., ed. Alison M. Jaggar and Paula S. Rothenberg (New York: McGraw-Hill, 1984), 380–85.

3. Christine A. Adamec, *There ARE Babies to Adopt: A Resource Guide for Prospective Parents* (Bedford, MA: Mills & Sanders, 1987), 150.

4. Deborah Work, "More Than Skin Deep: Can Adoptive Families Erase the Color Line?" *Sunshine* (14 October 1990): 6.

5. Sasha Khokha, "Unfolding the Complicated Layers of Racial and Cultural Identity," review of *Miscegenation Blues: Voices of Mixed Race Women*, ed. Carol Camper, *Sojourner* 20 (May 1995): 24.

6. Ibid.

7. Michelle McCalope, "Should White Families Adopt Black Children?" *Jet* (January 1991): 14.

8. Lois R. Melina, "Children Need Help Facing Negative Images of Their Countries of Origin," *Adopted Child* (February 1990): 2.

9. Peggy McIntosh, "White Privilege and Male Privilege: A Personal Account of Coming to See Correspondences Through Work in Women's Studies," in *Race, Class and Gender*, 2d ed., ed. Margaret L. Andersen and Patricia Hill Collins (Belmont, CA: Wadsworth, 1988), 79–81.

10. bell hooks, "Revolutionary Parenting," in *Feminist Theory: From Margin to Center* (Boston: South End Press, 1984), 144.

11. Phillips, "Closed Adoption is Child Abuse," 5.

12. See "Ethnic Images: A Primer for Adoptive Parents," *Ours* (May/June 1990): 18–21; Jan McFarlane, "Building Self-Esteem in Children and Teens of Color," *Ours* (March/April 1992): 26–31; Melina, "Children Need Help Facing Negative Images of Their Countries of Origin"; Lois R. Melina, "Advice for Parents of Children of Mixed Racial Heritage," *Adopted Child* 9 (May 1990): 4; Azzi Powell, "Raise Your Child with Ethnic Pride," *Ours* (November/December 1988): 26–29; and Francis Wardle, "Are You Sensitive to Interracial Children's Special Identity Needs?" *Young Children* (January 1987): 53–59.

13. Murray Ryburn, *Open Adoption: Research, Theory and Practice* (Brookfield, VT: Ashgate, 1994), 51.

14. Jeanne Warren Lindsay, *Open Adoption: A Caring Option* (Buena Park, CA: Morning Glory Press, 1987), 63.

15. Judith S. Modell, *Kinship with Strangers: Adoption and Interpretations of Kinship in American Culture* (Berkeley: University of California Press, 1994), 227.

16. Ruth McRoy, Harold D. Grotevant and Kerry l. White, *Openness in Adoption: New Practices, New Issues* (New York: Praeger, 1988), 113–118; Bruce M. Rappaport, *The Open Adoption Book: A Guide to Adoption Without Tears* (New York: MacMillan, 1992), 84–126; and Ryburn, *Open Adoption*, 77–89.

17. Modell, *Kinship with Strangers*, 57.

18. Ibid.

19. Ibid., 115.

20. McRoy, et al., *Openness in Adoption*, 115.

21. Lindsay, *Open Adoption*, 227; Kathleen Silber and Patricia Martinez Dorner, *Children of Open Adoption and Their Families* (San Antonio: Corona, 1990), 174–178.

22. McRoy, et al., *Openness in Adoption*, 117.

23. See, for example, Nancy Chodorow, *The Reproduction of Mothering* (Berkeley: University of California Press, 1978); Betty Friedan, *The Feminine Mystique* (New York: Dell, 1963); and Evelyn Reed, *Problems of Women's Liberation* (New York: Pathfinder Press, 1970).

24. Mina Davis Caulfield, "Imperialism, the Family and Cultures of Resistance," in *Feminist Frameworks: Alternative Theoretical Accounts of the Relations Between Women and Men*, 3d ed., ed. Allison M. Jaggar and Paula

S. Rothenburg (New York: McGraw-Hill, 1984), 442–47; Bonnie Thornton Dill, "Our Mothers' Grief: Racial Ethnic Women and the Maintenance of Families," in *Race, Class and Gender*, ed. Margaret L. Andersen and Patricia Hill Collins (Belmont, CA: Wadsworth, 1988), 215–37; Gloria I. Joseph and Jill Lewis, *Common Differences: Conflicts in Black and White Feminist Perspectives* (Garden City, NY: Anchor Books, 1981), 127–50.

25. Caulfield, "Imperialism, the Family and Cultures of Resistance," 444.

26. Modell, *Kinship with Strangers*, 60.

27. Ibid., 236.

28. Rappaport, *The Open Adoption Book*, 94.

29. See Dill, "Our Mothers' Grief," 219–234. Chinese sojourner families were a split-household family, wherein the father worked in the United States, but the wife and children (if any) remained in China, explicitly forbidden to form families in the United States by U.S. Immigration rules prior to the twentieth century. The man was seen as going on a "sojourn," with the goal of returning to China with enough money to buy land, although many never returned for more than infrequent visits.

Working on Redemption

MAUREEN T. REDDY

"Well, you can't change the world, you know?" My acquaintance looks at me expectantly, awaiting my nod of agreement. However, I do not agree.

We have been standing in the produce section of the local grocery store for the five or so minutes it took her to answer my casual question about her five-year-old son. She has decided to enroll him in a private school that touts its commitment to "diversity" but whose student population is almost entirely white. This woman knows that my husband Doug and I have decided not to send our son to that school because he is one of only two children of color admitted to their kindergarten for the coming year. She also knows that we told the school's admissions director why we were declining their offer of admission and stressed that we would reconsider only if they admitted significant numbers of so-called minority children. Since the school-age population of our city is more than 70 percent "minority," finding such children should not be difficult.

My acquaintance obviously feels guilty about her decision, hence the long, self-justifying tale. In addition to the maddening "you can't change the world" claim, she has offered a number of other clichés in support of her choice, including "everyone wants the best for their children." She has also assured me that she "understands" why the school would not be good for my son while being just fine for hers, because her son is white. I am so angry that I could happily push her into the tomatoes she is now examining, but I control myself.

"What bullshit! You *can* change the world," I say finally, "You've just chosen not to. Let's be honest, anyhow."

"Look, I'm not going to sacrifice *my* child for *politics*," she spits out, and stalks off. I am left to contemplate the produce along with the massive irony of a self-proclaimed feminist speaking of politics in such a disparaging way *and* believing she cannot change the world. Isn't one of the basic tenets of second-wave feminism "the personal is political"? And isn't feminism precisely dedicated to changing the world?

Seven years have passed since that conversation, and I have heard "you can't change the world" perhaps a thousand times since then, more lately than ever before. The phrase is sometimes spoken despairingly, sometimes self-righteously to justify easy but unethical choices. Your son says that boys in his class "hate" girls, he "hates" girls, and he will play only with other boys? *Sigh*. You can't change the world. Young black men express their anger and sorrow at the hostile treatment they receive from white police officers? Sad, but you can't change the world. I think that "you can't change the world" really means "I can't change the world entirely, alone, immediately, and therefore I abdicate my responsibility to try to change it at all. Instead, I accept the privileges that come my way and take comfort in knowing I'm a good person who *wishes* the world would change."

I have always believed I could change the world. Not the whole world, of course, and certainly not on my own or right this minute. My parents imbued me with the belief that people working together could, over a long period of time, accomplish something to change at least one little corner of the world. When my son was born, I realized how foundational this belief was in my family. Holding Brendan for the first time, my mother looked into his tiny face and said, "Maybe you will grow up to bring peace to the earth." Doug and I cracked up laughing at the grandiosity of this wish and teased my mother about it. What happened to the traditional grandmotherly desire that the new grandchild grow up to be a doctor, or president, or something "small" and reasonable like that? My mother's words have stayed with me, however, reminding me during the twelve intervening years to dream big while doing my own tiny part to change the world.

When I was a child, my mother did a lot of volunteer work, for which she often volunteered my siblings and me as well. One of my earliest memories involves me at five pulling a wagon loaded with my almost-two-year-old brother and flyers for John F. Kennedy's presidential campaign as my mother, carrying my baby sister, knocked on all our neighbors' doors, reminding them to vote. When Kennedy won, I felt personally responsible. I may even have expected an invitation to the inaugural ball. I remember countless hours devoted to making hideous gee-gaws for the Franciscan Missionary Sisters for Africa's annual Christmas bazaar and spring festival, and years of holidays spent with at least three mentally ill women, given day passes from the local asylum to enjoy a family celebration but lacking families of their own. I also remember going with my mother (admittedly with a very ill grace and a lot of whining on my part) to tenement houses that seemed horribly dark and smelly to deliver heavy bags of food to families my father had met through his work on an ad-hoc committee for low-income housing.

My family was Catholic, and a Catholic theme ran through my mother's various activities: Kennedy was Catholic, the nuns were of course Catholic, my mother met the mentally ill women through a Catholic hospital-visiting program, and I suspect that the food we delivered came from members of my parents' church. My mother's one area of non-Catholic volunteerism was the work she did for our local elementary school, including running the annual book fair (with which my siblings and I had to help, too).

In my early teens, I left the Catholic church and my mother's Catholic-based volunteering behind. I became active in anti-war protests and, a few years later, joined a feminist consciousness-raising group. I worked for George McGovern during my last year of high school, setting a pattern of volunteering for losing candidates that persists to this day. I finished college and went off to graduate school in the Midwest, firmly convinced that my life was very different from my mother's. After years of feeling stretched too thin across various projects, I devised a system for saying "no" to the representatives of various worthy causes who asked for my help. I would ask myself, "Does this group/cause/person promote feminism?" If not, I would decline to participate. If so, I would consider how I could help. Feminism became the theme that unified my activities, a parallel to my mother's Catholicism.

And then Brendan was born and my life totally changed, despite my resolve before his birth that my child would simply fit into my life, which I imagined would pretty much continue as it had been if I did not allow myself to become totally absorbed in motherhood. Becoming Brendan's mother gave me a new way of seeing, and that new vision led me to different ways of acting in the world. My crucial question—"does this group/cause/person promote feminism?"—began to seem inadequate and, eventually, downright mistaken in its assumptions.

I am exaggerating just a bit here: my life did not utterly change the moment Brendan was born. Instead, it happened in increments across two years or more. My husband is black; I am white. Before our son Brendan's birth, we had discussed race and racism in relation to children, trying to figure out strategies for explaining both to our child and, more importantly, for teaching him to resist racism. At two, Brendan started asking questions about race, and I quickly came to know that my education in race and racism was far from complete, despite nine years as half of an interracial couple and a vast amount of reading and listening about race. Brendan's questions challenged Doug's and my basic assumptions about race, alerting us to huge areas that we had left unexamined in our own lives.

I had known, or believed, that an important part of my child's life would be quite different from my own childhood: He would be black in a racist society, while as a white child I had been shielded from—and had unconsciously benefited by—that society's racism. What we had not considered was that our child's experience would also be different from Doug's, as Doug had two black parents, while Brendan did not. We had thought of Brendan as black, but it soon became clear that he was not *only* black and that having a white mother was an important element of his experience that differed from Doug's. His earliest questions were shaped by the differences he observed between us and the gap between what he saw at home and what he saw at day care and in books. He figured out quickly that race mattered, and that our family did not correspond to the most common images of families in his social world. We knew no interracial couples with children older than Brendan and could find nothing in print to help us to deal with Brendan's questions, so we struggled along on our own, never confident that we were doing the right thing.[1]

Although some of the racial issues we faced with Brendan were specifically related to his being biracial, many more pressing ones were the same faced by black children, particularly black boys, especially as he entered elementary school. While I had worked against racism so far as I had been aware of it before becoming a mother, I gained a more acute awareness of racism through mothering Brendan. Instead of thinking of racial justice as a broad social goal, I began thinking of it in relation to my own child. Racial justice became personalized: It was my beloved son's life that was threatened by racism, and consequently ending racism became urgent. Not that I ever imagined that I individually could end racism; I simply felt a more immediate responsibility for doing my part, however small, to contribute to racial justice. My new conception of myself as a mother of a black boy led me to change my basic question about political causes. My new question was "does this cause/ group/person promote antiracism and feminism?" I could answer affirmatively for astonishingly few groups; the feminist ones were not necessarily dedicated to antiracism, and the antiracist ones were not necessarily dedicated to feminism. Despite the much-remarked tension between women of color and white women, the people with whom I felt the strongest sense of comradeship were black mothers, feminist or not. Many black mothers I met had a sense of urgency about ending racism that was too often lacking among white mothers in general, including feminists. Black mothers of sons, in particular, faced struggles similar to my own. When our daughter Siobhan was born, eight years after Brendan, I began feeling that comradeship with black mothers of daughters as well.

While pregnant with Brendan, I had looked forward to joining a community of mothers. Virtually all my friends were connected in some way with the academic community, as I was in my fourth year of graduate school. Some of these friendships were becoming fraught with anxiety and a tense competitiveness as a group of us applied for scarce fellowships and even scarcer jobs. Having a child, I imagined, would admit me to other circles, centering around the playground, the daycare center, and such—all far in spirit if not in miles from the university. Getting to know women as mothers would be a relief, I thought, from this competition and anxiety. Naively, I thought making connections with other mothers would be easy: we would have shared concerns and experiences that would make establishing bonds between us simple.

Like almost everything else I imagined about mothering before I actually became a mother, this vision of a community of mothers turned out to be an attractive fantasy with little basis in reality. I did indeed meet mothers and even formed friendships with some. Establishing superficial bonds was easy enough through conversations about the minutia of daily life with children. Pushing past that superficial level was much more difficult. The chief barrier to forming a community of mothers was the definition of motherhood as private, within which most of the white mothers of white children I met situated their mothering work, seldom consciously; it was a definition I had shared without much thought until I began to feel restrained and alienated by it. Privatized mothering, it became clear, reinforced the racist, sexist status quo by encouraging—requiring, actually—competition rather than cooperation among mothers.

I encountered less competition among mothers of black children; however, I met far fewer of them. Making connections with black mothers was difficult not only because of the economic and racial segregation of the city where we then lived, but also because of the (understandable) suspicion with which my efforts to connect were frequently met. Until we moved to the Northeast and Brendan, at three, entered a daycare center that was predominantly black, I knew few mothers of black children around Brendan's age. But by that time, I had experience with one intriguing and, in my view, hopeful phenomenon. Whenever I took Brendan almost anywhere—playgrounds, meetings, daycare center,

YMCA, barber shop—black women would approach me, some out of curiosity, some to offer overtures of friendship, and some just to give advice, based on the assumption that no white woman would know how to raise a black child. Whatever their diverse motives, the women who approached me shared at least one thing: the belief that we had something important in common because we were raising black children.

Patricia Hill Collins has written persuasively about the tradition of "othermothering" and "community othermothering" in black communities.[2] According to Collins, African-American mothering is inclusive rather than exclusive, with black women more likely to recognize responsibility for other women's children than are white women. Historically, informal adoption and extended kin networks—whether blood-related or not—have been common among black people in the United States, a tradition that leads to what Collins describes as "othermothering": acting maternally toward a child not one's own by birth or formal adoption. "Community othermothering" is a logical extension of that tradition into a public realm, where women act politically on behalf of children in their community, broadly defined. For such women, *all* black children are "our children."

"Othermothering" is the antithesis of privatized, competitive mothering. Just as the latter supports a racist and sexist status quo, "othermothering" disrupts that status quo. "Othermothering" grew in part from the exigencies of resisting white supremacist attempts to undermine black families, but I think "othermothering" could serve as a model for antiracist work, which should *deliberately* seek to redefine "family" outside the repressive norms of white, patriarchal, nuclear entities. Developing an othermother consciousness demands that white women, in particular, be willing to start from scratch in order to remake our conceptions of mothering. At the very least, we need to acknowledge that no element of mothering can be separated from politics. Every choice we make as mothers is made within a political context and has political implications.

"Othermothering" requires us to challenge the conventional wisdom, used to excuse so many racist choices—that is, "everyone wants the best for their children"—by questioning that cliché. Does "the best" mean gaining privileges for one's own birth or adoptive children without regard for, or at the expense of, other children? By "the best" do people really mean that short-term privileges (such as an elite education) should be valued above long-term social goals (such as racial justice)? And, most importantly, who counts as "their children"?

Perhaps paradoxically, as a mother of black children, I began trying to develop an othermother consciousness from purely selfish motives. It was clear to me that my children's lives were intimately bound up with the lives of other black children; improving my own children's possibilities perforce included trying to improve other black children's lives. Seeing our children as some sort of exceptions, unrelated to other black people, never struck Doug and me as a desirable or even viable option. "The best" we wanted for our children, then, required action outside our family; working on behalf of our own children was impossible without working for all black children, except in the most limited, least effective ways.

Further, although there are increasing numbers of interracial families in the United States, we are still a tiny segment of the population and only sporadically visible in the media. Doug and I want our children to feel connected to other people, to see themselves not as isolated, comparatively powerless individuals but as participants in something bigger than themselves and hence powerful through collective action. Both Doug and I were raised in religions that were important to us as children and that gave both of us a sense of belonging; we have no religion now, but wanted to provide a context for our children that would give them a similar sense of belonging. Politics, especially small-scale community action, gives our children that grounding.

By the time Brendan entered elementary school, I had put in years of the common sorts of political/social service work: writing letters, making phone calls, canvassing neighborhoods, pressuring politicians, giving testimony at various hearings, protesting, giving and raising money, serving on committee after committee and board after board, and, of course, attending meeting upon meeting upon meeting. Some of the groups I worked with failed miserably, others enjoyed some success; none totally changed the world, but all changed something about some part of that world, if only one person's view of one issue.

On Brendan's first day of first grade, Doug and I accompanied him to school. We were overwhelmed by what seemed a sea of white faces punctuated by a very few children of color. We had known the school in which we had enrolled him was predominantly white, had even known the school's precise racial statistics, but I had not fully grasped what 15 percent so-called minority would *look* like in the context of 85 percent white. It was a shocker, especially coming on the heels of two years at a daycare center that was 75 percent "minority." I worried about how Brendan would fare in this context, but I also worried about the other children of color. Leaving the school with a friend—a black woman whose daughter was entering the second grade—I mentioned how stunned I had been by that sea of whiteness. She had the same feeling. We should do something. What? On the spot, we decided to form a support group for parents of "minority" children. Actually, my friend suggested we form a "black parents' support group," but agreed to expand it when I pointed out that I would not be included in that group.

Organizing this group took months, as we were blocked at several points by the school administration. First they refused to give us the names and addresses of the parents of "minority" students, citing confidentiality. Then they refused to distribute a notice about a preliminary meeting to the entire school, arguing that they could not help in any way with any group that was not 100 percent inclusive. When we opened the group to include anyone "interested in multicultural issues," we still met with stonewalling. This all made sense, since the administration realized that any such group was bound to stir up trouble. My friend and I finally organized the group entirely by word of mouth, with the help of a sympathetic teacher. At a preliminary meeting at my house, a small group of parents (basically everyone my friend and I already knew in the school) and the teacher brainstormed to list the names of all the "minority" children in the school, along with their parents' names if we knew them and the names of white people we thought would be supportive. We tracked down some of these parents using the phone book and a process of elimination, and reached others by haunting the school's halls in the mornings and afternoons, approaching any adults we saw with "minority" children and telling them of our plan to meet.

This group started out with a limited mission—to offer support to parents of "minority" children in this overwhelmingly white school—but changed almost immediately, when at our first large meeting we learned that problems each of us had thought of as isolated and minor were in fact shared by many of our children. We then set an ambitious agenda: to pressure the school to admit more "minority" students and to hire more "minority" teachers, to obtain financial aid specifically earmarked for "minority" students, and to change the school's curriculum from traditional and white-dominated to multicultural, all with the larger goal of making the school a more congenial place for children of color. We started working on small things—instituting a celebration of Black History Month, for instance, and volunteering ourselves for class projects and field trips—and, flush with our success in these areas, started a long, frequently demoralizing series of actions on our larger agenda. Some people dropped out of the group, others joined. We got into several ugly, tangled confrontations with teachers and with the established parents' organization. We had numerous internal squabbles. Our group splintered apart and reconstituted itself several times. On balance, we failed more than we succeeded, if measured by comparing our original, ambitious agenda to what actually changed in the school.

When Doug and I switched Brendan to a new school at the end of fourth grade, I felt like a deserter in a losing battle. Looking back now, nearly three years later, I am proud of this group's work, and can see the lasting impact it had, on the school itself but also, and more importantly, on some of the people who worked with the group, including myself. The group provided a safe place for parents to talk about race and racism as it affected their children, while also empowering people to act against that racism with group support, which is generally more effective than acting alone in a school. The group could take credit for the hiring of one "minority" teacher (of twenty-two teachers in all, but of just two new hires in the years we were working) and for the admission of more "minority" students. We were largely responsible for the school's instituting an annual Black History Month celebration, still ongoing. I think we also raised awareness of racial issues among some teachers, parents, and students, and improved the atmosphere for "minority" students.

Why, then, did most of the original group members feel that we had failed? I think the answer is that the successes we had were comparatively small and came slowly. Racism persisted, of course, in the school as in the wider society. Despite the group's including many veterans of civil rights and other long-term struggles, we wanted massive changes to happen quickly, and were disappointed when they did not. Our children would have, at most, seven years in the school. We wanted to improve those children's school years and, therefore, had a very short time in which to accomplish a great deal.

Being a feminist mother of a black boy in a school rife with racial tension and sexist to its core might have on its own caused me to look critically at my own position as a college professor. After leaving Brendan on that first day of first grade, when I was so shocked by the visual image of the school's overwhelming whiteness, I entered my own classes with new eyes. Of the thirty students in one women's studies class, two were Asian, four were black, two were Latina and the rest were white. Although the class had met twice already and although this racial breakdown was marginally better than the norm at my college, I suddenly saw it as intimidatingly, powerfully white. I know that working with the parents' group prompted me to hold fast to that view of whiteness as overpowering and to examine my teaching for ways to reduce the impact of that whiteness. Listening as both a mother and a professor to black mothers' stories about their own and their children's experiences in white-dominated schools and colleges forever changed my view of what I should be doing as a professor and caused me to bring some of that "othermother" consciousness to my own teaching.

After Brendan left that school, Doug and I became involved in a parents' group at his new school, and did more formal kinds of volunteering. I taught a mini-course at Brendan's new school, for instance, and we both worked on raising money for the school, which provides financial aid to 90 percent of its students and is itself desperately poor. I got involved with a daycare center that serves mainly a poor and "minority" clientele. And I worked for two (losing, of course) progressive candidates for political office, both antiracist and feminist. Doug and I felt like we were on a vacation from the hard work our old parents' group had done. We enjoyed the break, but we both knew we could do more, and felt vaguely guilty about the "vacation."

Two years after Brendan switched schools, I read a newspaper article about the disproportionate number of black and biracial children in state custody. The author noted that the majority of these children are in white foster homes or in institutions where the staff is predominantly white. Doug and I had already decided that we could not adopt or act as foster parents, given other demands on us, but we wanted to do something. We heard about a visiting program, which seemed modeled on the Big Brother and Big Sister programs, and looked into participating. After a lengthy application and vetting process, including some training, we were approved as visitors and looked forward to meeting a child.

Although we had asked to be matched with a particular black teenage boy, we were called to meet with a social worker about two younger children, Jessica and James, black siblings who were in institutional care. The children's social worker, a young white woman with a brisk manner, took just ten minutes to deliver, in a rapid monotone, a bruising narrative of nearly unimaginable loss and misery. To conclude our interview, she plucked a picture of the children from her bulletin board and handed it to us. "By the way," she said to me as we looked at the picture, "Jessica has a lot of trouble with white women, so don't expect her to warm up to you right away, and don't be hurt if she acts like she doesn't like you."

I was flabbergasted. The visiting program was supposed to be *fun* for the children, a break from their institutional routine and a chance to participate in family activities. Why compromise the whole point of the program by inflicting a white woman on a black girl who has "trouble with white women"? I tried to make this point to the social worker, but she misunderstood my concern. "Oh, I don't think she'll be mean to you or anything," she said by way of reassurance, "I'm just warning you she might not trust you."

"Look, I don't care if she *is* mean to me and I really don't see why she *should* trust me as soon as she meets me, if ever. My point is that I don't want to be an additional burden to this child. It sounds like her life is rough enough already. Why add one more problem? If she has trouble with white women, why force another white woman on her?"

The social worker looked at me blankly and then turned to Doug, reiterating that she doubted Jessica would be "mean." Both Doug and I tried to explain our reservations. Was there some reason that Jessica *must* like white women? Why was the social worker so determined to match us with these particular children if at least one of us was likely to be met with suspicion? The social worker simply continued to brush off our concerns. We tried a different angle, asking what led the social worker to think Jessica had trouble with white women. Well, Jessica did not trust her therapist, a white woman, nor had she warmed up to the social worker, also a white woman; therefore, Jessica must have trouble with white women. Doug and I looked at each other in amazement. We were both far from "warming up" to this social worker. Did that mean we had trouble with white women?

Eventually, we did meet the children and began a relationship with them that has added greatly to our family's life, while also filling me with despair about the child social services system. The children lived in a "home" reputed to be the best in the state, yet the more we learned about it the more we loathed it. The place was totally rule-bound, and about as unlike a real "home" as can be imagined. During one of our first visits, Jessica and James asked us about the rules for food in our house. What time is lunch? What time is snack? When we explained that we didn't really have set times for meals, and definitely not for snacks, they fell silent. Concerned they might think they would not be fed when they visited us, I added, "Just tell me when you're hungry, and I'll get you something to eat." This sent six-year-old James off into a fit of giggles. Jessica, two years older, said confidentially to us, "He probably thinks now that he can ask for a snack any time," and laughed knowingly. "That's right," Doug said. Back to stunned silence.

What Jessica and James did not know about ordinary daily life could have filled several volumes, and I found our first visits with them totally exhausting because *everything* had to be explained. After one entire day of fielding questions from Jessica and James, as well as from then-three-year-old Siobhan, I flopped on the couch with relief after we dropped them off at the "home." "Just think of it as spending the day with the guy from *Brother From Another Planet*," Doug advised me jokingly, although he too was tired. "Who is the brother from another planet?" Siobhan asked.

Some of the ignorance Jessica and James betrayed had me fuming silently at the workers at the "home." For instance, Jessica told me she would like to be a model when she grows up and mentioned that the houseparents said she could probably be a model. While it is true that she is quite pretty, modeling does not strike me as a very high ambition, and I told her so, mentioning that modeling is not usually a lifetime career choice, but limited to a few years, and that few models actually make enough money to support themselves. I did not want to destroy her fantasy entirely—after all, my own son once announced that he planned to be a unicorn when he grew up, and I did not burst that bubble—and so I said, "You know, Jessica, modeling might be a good way for you to earn money for college."

"What's college?" James and Jessica asked simultaneously. As I explained, they asked more questions, and I realized that no one had ever talked to these children about education. They had no idea what education of any sort is *for;* the most they could tell me was that "everybody has to" go to school and that it's good to know how to read. They also had no idea how schooling works. Jessica mentioned that she thought people were in school until they are "at least fifteen." James laughed derisively at this information, "Yeah right, Jessica! No way you're that old in school!" When I told them that I was in school until I was twenty-nine, they were amazed, and unsure whether to believe me. Maybe I was kidding them? Maybe I was not very smart and therefore had to stay in school for a long time? They did not know what to think.

Doug and I started talking to the children about education, trying to plant the idea that they should aim at college, thinking that perhaps in this one way we could have a positive impact on their lives. For both of us, this decision was specifically racial. The school drop-out rate among black children far exceeds that among whites, and fewer black students than whites are in college preparatory programs in high school. Recent research suggests that the early years in education are the most crucial and that family expectations are even more of a predictor of college attendance than is family income. Jessica and James did not have a family to give them such expectations. Doug and I were outraged that none of the many white people entrusted with Jessica's and James's care had noticed their intelligence enough to encourage them to see themselves as learners and, eventually, as college students. When I mentioned the first conversation about school to Jessica's therapist, a well-meaning but dim woman, she was taken aback: "Gee, that never occurred to me. I'll be sure to say something to her about college. That's a good point."

On another visit, a month or so after we first met Jessica and James, we took them, Brendan, and Siobhan to a restaurant for dinner to celebrate James's birthday. It was his choice of celebration, as he said he was "dying" to eat a lobster. Neither Jessica nor James had ever been to a restaurant fancier than McDonalds, and they were both wildly excited, bouncing on their chairs as they waited for their food. I got up to take Siobhan to the salad bar (it was not a *very* fancy restaurant), and heard James's voice across the restaurant, "Hey, Doug! How can you be a family? You are black and Maureen's white!" I certainly do not think this was the first time James had noticed our races. I think this racial difference had probably been on his mind for a while, but his tongue was finally loosened by the thrill of getting his wish for his birthday dinner.

Doug was still explaining when I got back to the table, while also trying to find out the basis of James's question. Did he think family members all had to be one color? Yes, he thought that was the law. "Don't they [unspecified] *make* you marry someone the right color?" James asked. Jessica was clearly mortified, and tried to prevent James from saying anything more. The subject made her terribly uncomfortable. I thought she might be worried that Doug and I would be angry and stop visiting with her and her brother, so I tried to reassure her. "Jessica," I said to her quietly, "it's okay to ask anything you want to ask. If we can't answer or don't want to answer, we'll tell you, but we'd never be angry about questions."

She seemed unconvinced. Looking close to tears, she said, "It's just so rude to talk about that stuff! You're not supposed to say 'black' or 'white.' That's racist."

"No, it isn't," Doug said from across the table. "Why do you think that?"

We learned that the staff at the "home" had instructed the children never to refer to race in any way, deeming all mentions of race "racist." Jessica had been racially name-called at the public school she attended while living at the group home, but had not been allowed to discuss the problem with anyone because reporting the racial insult earned her a punishment. Apparently, describing the offending child as "a white boy" was considered as "racist" as that same child's calling Jessica a "nigger." Jessica and James were under the supervision of the type of white people that I firmly believe are most responsible for the intransigence of racism. People who think racism cuts both ways, who confuse any interest in race with racism, who proudly assert that they (and their children) "don't see color; race doesn't matter to us." It does not matter to them because it doesn't have to; whiteness confers the great privilege of ignoring race whenever one wishes. Race does have to matter to black children, however, and denying the social significance of race does nothing to promote the end of racism. As Doug and I gave each other a where-do-we-start-to-deal-with-this look across the table, Brendan whispered, "Good luck, Mom," and left for the men's room.

We ended up talking a lot about race that day and on many other visits as well. We talk about race often in our family in any case, and so we just added Jessica and James in to those conversations. I recently told Jessica about a problem I had with Siobhan. When I went to pick up Siobhan at her preschool, she was arguing with another child about where to put some little figures. Her friend, Michael (a black boy), persisted in dumping all the figures into one box, which was too small to hold them all. Siobhan, instead of randomly dividing the figures and placing them in two boxes, was practicing segregation, insisting that Michael follow her lead by placing all the black figures in one box and all the white ones in another. When I asked why she was so set on this division, she said "These [black] people are one family, and these [white] people are a family. They should all be put away with their own families." The teacher, a black woman, said, "Siobhan, why do you think they are two families? Couldn't they be one family, like yours?" Absolutely not, according to Siobhan: "These are just ordinary people, not different like my family." When I relayed this incident to Jessica, curious about her reaction, she said, "That reminds me of James, when he thought people had to marry someone the same color as them. You better get Brendan to straighten Siobhan out." No anxiety, none of the discomfort Jessica had shown on the first occasion race came up. I was delighted; the year we have known Jessica has made some difference in her life.

Although Jessica and James are now in the process of being adopted, we are still involved with them and plan to continue to be part of their lives. We have also begun visiting with a thirteen-year-old boy who has been in state custody since he was three. He is now the only black child in his class and among the very few black children in the rural public school he attends. One of the white social workers we met with to discuss visiting with Henry claimed that racial imbalance was not a problem at all. "The other kids really accept Henry. In fact, he's just like their pet," he told us, smiling. "Their *pet?*" I asked incredulously, "This child is like a *pet* and you think that's okay?" Doug shot me a warning look, and I backed off. Later, he reminded me that we cannot have any positive impact on Henry's life if we cannot meet him because we get into a fight with the social workers. "We can fight them later," he commented. Good strategy.

Has our serving as visitors for these children changed the world? Yes, I would argue that it has. Our visits have changed Jessica's and James's worlds, at least a little bit, and they have changed our family's world as well. Changing the wider world is a long, collective, continuing process. My mother believed she could change the world, and tried hard to do so every day. Brendan has not yet realized her hope by bringing peace to the earth, but he's working on it, too, and now he has his sister, Siobhan, to share that responsibility. Brendan learned this week that his application to City Year's Young Heroes Program had been accepted. He danced around, waving the acceptance letter over his head, and punching the air with his other hand, yelling "Yes! Yes!" What was he celebrating? The opportunity to spend eleven spring Saturdays, 8:30 a.m. to 4:30 p.m., as part of a volunteer corps working on cleaning up vacant lots, tutoring, planting community gardens, painting daycare centers and the like. Was he sure he wanted to forgo baseball? Was he certain he could commit all those Saturdays to *work* (unpaid, even)? Yes, definitely. Why? He showed me the Young Heroes mission statement, which includes such assertions as "We, the youth of today, do hereby commit ourselves to positive social change" and "We understand that the problems of society will not go away until we take action."

"I really believe those things, Mom," he said, "and I think I'd be good at the stuff they do. I'm old enough to do something like that, don't you think?" Siobhan added, "I wish *I* were old enough! I'm sick of being too little for all the fun stuff."

When Brendan was six, he asked me what our religion was. "Politics," I answered, just partly joking. Politics do indeed stand in the place of my mother's Catholicism in my own life. I hope that Brendan and Siobhan do not leave this "church," but I know I cannot predict what their choices will be. For now, I'm proud of Brendan for taking action independently of Doug and me, choosing a group on his own that he thinks is worthy of his time and efforts. Will those eleven Saturdays change the world? Emphatically, yes.

Notes

1. I discuss these issues in greater detail in *Crossing the Color Line: Race, Parenting, and Culture* (New Brunswick, NJ: Rutgers Unviersity Press, 1994).

2. See Patricia Hill Collins, *Black Feminist Thought: Knowledge, Consciousness, and the Politics of Empowerment* (New York: Unwin Hyman, 1990), 119–130.

Bibliography

Adamec, Christine A. *There ARE Babies to Adopt: A Resource Guide for Prospective Parents.* Bedford, MA: Mills & Sanders, 1987.

Agosin, Marjorie, ed. *Surviving Beyond Fear: Women, Children, and Human Rights in Latin America.* Fredonia, NY: White Pine Press, 1993.

Allen, Jeffner. "Motherhood: The Annihilation of Women." In *Feminist Frameworks: Alternative Theoretical Accounts of the Relations Between Women and Men.* 3d ed., edited by Alison M. Jagger and Paula S. Rothenberg. New York: McGraw-Hill, 1984.

Alvarado, Elvia. *Don't Be Afraid, Gringo: A Honduran Woman Speaks from the Heart,* translated and edited by Medea Benjamin. New York: HarperPerennial/Harper & Row, 1989.

Anonymous. "Ethnic Images: A Primer for Adoptive Parents." *Ours* (May/June 1990).

Appiah, Kwame Anthony. "Racisms." In *Anatomy of Racism,* edited by David Theo Goldberg. Minneapolis: University of Minnesota Press, 1990.

Bakhtin, Mikhail. *The Dialogic Imagination,* edited by Michael Holquist, translated by Michael Holquist and Caryl Emerson. Austin: University of Texas Press, 1981.

Bell, Derrick. *Faces at the Bottom of the Well: The Permanence of Racism.* New York: Basic Books, 1992.

Bell-Scott, Patricia, et al. *Double Stitch: Black Women Write About Mothers and Daughters.* New York: HarperPerennial, 1993.

Blau, Eric. *Stories of Adoption: Loss and Reunion.* Portland, OR: New Sage Press, 1993.

Boxhill, Bernard. *Blacks and Social Justice.* Lanham: Rowan & Allanheld, 1984.

Boyarin, Jonathan. *Storm from Paradise: The Politics of Jewish Memory.* Minneapolis: University of Minnesota Press, 1992.

Boyd, Julia A. *Girlfriend to Girlfriend: Everyday Wisdom and Affirmations from the Sister Circle.* New York: Dutton, 1995.

Brophy, Nanette. *The Color of My Fur.* Nashville: Winston-Derek, 1992.

Brown, Elsa Barkley. "African-American Women's Quilting: A Framework for Conceptualizing and Teaching African-American Women's History." In *Black Women in America: Social Science Perspectives*, edited by Micheline R. Malson, et al. Chicago: University of Chicago Press, 1990.

Bunch, Charlotte. "Making Common Cause: Diversity and Coalitions." In *Passionate Politics*. New York: St. Martins, 1987.

Caruth, Cathy, ed. *Trauma: Explorations in Memory*. Baltimore: Johns Hopkins University Press, 1995.

Caulfield, Mina Davis. "Imperialism, the Family and Cultures of Resistance." In *Feminist Frameworks: Alternative Theoretical Accounts of the Relations Between Women and Men*. 3d ed., edited by Alison M. Jagger and Paula S. Rothenberg. New York: McGraw-Hill, 1984.

Chodorow, Nancy. *The Reproduction of Mothering*. Berkeley: University of California Press, 1978.

Cole, Johnetta B. "What If We Made Racism a Woman's Issue . . . " *McCalls* (October 1990).

Collins, Patricia Hill. "Shifting the Center: Race, Class, and Feminist Theorizing About Motherhood." In *Mothering: Ideology, Experience, and Agency*, edited by Evelyn Nakano Glenn, Grace Chang and Linda Rennie Forcey. New York: Routledge, 1994.

———.*Black Feminist Thought: Knowledge, Consciousness and the Politics of Empowerment*. New York: Unwin Hyman, 1990.

Comer, James P., and Alvin F. Poussaint. *Raising Black Children*. New York: Plume, 1992.

Commission, Wilesse A.F. *The Best Face of All*. Chicago: African American Images, 1991.

Curry, Blanche Radford. "Racism and Sexism: Twenty-First Century Challenges for Feminists." In *Overcoming Racism and Sexism*, edited by Linda A. Bell and David Blumenfeld. Lanham: Rowman & Littlefield, 1995.

Dance, Daryl Cumber. *Shuckin' and Jivin': Folklore from Contemporary Black Americans*. Bloomington: Indiana University Press, 1978.

Delancy, Dayle. "Motherlove Is a Killer: *Sula, Beloved*, and the Deadly Trinity of Motherlove." *Sage* 8, 2 (1990).

Dill, Bonnie Thornton. "Our Mothers' Grief: Racial Ethnic Women and the Maintenance of Families." In *Race, Class and Gender*, edited by Margaret L. Andersen and Patricia Hill Collins. Belmont, CA: Wadsworth, 1988.

Du Bois, W.E.B. *The Souls of Black Folk*. New York: Viking, 1903.

Duncan, Sydney. "Healing Old Wounds." Paper presented at the North American Conference on Adoptable Children, St. Louis, MO, 1988.

Ezorsky, Gertrude. *Racism and Justice: The Case for Affirmative Action.* Ithaca: Cornell University Press, 1991.

Fanon, Franz. "The Fact of Blackness." In *Anatomy of Racism,* edited by David Theo Goldberg. Minneapolis: University of Minnesota Press, 1990.

Felman, Shoshana. "Education and Crisis, or the Vicissitudes of Teaching." In *Trauma: Explorations in Memory,* edited by Cathy Caruth. Baltimore: Johns Hopkins University Press, 1995.

Felsen, Henry Gregor. *To My Son in Uniform.* Cincinnati, OH: Dodd, Mead & Company, 1987.

Franklin, John Hope. *From Slavery to Freedom.* New York: Knopf, 1980.

Freire, Paulo. *Pedagogy of the Oppressed.* New York: Continuum, 1993.

Friedan, Betty. *The Feminine Mystique.* New York: Dell, 1963.

Gaines, Ernest J. *A Lesson Before Dying.* New York: Vintage, 1993.

Goldberg, David Theo, ed. *Anatomy of Racism.* Minneapolis: University of Minnesota Press, 1990.

Gravel, Jane. "Agency-Parent Panel Speech." Paper presented at Seminar on Adoption of Special Needs Children, Conference on Adoptable Children, Orlando, FL, 1982.

Green, Judith M., and Blanche Radford Curry. "Recognizing Each Other Amidst Diversity: Beyond Essentialism in Collaborative Multi-Cultural Feminist Theory." *Sage* 8, 1 (1991).

Greenman, Nancy P., Ellen B. Kimmel, Helen M. Bannan and Blanche Radford Curry. "Institutional Inertia to Achieving Diversity: Transforming Resistance into Celebration." *Educational Foundations* 6, 2 (1992).

Gwaltney, John. *Drylongso.* New York: New Press, 1993.

Hampl, Patricia. "The Tenacity of Ruin." *New York Times Book Review.* 14 January 1996.

Harding, Vincent G. "Healing at the Razor's Edge: Reflections on a History of Multicultural America." *Journal of American History* 81, 2 (1994).

Harris, Leonard, ed. *The Philosophy of Alain Locke: Harlem Renaissance and Beyond.* Philadelphia: Temple University Press, 1989.

Hartman, Geoffrey. "Public Memory and Its Discontents." *Raritan* 8, 4 (1994).

Hoffman, Eva. *Lost in Translation: A Life in a New Language.* New York: Penguin Books, 1989.

Hoffman, Mary. *Amazing Grace.* Illus. Caroline Binch. New York: Scholastic, 1991.

hooks, bell. *Feminist Theory: From Margin to Center.* Boston: South End Press, 1984.

———. *Sisters of the Yam: Black Women and Self-Recovery.* Boston: South End Press, 1993.

———. *Talking Back: Thinking Feminist, Thinking Black.* Boston: South End Press, 1989.

———. *Yearning: Race, Gender, and Cultural Politics.* Boston: South End Press, 1990.

Hopson, Darlene, and Derek Hopson. *Different and Wonderful: Raising Black Children in a Race-Conscious Society.* New York: Simon & Schuster, 1992.

Jones, Jacqueline. *Labor of Love, Labor of Sorrow.* New York: Vintage, 1986.

Joseph, Gloria I., and Jill Lewis. *Common Differences: Conflicts in Black and White Feminist Perspectives.* Garden City, NY: Anchor, 1981.

Killens, John Oliver. *Youngblood.* Athens: University of Georgia Press, 1982.

King, Coretta Scott, comp. *The Words of Martin Luther King, Jr.* New York: Newmarket Press, 1983.

King, Martin Luther, Jr. *Where Do We Go From Here: Chaos or Community?* New York: Harper & Row, 1967.

Langer, Lawrence L. *Admitting the Holocaust: Collected Essays.* New York: Oxford University Press, 1995.

de Lauretis, Teresa. *Technologies of Gender.* Bloomington: Indiana University Press, 1987.

Lawson, Bill E., ed. *The Underclass Question.* Philadelphia: Temple University Press, 1992.

Lazarre, Jane. *Beyond the Whiteness of Whiteness: Memoir of a White Mother of Black Sons.* Durham, NC: Duke University Press, 1996.

Lester, Joan Steinau. *The Future of White Men and Other Diversity Dilemmas.* Berkeley: Conari Press, 1994.

Lindsay, Jeanne Warren. *Open Adoption: A Caring Option.* Buena Park, CA: Morning Glory Press, 1987.

Lorde, Audre. *Sister Outsider.* Freedom, CA: The Crossing Press, 1984.

McCalope, Michelle. "Should White Families Adopt Black Children?" *Jet* (January 1991).

McFarlane, Jan. "Building Self-Esteem in Children and Teens of Color." *Ours* (March/April 1992).

McIntosh, Peggy. "White Privilege and Male Privilege: A Personal Account of Coming to See Correspondences Through Work in Women's Studies." In *Race, Class and Gender: An Anthology.* 2d ed, edited by Margaret Andersen and Patricia Hill Collins. Belmont, CA: Wadsworth, 1995.

——."White Privilege: Unpacking the Invisible Knapsack." *Peace and Freedom* (July/August 1989).

McLaren, Peter and Kelly Estrada. "A Dialogue on Multiculturalism and Democratic Culture." *Educational Researcher* 22, 3 (1993).

McRoy, Ruth G., Harold D. Grotevant and Kerry L. White. *Openness in Adoption: New Practices, New Issues.* New York: Praeger, 1988.

Melina, Lois R. "Children Need Help Facing Negative Images of their Countries of Origin." *Adopted Child* 9 (February 1990).

——."Racial Identity of Children of Mixed Heritage Still Controversial." *Adopted Child.* 9 (May 1990).

——."Advice for Parents of Children of Mixed Racial Heritage." *Adopted Child* 9 (May 1990).

Modell, Judith S. *Kinship with Strangers: Adoption and Interpretations of Kinship in American Culture.* Berkeley: University of California Press, 1994.

Morales, Rosario. "We're All in the Same Boat." In *This Bridge Called My Back,* edited by Cherríe Moraga and Gloria Anzaldúa. New York: Kitchen Table: Women of Color Press, 1983.

Morrison, Toni. *Sula.* New York: New American Library, 1973.

——. *The Bluest Eye.* New York: Holt, 1970.

Naylor, Fred. "Freedom and Respect in Multicultural Society." *Journal of Applied Philosophy* 8, 2 (1991).

Park, Shelley M., and Michelle A. LaRocque. "Feminism, Multiculturalism and the Politics of the Academy." Paper presented at the South Eastern Women's Studies Association Conference, Tampa, FL, 1992.

Pharr, Suzanne. *Homophobia: A Weapon of Sexism.* Little Rock: Chardon Press, 1988.

Phillips, Randa. "Closed Adoption is Child Abuse." *Sojourner* 20 (May 1995).

Pope, Raechele L. "Multicultural-Organization Development in Student Affairs: An Introduction." *Journal of College Student Development* 34 (1993).

Powell, Azizi. "Raise Your Child with Ethnic Pride." *Ours* (November/December 1988).

Rappaport, Bruce M. *The Open Adoption Book: A Guide to Adoption Without Tears.* New York: MacMillan, 1992.

Ravitch, Diane. "Diversity and Democracy: Multicultural Education in America." *American Educator* 14 (1990).

Reddy, Maureen T. *Crossing the Color Line: Race, Parenting, and Culture.* New Brunswick: Rutgers University Press, 1994.

Reed, Evelyn. *Problems of Women's Liberation.* New York: Pathfinder Press, 1970.

Rensberger, Boyce. "Racial Odyssey." In *Applying Anthropology: An Introductory Reader,* edited by Aaron Podolefsky and Peter J. Brown. Mountain View, CA: Mayfield, 1992.

Rich, Adrienne. *Of Woman Born: Motherhood as Experience and Institution.* New York: W.W. Norton, 1986.

Ringgold, Faith. *Aunt Harriet's Underground in the Sky.* New York: Random House, 1993.

Ruddick, Sara. *Maternal Thinking: Toward a Politics of Peace.* Boston: Beacon, 1989.

Ryburn, Murray. *Open Adoption: Research, Theory and Practice.* Brookfield, VT: Ashgate, 1994.

Schaefer, Charles E., and Theresa DiGeronimo. *How to Talk to Your Kids About Really Important Things.* San Francisco: Jossey-Bass, 1994.

Silber, Kathleen, and Patricia Martinez Dorner. *Children of Open Adoption and Their Families.* San Antonio: Corona, 1990.

Smith, Barbara, and Beverly Smith. "Across the Kitchen Table: A Sister-to-Sister Dialogue." In *This Bridge Called My Back,* edited by Cherríe Moraga and Gloria Anzaldúa. New York: Kitchen Table: Women of Color Press, 1983.

Stack, Carol B. *All Our Kin: Strategies for Survival in a Black Community.* New York: Harper & Row, 1974.

Steady, Filomina Chioma, ed. *The Black Woman Cross-Culturally.* Rochester, VT: Schenkman Books, 1981.

Steptoe, John. *Mufaro's Beautiful Daughters*. New York: Lothrop, Lee & Shepard Books, 1987.

Takaki, Ronald. *A Different Mirror: A History of Multicultural America*. Boston: Beacon, 1993.

Taylor, Charles, and Susan Wolf. *Multiculturalism and the Politics of Recognition*. Princeton: Princeton University Press, 1992.

Walker, Alice. *In Search of Our Mothers' Gardens*. San Diego: Harcourt, Brace & Jovanovich, 1983.

——. *Meridian*. New York: Pocket Books, 1986.

Walkerdine, Valerie, and Helen Lucey. *Democracy in the Kitchen: Regulating Mothers and Socialising Daughters*. London: Virago Press, 1989.

Wardle, Francis. "Are You Sensitive to Interracial Children's Special Identity Needs?" *Young Children* (January 1987).

Washington, Valora. "The Black Mother in the United States: History, Theory, Research, and Issues." In *The Different Faces of Motherhood*, edited by Beverly Birns and Dale F. Hay. New York: Plenum Press, 1988.

West, Cornel. *Race Matters*. Boston: Beacon, 1993.

Williams, Patricia J. *The Alchemy of Race and Rights*. Cambridge: Harvard University Press, 1991.

Work, Deborah. "More Than Skin Deep: Can Adoptive Families Erase the Color Line?" *Sunshine* (14 October 1990).

Yamato, Gloria. "Something About the Subject Makes It Hard to Name." In *Race, Class and Gender: An Anthology*. 2d ed, edited by Margaret Andersen and Patricia Hill Collins. Belmont, CA: Wadsworth, 1995.

Zack, Naomi. *Race and Mixed Race*. Philadelphia: Temple University Press, 1993.

Contributors

Marguerite Guzman Bouvard is the author of four books of poetry as well as books in the fields of psychology, politics and sociology. Her most recent book, *Revolutionizing Motherhood: Mothers of the Plaza de Mayo,* appeared in 1994, and her book *Women Reshaping Human Rights from the Local to the Global,* is forthcoming in 1996. Bouvard, a professor of political science and poetry for twenty-five years, has taught poetry at the Radcliffe Seminars and has been a writer in residence at the University of Maryland. She is a resident scholar with the Women's Studies Program at Brandeis University.

Nancy Butcher is a Japanese-American writer whose work has appeared in *Short Fiction by Women,* the anthology *Love's Shadow* (The Crossing Press), and the *Baltimore Sun.* She also writes books for several children's mystery series, including *Ghostwriter.* Butcher lives in Saratoga Springs, New York, with her husband, Philip, and their son, Christopher.

Blanche Radford Curry is an associate professor of philosophy at Fayetteville State University. She earned her Ph.D. in philosophy at Brown University. Her research and teaching areas include moral and social value inquiry, multicultural theory and feminist philosophy. She is an assistant editor of the American Philosophical Association's "Newsletter on Philosophy and the Black Experience" and is on the editorial board of *Hypatia: Journal of Feminist Philosophy.* Her publications include articles on transformative philosophy, feminist philosophy and multicultural theory.

Eileen de los Reyes has lived in the United States with her family since 1972. She teaches in the Interdisciplinary Studies Department at Salem State College in Massachusetts. De los Reyes teaches in the Women's Studies Program and directs the Language Intensive Interdisciplinary Program for students for whom English is a second language. She is also a visiting lecturer at the Harvard School of Education, where she teaches the course Education for Social and Political Change.

Shawn Riva Donaldson received her B.A. and M.A. from the University of Pennsylvania and her Ph.D. in sociology from Rutgers University. A faculty member at the Richard Stockton College of New Jersey since 1980, Donaldson has served as the coordinator of African-American Studies, chair of the Sexual Harassment Subcommittee, president of the Council of Black Faculty and Staff and advisor to numerous student organizations. In addition, she has been active with local civic groups, such as the Pleasantville public school district and recreation advisory board. Recently promoted to associate professor, Donaldson teaches courses in sociology, African-American studies and women's studies.

Julia Epstein is Barbara Riley Levin professor of comparative literature at Haverford College. She is the coeditor, with Kristina Straub, of *Body Guards: The Cultural Politics of Gender Ambiguity* (1992). Epstein is the author of *The Iron Pen: Frances Burney and the Politics of Women's Writing* (1989) and of *Altered Conditions: Disease, Medicine, and Storytelling* (1995).

Phyllis Gray-Ray is an associate professor of criminal justice at North Carolina Central University. She received her Ph.D. in sociology from Iowa State University. Her areas of specialization focus on criminology, deviance, race relations and rural sociology. Gray-Ray has published in such journals as *Youth and Society, The Journal of Research on Crime and Delinquency* and *Rural Sociology.*

Daryl LaRoche lives in Jacksonville, Florida, with her teenage daughter. She is currently at work on her first book.

Jane Lazarre is the director of the Writing Program at the Eugene Lang College at the New School for Social Research in New York City, where she is a member of the faculty in writing and literature. Her published books include two works of nonfiction—*The Mother Knot* and *On Loving Men*—and three novels—*Some Kind of Innocence, The Powers of*

Charlotte and *Worlds Beyond My Control.* Her new memoir, *Beyond the Whiteness of Whiteness: Memoir of a White Mother of Black Sons,* is published by Duke University Press. Lazarre is a recipient of a National Endowment for the Arts award and a New York Foundation for the Arts award, both in fiction. Her work has been widely anthologized and published in magazines and periodicals.

Gary Lemons is a professor at the Eugene Lang College at the New School for Social Research in New York City. As a committed advocate of feminist movement, the liberation of black people and all people who struggle to be free, he teaches courses in African-American literature, gender and feminist studies, as well as cultural studies that speak to the practice of education as freedom.

Lynda Marín orchestrates a family, teaches part-time at the University of California, Santa Cruz, always plants too many tomatoes and spends more time than she would like driving her car. She is active in a number of groups organized around issues that pertain to women and children in the United States, Latin America and the Middle East. She is a drummer.

Jennifer E. Morales is a mother, poet, childbirth assistant, and activist living in Wisconsin with her husband and two sons. She was formerly the editorial assistant and grantwriter at the antiracist educational journal *Rethinking Schools.* Morales graduated from Beloit College in Beloit, Wisconsin, in 1991 with a B.A. in modern languages and literatures.

Yolanda Flores Niemann was raised in San Antonio, Texas, and received her Ph.D. in psychology from the University of Houston. Her research centers on the effects of stereotypes on person perception and on interethnic group relations. In addition to her faculty responsibilities at the University of Houston, Niemann is also director of the Division of Ethnic Diversity Issues for the Texas Psychological Association and a member of the Interethnic Forum of Houston, an organization that monitors race relations in the city of Houston. Her favorite activities involve her husband and their two teenage children.

Andrea O'Reilly teaches in the departments of English, humanities and women's studies at York University, Toronto, Canada and has developed courses for the women's studies curriculum there. She has published articles on Constance Beresford-Howe, Nicole Brossard, Charlotte Brontë and Toni Morrison, and her article on designing and teaching a motherhood course appears in *Feminism and Education* (CWSE Press, 1994). She is currently completing her dissertation on mothering as portrayed in the novels of Toni Morrison and writing a book on motherhood in contemporary feminist thought. O'Reilly is the mother of three young children and lives with her family in the country, north of Toronto.

Shelley Park is a white, middle-class, almost-middle-aged, heterosexual Canadian who lives and works in Orlando, Florida. She and her partner are the proud and overtired parents of two American-born preschool daughters. Park is assistant professor of philosophy at the University of Central Florida, where she teaches feminist theory, and is a member of UCF's Women's Studies Steering Committee and Cultural Diversity Task Force. Her research focuses on feminist issues, including the position of women in higher education, the debate over "false memory syndrome," and adoption. She and a colleague are currently collaborating on an anthology discussing adoption from diverse women's perspectives.

Martha Roth, born in Chicago in 1938, has been married to Marty Roth since 1957. They have three children. She has worked as a switchboard operator, actor, medical and scientific editor, publicist, waitress and market-research interviewer, and, as Martha Vanceburg, she cowrote several meditational guides. She is a coeditor of *Mother Journeys: Feminists Write About Mothering* (Spinsters Ink, 1994) and *Transforming a Rape Culture* (Milkweed Editions, 1993), and is a cofounder of *Hurricane Alice: A Feminist Quarterly.* Her novel *Goodness* was published by Spinsters Ink (1996).

Pauline A. Santos is mother (step, adoptive, biological) of six and grandmother of seven. She has worked at various Providence, Rhode Island, law firms for more than twenty-five years as a legal secretary/legal assistant. While working full-time, Santos earned a degree in human services, counseling, and family studies at the University of Rhode Island in 1993 at the age of forty-seven, and is currently a graduate student at the Rhode Island College School of Social Work. Santos grew up in the 1950s in a small New England town where there were fewer than a half dozen families of color. Being born to parents of black and white has colored her life as anything but.

Martha Satz, assistant professor of English at Southern Methodist University in Dallas, adopts children at eighteen-year intervals. Her teaching, which experiments with incorporating computer technology and volunteerism into the classroom, concentrates on minority literature, women's studies and nineteenth- and twentieth-century British literature. Satz's academic writing exploits her dual background in philosophy and literature. She has published on such subjects as Jane Austen, Mary Wilkins Freeman, Holocaust literature and the pedagogy of black literature. She is currently at work on a book, *What Can a Woman Know? What Should a Woman Do: Epistemological and Ethical Paradigms in Female Fiction.*

Linda H. Southward is an associate professor and director of the undergraduate Social Work Program and Chair of the Women's Studies Program at Mississippi State University. She received her Ph.D. in social work from the University of Alabama. Southward has nine years of social work practice and supervision experience in Mississippi. Her scholarly interests are in the area of social work in health care, with a particular research focus on violence against women.

Staci Swenson, a white lesbian mother in her late twenties, spent her teenage and initial adult years in the mountains of rural, white Appalachia, and first became aware of multicultural feminist politics at the age of twenty-one. She teaches a multicultural interdisciplinary course in the Department of Women's Studies at Ohio State University. Her course emphasizes the intersections of gender with race, class, sexual orientation, age and ability. She also works as a patient advocate for women and girls with unplanned pregnancies. Currently living in Columbus, Ohio, with her daughter and her partner, Swenson is completing her M.A. in women's studies before continuing her education in counseling.

About the Editor

Maureen T. Reddy is a professor of English and director of the Women's Studies Program at Rhode Island College. Her previous books include *Crossing the Color Line: Race, Parenting, and Culture* (Rutgers University Press), *Mother Journeys: Feminist Write About Mothering* (coedited with Martha Roth and Amy Sheldon; Spinsters Ink), and *Sisters in Crime: Feminism and the Crime Novel* (Continuum).

Selected Titles from Seal Press

Parenting

THE ADOPTION READER: *Birth Mothers, Adoptive Mothers and Adopted Daughters Tell Their Stories*, edited by Susan Wadia-Ells. $15.95, 1-878067-65-6.

THE SINGLE MOTHER'S COMPANION: *Essays and Stories by Women*, edited by Marsha R. Leslie. $12.95, 1-878067-56-7.

WHAT PARENTS NEED TO KNOW ABOUT DATING VIOLENCE, by Barrie Levy and Patricia Occhiuzzo Giggans. $10.95, 1-878067-47-8.

THE LESBIAN PARENTING BOOK: *A Guide to Creating Families and Raising Children*, by D. Merilee Clunis and G. Dorsey Green. $16.95, 1-8780670-68-0.

PAST DUE: *A Story of Disability, Pregnancy and Birth* by Anne Finger. $10.95, 0-931188-87-3.

Popular Culture and Feminist Studies

LISTEN UP: *Voices from the Next Feminist Generation*, edited by Barbara Findlen. $12.95, 1-878067-61-3.

WIRED WOMEN: *Gender and New Realities in Cyberspace*, edited by Elizabeth Reba Weise. $16.00, 1-878067-73-7.

SURFERGRRRLS: *Look Ethel! An Internet Guide for Us* by Laurel Gilbert and Crystal Kile. $15.00, 1-878067-79-6.

CLOSER TO HOME: *Bisexuality and Feminism*, edited by Elizabeth Reba Weise. $14.95, 1-878067-17-6.

SHE'S A REBEL: *The History of Women in Rock & Roll* by Gillian G. Gaar. $16.95, 1-878067-08-7.

Young Adult and Children

GETTING THE REAL STORY: *Nellie Bly and Ida B. Wells* by Sue Davidson. $8.95, 1-878067-16-8.

A HEART IN POLITICS: *Jeannette Rankin and Patsy T. Mink* by Sue Davidson. $9.95, 1-878067-53-2.

MOMMY AND DADDY ARE FIGHTING: *A Book for Children About Family Violence* by Susan Paris. $8.95, 0-931188-33-4.

IN LOVE AND IN DANGER: *A Teen's Guide to Breaking Free of Abusive Relationships* by Barrie Levy. $8.95, 1-878067-26-5.

NO MORE SECRETS by Nina Weinstein. $8.95, 1-878067-00-1.

Fiction and Poetry

WHERE THE OCEANS MEET by Bhargavi C. Mandava. $22.95, 1-878067-86-9.

NOWLE'S PASSING by Edith Forbes. $21.95, 1-878067-72-9.

AN OPEN WEAVE by devorah major. $20.95, 1-878067-66-4.

IF YOU HAD A FAMILY by Barbara Wilson. $12.00, 1-878067-82-6.

WORDS OF FAREWELL: *Stories by Korean Women Writers* by Kang Sok-kyong, Kim Chi-won and O Chong-hui. $12.95, paper, 0-931188-76-8; $20.95, cloth, 0-931188-77-6.

NERVOUS CONDITIONS by Tsitsi Dangarembga. $12.00, 1-878067-77-X.

EGALIA'S DAUGHTERS: *A Satire of the Sexes* by Gerd Brantenberg. $11.95, 1878067-58-3.

ANOTHER AMERICA/OTRA AMERICA by Barbara Kingsolver. $10.95, 1-878067-57-5.

DISAPPEARING MOON CAFE by SKY Lee. $10.95, paper, 1-878067-12-5; $18.95, cloth, 1-878067-11-7.

General Nonfiction

SEASON OF ADVENTURE: *Travel Tales and Outdoor Journeys of Women Over 50*, edited by Jean Gould. $15.95, 1-878067-81-8.

DHARMA GIRL: *A Road Trip Across the American Generations* by Chelsea Cain. $12.00, 1-878067-84-2.

CROSSING THE BOUNDARY: *Black Women Survive Incest* by Melba Wilson. $12.95, 1-878067-42-7.

THE ME IN THE MIRROR by Connie Panzarino. $12.95, 1-878067-45-1.

Ordering Information

Individuals: If you are unable to obtain a Seal Press title from a bookstore, please order from us directly. Enclose payment with your order and 16.5% of the book total for shipping and handling. Washington residents should add 8.2% sales tax. Checks, MasterCard and Visa accepted. If ordering with a credit card, don't forget to include your name as it appears on the card, the expiration date and your signature. Please keep in mind that we are unable to accept returns.

Seal Press
3131 Western Avenue, Suite 410
Seattle, Washington 98121
1-800-754-0271 orders only
(206) 283-7844 / (206) 285-9410 fax
sealprss@scn.org